The Cultural Roots of National Socialism

HERMANN GLASER

Translated, with an Introduction and Notes by
ERNEST A. MENZE

UNIVERSITY OF TEXAS PRESS, AUSTIN

Originally published in 1964 as *Spiesser-Ideologie: Von der Zerstörung des deutschen Geistes im 19. und 20. Jahrhundert*

International Standard Book Number 0-292-71044-5
Library of Congress Catalog Card Number 77-89144
Translation copyright © 1978 by Croom Helm Ltd.

Printed in England

CONTENTS

Still trembling, I laughed and laughed and said with uncertain heart:
Here dwell all impostors. With blotted faces and limbs there you sit
and amaze me, you men of the day! Surrounded by fifty-odd echoes
which tickle your fancy and ape your airs! Truly, no better mask
than your own face could conceal your fraud. Who can know — you!
From those who deign to know you you hide behind the runes of
the past and more recent scars. And even those who see the core fail
to grasp it: for who would believe that there is one!
Façade and plaster seem your substance.
Your bearing flimsily reflects all ages and nations. Remove your
veils and cloaks, your paint and pose, and what is left but a
scarecrow. Truly, I am the feathered victim who saw you raw and
bare; and I flew away as the skeleton beckoned me with love.

Friedrich Nietzsche

PREFACE

It is characteristic of the paradoxical nature of this study that Nietzsche's words appear as its epigraph; for these are the words of a philosopher some of whose thought, in so far as it was confused and confusing, substantially aided in imperilling and destroying the German intellect, morality and culture. On the other hand, it was particularly this thinker who, faced by the perennial abyss, fearlessly gazed downward and began to survey its depth. A third factor makes his fate exemplary: his life and work were subjected to a misinterpretation which bordered on deliberate distortion. This was a tendency found time and again in the intellectual and cultural history of the nineteenth and twentieth centuries. 'Nietzsche's case', therefore, may well serve to illustrate the reflections contained in the following chapters.

The past century and a half was a period of intellectual confusion, many instances of which will be shown in this study. Yet they will only amount to a small selection from the monstrous catalogue of *Weltanschauungen* that were prevalent during the recent and more remote past. Büchner had already grasped this terror when he reminded us in *Woyzeck* that 'everyman is an abyss and it is dizzying to contemplate the chasm'.

Misinterpretation and distortion play important roles in all these examinations of the past. German culture, regardless of the period in question, whether it be the Classical age, the Romantic, or the Age of Enlightenment, cannot be made responsible for the year 1933. Neither the Romantic age, the Classical age, nor any other time were 'tragic' periods in German history; true culture can never be a disaster! It must also be remembered that the Classical and Romantic ages were no more susceptible to misinterpretation than any other period. They were victimized because they were nearer in time. The concluding phase of the Romantic age actually parallelled the rise of its earliest unimaginative imitators. But the Classical and the Romantic periods were also victimized because, as extremely fruitful epochs of German intellectual and cultural life, they were most flagrantly abused as façades of culture. The national tragedy rests on the fact that prime elements of German culture, especially Classicism and Romanticism, were perverted, distorted, twisted into opposites and yet nominally retained. What remained were lifeless, resentful words deprived of their meaning. Culture became façade, and *Logos* (the word; meaningful speech and reason *per se*) was destroyed and replaced by a confused myth, which in itself was a distortion of the word *Mythos.* This repression of intellect, reason and truth brought about emotional attitudes which must be interpreted on the basis of a psycho-pathological examination; we encounter a conglomeration of complexes which again produced a host of disparate and deranged ideas.

The Nietzschean epigraph can be related to the intellectual intent in every aspect of this study; methodological as well as textual introductory remarks, therefore, are best included in the framework of this *ad hoc* exegesis.

> Still trembling, I laughed and laughed and said with uncertain heart:
> Here dwell all impos͓ rs. With blotted faces and limbs there you sit
> and amaze me, you men of the day! Surrounded by fifty-odd echoes
> which tickle your fancy and ape your airs!

Whoever explores the manifestations of the 'official' German mentality of the nineteenth and twentieth centuries finds himself enmeshed in a cabaret of culture, verse and thought that seems to have no end; he stands transfixed, gaping in the face of *Weltanschauungen* that were 'conceived on Victorian velvet and realized in the gas ovens of Auschwitz and Theresienstadt' (Hühnerfeld).

The concept of *Weltanschauung* must be parenthesized and used with care: at best it represents a *mélange.* Nietzsche speaks of blotted faces, and such is the *Spiesser's*[1] plumage today and yesterday. The concept *Spiesser* must not be understood sociologically as relating to profession, income or standard of living; rather, it is meant to portray a psychological and anthropological condition. The term petit bourgeois signifies a quite specific form of spiritual and intellectual behaviour, a mode of conduct which is called *Spiesser*- ideology here; the description and documentation of its manifold aspects will be attempted in this study. On the whole the petit bourgeois is mediocre and provincial, fanatical and brutal, narrow-minded and full of resentment; but he is also 'sensitive' and given to 'sentiment'. He is very much a part of everyone's environment. The separate strands of his make-up permeate the texture of our 'great society': Victorian velvet in the neon age, Hitler still alive in us. Some of the speeches quoted could well be given today, and some still are. This study is limited to the past for reasons of methodological convenience. Contemporary culture therefore will not be taken into account.

Truly, no better mask than your own face could conceal your fraud! Who can know — you! From those who deign to know you you hide behind the runes of the past and more recent scars. And even those who see the core fail to grasp it: for who would believe that there is one! Façade and plaster seem your substance.

It is not an easy task to penetrate and unmask the petit-bourgeois attitude to life. Even among the petit-bourgeois élite, mediocrity is not a pretence like a propagandistic gesture: it is reality. Their mediocrity is existential, not accidental. Only rarely will one be able to raise the charge of hypocrisy. Lying, vulgarity and crime, preposterously pretentious art appreciation and ominously idyllic 'inwardness', all these traits are most genuine. Whoever interprets them is bound to err here and there, to over- or even underestimate their importance. The origin of the slogans and streamers which characterize or envelop these petit-bourgeois beings (unwrap them and search in vain for a core or substance: 'For who would believe that there is one!') is disputable, and considerably varying opinions may be held about them. The provocative nature of this study should, therefore, be understood by the reader to be a challenge to discussion.

All times and nations are reflected in your many-hued veils; and mores and faiths speak animatedly in your gestures.

The determining of the specific characteristics of the petit-bourgeois species is not just a concern of German anthropology. The reasons for concentrating on Germany are primarily methodological in nature: a manageable area of investigation was chosen which is especially relevant to Germans. Besides, if the petit-bourgeois were treated as a supra-national anthropological concept, the peculiarly chauvinistic nature of the petit-bourgeois mentality could not be properly valued. Most importantly, it should not be forgotten that in other nations petit-bourgeois character and behaviour never assumed the proportions they did in Germany. We must face the fact that the masses joyfully trod the path to 'cultural despair' — a flock of sheep following an ass, as one might pointedly phrase it. We must face the fact that the German people have never been effectively divided over questions of political ideology, but instead found themselves more or less united in their assent to political perversions of the most varied kinds. The opposition to this 'official' trend was isolated in small groups in self-imposed exile at home or abroad. Viewed typologically and anthropologically, as modes of being rather than as historical periodization, such great counter-currents as Realism, Naturalism, Expressionism and Surrealism were repressed, not acknowledged and then ridiculed. The exile of Büchner,[2] Marx, Heine,[3] the withdrawal of Stifter,[4] Grillparzer,[5] or Fontane,[6] the proscription of Hauptmann,[7] the despair of Trakl,[8] all these are symptomatic. Theodor Mommsen[9] asserted in his political testament:

> In my innermost being, and by that I mean with the best I have within me, I have always been an *animal politicum,* and wanted to be a good citizen. This is not possible in our nation, where the individual, even the best, never transcends service in the rank and file of political idolatry. This internal alienation from the people to whom I belong has determined me to refrain as far as possible from appearing in person before a German public which I do not respect.

That should make it clear that this volume is not concerned with the real German intellect and culture of the nineteenth and twentieth centuries, a culture and intellect that could be denied only by fanatical Germanophobes. This is not an exercise in self-denigration; rather, it is a lament that the self was not nurtured and that it was permitted to fall from culture into barbarism. In other words, the outstanding and truly great performances and accomplishments of the German artistic and political genius were 'officially' unacknowledged. Worse yet, it is part of the perversion of culture that one can hardly use words such as great, exalted, or other justifiable words of praise any longer in good conscience. 'Official', as used here and elsewhere, means the taste of the masses as it was guided, supported, promoted or − on account of the lack of opportunity to choose or to make comparisons, that is, because of the suppression of pluralistic taste − created in the first place by state authority. It is precisely in this connection that one can speak of the enormous guilt of those responsible. They cannot excuse themselves by claiming to be the victims of an unfortunate historical constellation or captives of a one-way street. They consciously turned the highway signs in the wrong direction and twisted the guideposts of the German spirit. The 'submissive'[10] judges, clerics, officers, bureaucrats, professors, teachers and journalists who thus became 'pillars of society' are the accused.

Why did all this happen? Why were the ideas of democracy and liberality, of evolutionary socialism and cosmopolitanism, of an intellectual and spiritual culture unable to make much impression, even though so many Germans were their creators, advocates and representatives? Various answers will be advanced in the course of this study. In the final analysis an answer without recourse to metaphysics will not be possible; but the present writer will not hazard an excursion into this field. Our principal concern is in the realm of phenomenology. *Phainomenon* means that which manifests itself, that which appears, and manifestations will be described here. An inventory of this kind must, of course, give rise to moral impulses; Nietzsche demanded these when he said: 'I will make up to my children that I am the child of my fathers: and this day shall be eternity!'

This study should not be mistaken for a historical work, a *Geistesgeschichte* bound by the principle of chronology. Recognized traits will be compared frequently without regard to chronology and repeatedly portrayed from various points of view. This study asserts and attempts to substantiate the thesis that the history of 'official' German culture during the last 150 years was not marked by development, but resembled a monotonous rotation around unchanging ideological distortions and perversions of reality; thus Fichte[11] appears as a Nazi professor, Menzel[12] as a 'new-German' student leader, Jahn[13] as the national sports administrator, Hitler as an author of the Gartenlaube[14] or a racist Ganghofer,[15] Rosenberg is emulating Wagner, and Goebbels is a kind of Wilhelm II. What may now appear as a journalistic gag will be substantiated in the course of the study.

> Truly, I am the feathered victim who saw you raw and bare; and
> I flew away as the skeleton beckoned me with love.

Camus tells us in *L'Etat de siège* that profanity revolts, while stupidity disheartens. Reflection on the nineteenth and twentieth centuries revolts, disheartens, even terrifies the beholder. The author cannot remain neutral. He cannot reject German warmth, German spirit and German culture. He cannot deny those two great Germans, Goethe and Schiller. He still believes in the idyll that was the sentimental *Biedermeier* period and the moonlight madness of Romanticism with its delightful and perceptive irony. But when these things beckon the beholder as 'skeletons' he must 'fly away'. Today it is impossible to accept any of these values without qualms of conscience. We have not lost this culture, it is true; but we have lost our joy in it. Before we can claim it again, we must clear away the ideological rubble or must wade through the watershed of intellectual catharsis.

After all that had happened, National Socialism was not an accident of German history. Rather, it was the terminus of a broad and invitingly laid-out path; alternative paths were travelled only by a few. Hitler's rise to power did not initiate the crisis; it made it apparent — visible to one and all and favoured by the politico-economic situation. It is therefore wrong to make the political and economic conditions of the Weimar Republic responsible for the development and success of National Socialism. They destroyed the forces of resistance, it is true, and thus enabled the disease (whose long incubation period will be described in this volume) to spread so speedily and with such devastating results. The crisis would have come to a head even without Hitler, or else it would have taken prolonged therapy to neutralize the poisonous seeds of the nineteenth and twentieth centuries, which had already caused widespread contamination. A victorious war would not have freed the forces necessary for this process; it would only have meant the continuation of Wilhelminian autocracy. But in this case the existing anti-democratic and anti-humanitarian currents would probably not have assumed the degree of brutality they developed under Hitler's National Socialism.

Hitler was a petit bourgeois surrounded by petit-bourgeois paladins.

These were not demons who struggled fiercely to reach the top and ultimately succeeded; they were more or less average citizens. They succeeded not because they were different, but because of their conformity. . .It is not only men of character who make history; hooligans do too, because they can sense the desires and cravings of the masses and set them in motion with dynamic and epoch-making power. It takes only a small pebble to create mighty waves [Heiber] .

The National Socialist view of the world was, in the final analysis, *Spiesser* ideology. Frequent examples from the national Socialist era, especially from *Mein Kampf,* therefore fit well into the context of this study and assist our analysis. A commentary on Hitler's *Mein Kampf,* an examination of its anthropological, sociological and psychological contents show that this book was nothing but a reservoir of currents arising chiefly from the misinterpretation of Classicism and Romanticism during the nineteenth century. These currents of thought had long been paving the way for Germany's doom; they culminated in the destruction of German culture, morality and politics. It has been said that the importance and influence of *Mein Kampf* should not be over-estimated, since the book, though widely distributed, was rarely read. That may be true; but from this observation one could draw a conclusion which may, at first sight, seem paradoxical: the book did not have to be read to become a success. The consciousness and outlook of most Germans were reflected in Hitler's book. Its contents, propagated in thousands of pamphlets, newspapers and journals, reflected the *Spiesser's* heart and soul: abysmal vulgarity, overworked verbal blancmange, resentments couched in oblique metaphors, endless tirades, rhetorically painted platitudes and shallow, 'arty' dilettantism. *Mein Kampf* thus appears as the *Spiesser's* mirror *par excellence.* Hitler possessed the genius of mediocrity. His 'Averageness' was above average; so it was his mediocrity that became the destiny of a nation, a nation that permitted itself to be led, step by step, away from the theory and practice of humanity.

Notes

1. For a definition of the term *Spiesser* see Ernest A. Menze's Introduction.
2. Georg Büchner (1813-37), revolutionary dramatist of major talent to whom maturity came early and whose incomplete work was rediscovered by later generations; it anticipated modern developments in the drama.
3. Heinrich Heine (1797-1856), major poet and writer of Jewish descent whose life and work were dedicated to mediation between German and French intellectual life and whose tragic death in exile was an omen of Germany's future alienation from the West.
4. Adalbert Stifter (1805-68), Austrian poet, painter and school official who attempted a synthesis of German Romanticism and Classicism; he sought to master the tensions of the age by emphasizing Christian-humanist themes.
5. Franz Grillparzer (1791-1872), major Austrian writer and dramatist.
6. Theodor Fontane (1819-98), major German poet and novelist.
7. Gerhart Hauptmann (1862-1946), German poet and dramatist, one of the principal figures of modern German literature whose work combined stylistic innovation with powerful themes of social criticism.
8. Georg Trakl (1887-1914), poet of the pre-First World War period who matured while still young and whose work reflects the anxiety of impending doom.
9. Theodor Mommsen (1817-1903), the dean of historians of Roman antiquity, an outstanding individual of far-ranging influence.
10. German *untertänig,* prone to a subject mentality.
11. Johann Gottlieb Fichte (1762-1814), one of the major German idealist philosophers, whose work was of world-wide significance in its influence on Romanticism and the theory of knowledge; his political writings reflect strong nationalist tendencies.
12. Wolfgang Menzel (1798-1873), writer, editor and historian who was jailed for his involvement in the German student movement of the post-Napoleonic period and who stressed moral and political convictions as standards in the evaluation of achievement in art and literature.
13. Friedrich Ludwig Jahn (1778-1852). Berlin high-school teacher and German patriot active in the liberation movement against Napoleon; he advocated sound minds in sound bodies in the struggle for the fatherland and to this end he organized gymnastics courses. Jahn's ideas were instrumental in the

nation-wide Turner movement, which was also taken to America by German immigrants.

14. The *Gartenlaube*, German weekly family journal established at Leipzig in 1853; initially liberal, it followed the trend of increasing vulgarization of culture and politics and eventually became the reflection of the lowest common denominator of the propertied middle class.

15. Ludwig Ganghofer (1855-1920), Austrian writer and editor who moved to Munich in 1895 and became famous for his romantic stories of country life and the mountains – popular idealizations of the naïveté, warmth and piety of life.

INTRODUCTION

Ernest A. Menze

Mr Glaser's pointed and pitiless indictment of the forces he deems responsible for the destruction of German *Kultur* speaks for itself. The impact of Glaser's words at the time of publication may be measured by the intensity of the immediate response in the press. *Spiesser-Ideologie*, the title of the German original, has meanwhile become a widely accepted term designating the particular attitude of mind that is the subject of this work. The long-term validity of Glaser's analysis will be determined by the judgement of history. But one conclusion can already be drawn. More than thirty years after Hitler's *Götterdämmerung* and many years after their composition the sting of his words has not abated and new aspects of their comparative applicability to other societies are constantly becoming apparent.

To be sure, Glaser's work is not addressed to other societies, nor does its content permit facile analogies. It was and is an invitation to discuss the causes and consequences of cultural developments that made the most tragic period of German history possible. The scholar and student of German history will find much food for thought, but also a good deal of provocation in Glaser's challenge to his countrymen. By focusing his analysis on Germany, Glaser did not imply that the phenomena of cultural decay so prominent in Germany do not manifest themselves in other societies. Though his remarks concerning Germany do not need an introduction, their relevance to situations elsewhere might benefit from one.

These introductory remarks, then, aside from serving to define the *Spiesser* in his German setting and to discuss the critical reaction to Glaser's book, are principally concerned with drawing analogies between problems which afflicted Germany and are being repeated in America. America serves as a model only — the list of societies subject to the crises examined by Glaser is limited only by the relative stage of their development. An excursion into comparative analysis is undertaken in full awareness of the limitations of that method in relation to something so uniquely German as the *Spiessertum* and its historical consequences. If the comparative method is applied here, it is done not least to counteract the 'reverse' type of historicism which has insisted on the uniqueness of the 'German problem'. The specific

conditions that render some aspects of a nation's culture so different
from all others are legitimately stressed in the study of history. But
their significance can become truly apparent only when they are judged
in the context of broader perspectives and when their ever-present
common human undercurrents are revealed in the process.

The term *Spiesser* itself is not rendered easily in English. The
dictionary version of 'philistine' is a 'loan' from the past rather than an
adequate translation. No doubt the *Spiesser* shares some traits with the
philistines of myth and history. Like Webster's philistine he is
'temperamentally inaccessible to' or 'afraid of new ideas, esp. of ideas
whose acceptance would involve change';[1] he is actively or passively
opposed to progress or progressive ideas, 'antagonistic to those of
artistic or poetic temperament', in short, again with Webster, 'a prosaic
person'. The modern academic usage of the term as opprobrium —
dating from the seventeenth century — and alternately conceiving of the
philistine as a former student confined to bourgeois life or simply as the
'unacademic' person had its genesis as much in biblical allusions as did
the uncomplimentary references to him in Origen, Abelard and others.
The negative characteristics of the philistine are largely the fruit of
myth. But even myth does not suffice as a synonym for the German
Spiesser.

The German *Spiesser,* as Glaser depicts him, is a product of the
nineteenth century whose roots lie deep in German social history. The
'everyman' of the swiftly expanding middle class, his domicile is not to
be sought in one particular income group. His kind of middle-class
mentality extended from the ranks of workers climbing the social
ladder to the footsteps of the throne. Conceiving of himself as the
representative of his nation's culture, he was not aware of the fact that
his understanding of culture was a perversion, his representation of it
an empty and distorted shell. Caught in the midst of rapid change, the
average middle-class man found his own limited cultural resources taxed
by the increasing demands of his environment. Lacking the leisure,
education and often the perception to make the cultural heritage
of mankind part of his own life, he substituted nationalist catch-phrases
made readily available by the advocates of 'national culture', the
modern apostles of mediocrity.

Rather than raising the eye of the uninitiated to the humanity of the
representatives of classical German culture, these apostles of mediocrity
cheapened the Classicists until they were on a level with the masses.
They helped to throw up cultural façades where genuine culture might
gradually have been fostered. The *Spiesser* was encouraged to confiscate

the legacy of Goethe, the cosmopolitan, to serve his nationalistic needs. The removal in thought from the age of Goethe was matched by the political transformation of the people into a nation. The ideals of the past had to be reinterpreted to become the new idols. In the end, it was because of a profound misunderstanding of the values which alone can lay claim to German greatness, that the cultural Weimar of Goethe was divorced from the political Weimar of the 'November criminals' of 1918 and linked with the 'noble heritage' of Potsdam. In other words, the Weimar Republic, the sole political creation of modern German history truly consonant with the tenor of the Western world, conceived and called into existence in immediate reference to the classical and humanistic Weimar of old, was relegated to the garbage heap of liberal illusions and replaced by the 'positive' memory of the Prussian kings. Defenceless, 'classical' Weimar — now even more deprived of its inner content — continued in the *Spiesser*'s possessive embrace. When the drama of national power and glory were defeated on the battlefield, he needed the consoling image of his nation's splendid past even more. Eventually a synthesis with a new tomorrow would be forged. Hitler's 'thousand-year Reich' was to be the fulfilment of collective memories and aspirations for the *Spiesser*. At each stage of this journey he was sincere in his commitment to a better and greater Germany as he understood it.

Here rests one of the principal problems in an evaluation of the *Spiesser* and his kind. The very genuineness of his commitment, his unswerving adherence to 'values', the touch of righteousness in all his doings make it difficult to ascribe villainy to him. The demands for the portrayal of 'healthy' motifs of art, for 'clean lines' and 'clarity' in art and literature find echoes everywhere. Glaser's association of the idyllic with the murderous in SS figures such as Rudolf Höss, the Commandant of Auschwitz, and Eichmann only spells out the most abhorrent of these uncomfortable truths. It is the *Spiesser*'s touching ignorance as much as his demonstrative sense of order that makes him invulnerable to the charge of villainy. How could the nation's most loyal servants be called the destroyers of its culture? How can one whom Schiller's 'sacred words' caused breathless shudders be accused of their perversion? Schiller's language lends itself so well to the expression of the most sublime dreams; but is not this very quality also often abused, to cheat by fancy's flights the sober troops of reason? Glaser's striking array of quotations serves better than any summary definition as a display of the *Spiesser*'s idiom.

The stern and persistent indictment contained within Glaser's treatise tends to present the process of cultural decay as a series of acts, but the actors were victims rather than executors of destiny. As the 'people's attorney' of a generation of betrayed heirs he is compelled to identify the sources of the Germany tragedy. A thorough reading of his book, however, shows that he is well aware of the ground-swells of history that impelled the actors, and the effect of their actions in the world at large. If tne author remained true to his task as prosecutor of the German case to the end, he did not thereby discharge his readers from the duty of seeing the broader perspective. The German *Spiesser*'s romanticism, his prettying of life's dimensions, his escape into myth and his envious degrading of intelligence have almost international application. 'Decadent', 'professor', 'liberal democrat', 'socialist criminal' and 'shopkeeper mentality' easily form chains of words that roll in ready reproof from many tongues. The bigot's pride of race and nation, the firm commitment to the destiny of the fittest, insistence on the scapegoat's guilt and yearning for the 'great synthesis' are traits of the upright bourgeois everywhere. His image — mirrored in the German *Spiesser*'s fate — deserves a closer look. To begin with, however, the accuracy of Glaser's indictment should be measured against the critical reaction of his countrymen.

The critical reaction to Glaser's book has been intense from the beginning and the discussion is not over yet. The many positive voices stress first of all its value as a stimulant to self-critique and discussion. To Wolfgang Bartsch in the Frankfurter *Rundschau* (13 June 1964) it was proof that Hitler was no accident. It is a book that 'does not only belong in teachers' libraries'. To write it, Bartsch continues, Glaser must have read enormous amounts of material, but he must also possess a strong stomach to resist the sickening effects of wading for years through the ghastly muck of German 'literary' efforts. Depressing as it is, the book must be read, said Ernst Johann in the *Frankfurter Zeitung* (30 June 1964) 'because the *Spiesser-Ideologie* of the German past remains the enemy of the German future'. The reviewer made the important distinction — not acknowledged by many critics — that Glaser writes as a critic of culture, not as a historian. Disregarding chronology, Glaser links those strands of German culture which in his view formed the destructive pattern. Further, by the use of judicious contrast and comparison, he shows clearly — if in briefer passages — those elements of genuine greatness in German culture which were not part of the *Spiesser*'s world.

With all its flaws, Harry Pross concludes in an article in the *Süddeutsche Zeitung* (27/28 June 1964), that Glaser's book is a must because of the material it contains. 'Not for a moment does the reader lose the conviction that this is the work of a man who really wants to know, who has the courage to see the uncomfortable perspective. Such virtue is rare.'

One of the principal contentions of Glaser's critics is that he has failed to present the developmental aspects of the issues he raises. Glaser's purposeful and yet seemingly arbitrary crossing of chronological barriers to show that there *was* no significant development of German culture and psyche during the past 150 years irritates them. Glaser's 'phenomenological' approach does not fit into the historian's framework of reference. With refreshing disrespect for the traditional frontiers of Academe his work is a *tour de force* in interdisciplinary research.

Glaser's main thesis, that National Socialism in Germany was not an accident of history, but 'the terminus of a broad and invitingly laid-out path' ('Preface', p.14) and that 'the history of "official" German culture during the last 150 years was not marked by development, but resembled a monotonous rotation around unchanging ideological distortions and perversions of reality' ('Preface', p.13), are borne out throughout the book. Glaser's insistence that his book is not intended to be an intellectual history or an exercise in metaphysics, but a 'phenomenology' — that is, the listing of symptoms without observance of chronology — should have disarmed his critics; but some of them insist on castigating as serious oversight what is serious method to him.

A recurrent charge of Glaser's critics deals with the 'arrangement of his evidence'. One of them saw it as no more than a staged 'carnival display of terror in perverted thought'.[2] To be sure, the evidence is arranged, but it is arranged as a multitude of examples drawn from related occurrences which — space permitting — could be documented *ad infinitum.* The juxtaposition of related phenomena — even if they were separated in time by years or centuries — carried out within the context of clearly defined methodological and substantive limits of comparative analysis need not — as some of the reviewers thought — lead to a static, unhistorical result, but adds dimensions to historical understanding unattainable in the confines of traditional *Historismus.*

A serious and substantial shortcoming of Glaser's book compared with traditional scholarly monographs is in the absence of exhaustive and fully documented background studies of the principal figures and issues discussed. Such research, it is felt, would have revealed the complex motivation behind the work of authors vacillating between the rational and irrational. More extensive probing into the motives of the individuals discussed by Glaser would indeed make fascinating intellectual fare: Glaser himself would welcome it heartily. But the point of the matter is that the scope of the book was limited to the raising of issues and tentative hypotheses. That it has done. However, this limitation of scope should not be construed as a conspiracy to deceive the reader. Rather, the whole book is an invitation to others to continue the investigation. Glaser challenged his countrymen to help him remove the rubble of the past. His exemplary work in doing just that has earned him the opprobrium of one 'who fouls his nest' *(Nestbeschmutzer)*.

An evaluation of the thought of those who are frustrated by the attempts of Glaser and others to 'overcome' the past can easily lead to unnecessary insinuations. Glaser's tone and method do not spare the already strained sensitivities of German nationalists. Agonized by the tragic ideological and physical division of their land and nervously over-reacting to the ever-present charge of association with the Hitlerian past, they lash out wildly at those who find fault with pre-Hitlerian Germany. It seems unbearable to them that not only the aberrations of the twentieth century, but aberrations throughout the long trail of German history have contained elements that funnelled national energies in the direction of self-destruction. Surprisingly, they overlook the clear insistence of the *Vergangenheitsbewältiger*[3] that this development was by no means inevitable, that it was its very 'evitability' which forms the substance of the tragedy. The maligned conservative insists that his opponent is fundamentally alien to the 'national tradition', that his 'negativism' makes him constitutionally incapable of recognizing the 'organic' and 'positive' values of society and forces him to 'foul his nest' by attributing to 'his own kind' hereditary and inescapable character flaws.

The intellectual acuteness of some liberal critics and their somewhat cynical 'stripping' of national myths probably arouses anti-intellectualism in most societies. More about this will have to be said later. In the German context and, specifically with reference to the issues raised in this book and other works by Glaser, these irreconcilable animosities, fomented by both sides, should not be overlooked. On the political left they deteriorate into hysterical polemics and violence of the most extreme order — unfortunately causing a backlash where society can least afford it. On the right they find full-throated expression in the paladins of the eternal yesterday.

Glaser emphasizes that right-wing irrationalism and its consequences were dictated by the course of German history. However, there can be no mistaking that his message applies to irrationalism wherever it raises its head. That the autnor has found the mark is borne out by the reaction of his critics.

The application of Glaser's analysis to other societies is made difficult because of the specifically German milieu from which all his evidence is drawn. Careful comparative analysis of phenomena relating to the complex of questions raised by Glaser is, however, possible. The United States of America is only one — but a surprisingly revealing — example of the many societies with which this comparative analysis can be undertaken. Fate has been kind to America in sparing it the kind of predicaments that twisted the course of German history; Clio has been kind to Americans by helping to foster the illusion that their country is 'God's country'. They have difficulty in realizing that they are not immune to the diseases of others. The comparability of German and American phenomena within Glaser's terms of reference is perhaps best brought out if they are analysed in line with the contextual sequence of this book. 'True culture can never be a disaster', Glaser observed as he set out to define the purpose of his work ('Preface', p.9). His attack, then, is directed against the misinterpretations and perversions of German culture during the past century and a half. 'Culture as façade', consists of a nostalgic appeal to a yesterday that never was. The *Spiesser* equipped the great men in German culture with characteristics fitting his own mediocrity, but he instinctively avoided the painful necessity of coming to grips with the contradictions and conflicts that are the attributes of greatness.

To the 'silent American' there is a majestic consistency in the character and works of his founding fathers. Blasphemous indeed is the man who dares to question their motives. When the 'national monument' of the Constitution was attacked by Charles Beard and others as the product of partisan interest, it seemed an incredible charge to make; to the majority it never made sense. Historians have not ceased to debate the issue. Much has been done in the interests of clarification and partisan simplicity on this level is no longer possible. But the myth of the Constitution and its pristine qualities continues to exist undiminished in the hearts of Americans; the widespread conviction of America's uniqueness depends a good deal on it.

Just as the Germans derive their boundless confidence in the uniqueness of their *Kultur* from the German *Klassik* and its masters, Americans see the roots of their heritage in a chronologically parallel classical period of great achievements.

In a land overwhelmingly protestant in its formative years, with widespread Messianic overtones in religious life, the cultural façade of America's mainstream was bound to have a strong veneer of righteous religiosity. Divorced from the 'decadence' of the Old World, the New erected a cultural façade that claimed a purity all its own. The real achievements that formed the pillars of this creed, the steady advance of democratic processes and social equality, served to deepen the conviction that it was unique. As the Germans burrowed deeper into cultural chauvinism, proudly pronouncing how different they were from the merely civilized traditions of the West, the Americans, so deeply in the 'cultural tow' of Western Europe, began to embrace their own distinctiveness with passion. Critics of this cultural fetishism remained prophets in the wilderness there as well as here in Europe.

Henry Adams, 'an *émigré de l'intérieur*', 'a born critic rather than a born leader', was just such a prophet in the wilderness in the estimation of D.W. Brogan.[4] When the catharsis of the Civil War — the great attempt at purification and national synthesis — was followed by the vulgarity of the Gilded Age, his idealism turned into 'cultural despair'. Adams, who had 'hitched his wagon', in Emerson's words, 'to the star of reform'

. . .fresh from the cynicism of European diplomacy, had expected to enter an honorable career in the press as the champion and confidant of a new Washington, and already he foresaw a life of wasted energy, sweeping the stables of American society clean of the endless corruption which his second Washington was quite certain to breed.

'The country might outlive' what he then called 'one dirty cesspool of vulgar corruption. . .but not he'.[5]

'Society laughed a vacant and meaningless derision over its own failure', and shrouded itself in the myth of success.[6] If even at Harvard the craving for conformity was already so strong that 'no irregularity shocked the intellectual atmosphere so much as contradiction or competition between teachers', how hopeless must the rest of American society have looked to Adams.[7]

The American character showed singular limitations which sometimes drove the student of civilized man to despair. Crushed by his own ignorance — lost in the darkness of his own gropings — the scholar finds himself jostled of a sudden by a crowd of men who seem to him ignorant that there is a thing called ignorance; who have forgotten to amuse themselves; who cannot even understand that they are bored.[8]

Doomed to go on amidst the 'mental inertia of sixty or eighty million people',[9] he would have liked to escape to the east, 'if it were only to sleep forever in the tradewinds under the southern stars',[10] for he was tired of a world he no longer understood. 'Since 1871 nothing had ruffled the surface of the American world', all was 'busyness' and contentment, but this unruffled façade troubled the American visionary.[11]

Richard Hofstadter's association of Adams's '. . .indictment of post-Civil War America as a coarse, materialistic society' with the alienation of the post-First World War intellectuals highlights the universality of the estrangement between the thinking critics and their society.[12]

Based on firmer foundations and feeding on deeper springs of reason than the precarious 'borrowed' Enlightenment *(Aufklärung)* in Germany, the American critique of thoughtless conformity stimulated a correspondingly massive anti-intellectual response, which drew on powerful traditions of its own. It is in this response to criticism rather than in the idylls sketched in the first part of Glaser's work that the American equivalent of the *Spiesser* mentality reveals itself. Whereas the intellect in Germany — as in Europe generally — enjoyed abstract respect except where its 'negative', i.e. 'decadent-critical', aspects were concerned, in America it was subject to a much more sweeping rejection.[13] This rejection — though modified by the sobering demands of modern technology — extends into our day; from President Nixon's disgust with the 'self-appointed intellectual élite'[14] to the numb resentment of the man in the street. Broadly based and uniquely American though it is, this anti-intellectualism clearly corresponds to some of Glaser's categories summarized under the heading *'Mythos* and *Logos'*. The myth as a weapon against the discomfort of reason has universal application. Glaser makes a strong case for its fatal power in German history. But its webs were also finely spun in America's past. Glaser's references to German indictments of intellect as 'the adversary of the soul', of rationalism as the product of 'nervous perspiration', and of — generally Jewish — 'disgusting intellectuals with long hair, horn-rimmed glasses and a 5 o'clock shadow' strikes familiar cords in those conversant with the vocabulary of American anti-intellectualism. The 'effete snobs' of the present — though racially castigated only in the most extreme cases — are the objects of the same frustrated and deriding contempt that beset their counterparts (and not infrequently their fathers) in Germany.

One does not have to go far in America to encounter the word 'decadence' as the ultimate in the derogatory exchanges of contending sides. Glaser shows the cost of this arrogance in the alienation of German society from Western values. His allusion to the quarrel between Thomas and Heinrich Mann as an elevated example of the problem is heavy ammunition indeed. But his catalogue of the blows inflicted by the 'judges of decadence' on the memory of Heine's free spirit cuts to the core. Those who refuse to conform are decadent. Those who are critical of and wish to segregate themselves from society must be decadent. The American 'Yippie' was not allowed to withdraw from the tyranny of the majority; and de Tocqueville had already given warning about this overbearing majority in the nineteenth century.[15] The Yippie was, of course, only an extreme example whose fate is not likely to evoke much sympathy even among the most liberal of the conglomerate majority. For the point of the matter is just that: the charge of decadence comes from society at large, not just from the political right.

'Compromise with power' is the key phrase in Glaser's critique of the conduct of German professors after the failure of the revolution of 1848. The corrupting influence of the consciousness of increasing national power of the German professoriate, from the initial endorsement of Bismarck's methods over the wholehearted approval of their results to the subsequent rationalization of and eventual surrender to the excesses of the twentieth century, is well documented. In view of the present alienation of the academic community from the sources of political power in America, it may seem fatuous to draw an analogy to the liaison German Academe entertained with power. However, the progressive interweaving of public funds and university research and the trend to increased governmental supervision and financing of education in general have created submerged dependencies in relation to which the surface alienation is only the tip of the iceberg. Here it should not be forgotten that the substance of power in American higher education still rests with the boards of trustees, and their relationship to established authority does not need to be belaboured. Though the American academic community on the whole has been infinitely more critical of society than its German counterpart, its secondary school substructure has been, and to a large degree still is, subservient to the mandates of national power. If that national power has so far largely been used to ends that compare favourably to its abuse in Germany,

recent history has again shown that the pitfalls of power spare none
that possess it. The increasing interlinking of government and education
and the resultant dependencies in America therefore constitute a threat
to the safeguards of society that cannot be concealed by the temporary
alienation of intellectuals from one administration or the other.
Concentration on the 'stars' and prestige campuses of American
intellectual life has served to grossly exaggerate the extent of this
alienation anyhow.

If the juxtaposition of academic life and political power seemed
strained, the attempt to apply Glaser's category of 'Heroes, Hawkers
and Democrats' to the American scene appears even less justifiable.
American history is testimony to the durability of its democratic
institutions and the depth of its democratic tradition. Glaser's gallery
of undemocratic figures who damn democracy as 'un-German' have no
match in America. However, there are some resemblances: in the section
'Heroes, Hawkers and Democrats' (p.118). Ludwig Marcuse is quoted
lamenting the 'tragic alliance of Athens and Agadir' as the downfall of
humanistic education; this retrospective myth-making has eerie echoes
in America, where modern epigones have lent heroic dimensions to the
'founding fathers' and dressed them in robes of martial glory.

The *Spiesser*'s loathing of socialists as pernicious corrupters of
society has more relevance to the American scene. If anything, German
Social Darwinism and the deep-seated anti-socialist phobia of the
propertied fall short of their more broadly based equivalents across
the ocean.[16] Hofstadter's puzzled description of American Social
Darwinism as '. . .a conservatism so utterly progressive. . .' in reference
to William Graham Sumner's sober farewell to the reign of status[17]
points to a significant difference between the German and the American
brands.[18] Where American history and social conditions made a
consistent application of the implications of Darwin's theories possible,
Germans, still confined by the reign of status, used them selectively and
ambiguously. They would curse those sympathizing with the workers'
lot as sentimentalists, but at the same time sentimentally cling to status
relationships. In America both kinds of sentimentality were castigated
by the Social Darwinists. Hofstadter's analysis of the historical
association of American political conservatism with economic and
social innovation on the one side and of moderate 'leftism' with schemes
to restore and conserve old values on the other side is a useful example
of the difficulties encountered in a comparative study of the Old and
the New Worlds.[19] However, the point is not really which brand of
Social Darwinism deserves the term 'peculiar', but rather that Social

Darwinism served the *Spiesser* on both sides of the Atlantic, and that his politics were to the left and right of the political watershed on both sides of the Atlantic too. The endless varieties of liberalism and conservatism were convenient vehicles for the changing requirements of the bourgeoisie. In their attitude to the 'lesser' classes they were differentiated only by the degree of pity they exhibited, which again depended on the degree of economic security they had attained. Drifting in the lower echelons of the bourgeois world, the *Spiesser* compensated for his fear with rabid if forced contempt. In America his anti-socialism has become a conviction of religious intensity. It is not difficult to find American parallels to Wilhelm II's socialists, who were 'fellows owning to no country', and to Hitler's socialists, 'hyenas' unable to 'abandon the carcass' — even if the German phraseology is unique. The frightening aspect of this phobia in America is that it has far transcended the limits of what once was the bourgeoisie and has penetrated virtually all of society save the intellectuals, the poorest of the poor, and the young — as long as they remain so. Should a new kind of realism — discernible in American foreign policy — pervade society as a whole and take the place of the manifold escape roads into yesterday, a change could possibly come about.

Glaser calls German conservatism 'the ideology of the unreal'. In Hofstadter's view, for 150 years American conservatism was a peculiar blend of political aristocracy and economic realism. Only with Franklin D. Roosevelt did American liberalism jettison its own 'ideology of the unreal' and link realistic socio-economic politics with its historical political progressivism. And it is since that time that American conservatism has increasingly taken up the backward-looking stance abandoned by the liberals and thereby come closer to the German 'ideology of the unreal'. This transformation in conservative thought was accompanied by changes in the ranks of its supporters. Historically, American conservatism was an aristocratic minority current, flowing from rational sources, but its transition has broadened its appeal, vulgarizing it and opening the way to irrationalism as well. This does not mean that right-wing extremism is something new to America;[20] what it does mean is that the excesses of the past are becoming the rule of the day, even if the explosiveness of the noise they make is cushioned by the broad mass who support them. The silent majority has become the launching pad of extremes: it has left its liberal moorings and is drifting to the right. The new conservatism is becoming a mass movement, the political consequences of which are as yet only vaguely outlined — and unfortunately the hope that the new young voters may reverse this trend is proving to be an illusion. Naturally, much depends on the role of leadership.

In Glaser's Germany the most important ingredient of leadership was Hitler's determination to be *Führer* and the matching determination of the petit bourgeois to let his peer become leader (p.134). Hitler's madness and vulgarity cannot be surpassed anywhere, nor can the historically conditioned subject mentality of the German *Spiesser*. But Hitler's 'clever political technique' of leading by choosing the low road was the eternal detour of the demagogue, practised everywhere and at all times and finding wide acceptance in modern American politics too. The triumph of mediocrity may be an unavoidable by-product of democracy, but it is richly compensated for if democracy is real. However, if identification with mediocrity becomes a tool of leadership to abuse democracy, to establish through tyranny by the many the dominance of the few — as it did with Hitler, and as tends to be the case with latterday leaders — growth ceases and the destruction of culture becomes inevitable. The railing of the American leadership against the 'house of intellect' and the simultaneous identification of the leaders with the 'healthy' and 'positive' instincts of the masses is a sad caricature of the guidance imparted to the American people by the men who made the Republic and who — presumably — serve as models for these modern politicians.

Schiller's maxim, 'Only in his physical state does man suffer the oppression of nature; assuming his aesthetic nature he escapes this oppression. His moral nature overcomes it', serves Glaser as a yardstick to measure the progressive brutalization of man in Germany (p.136). The adoration of the physical has been a recurrent feature of modern German culture; the heroic 'blond beast' (p.138) was only its ultimate perversion. The brutality of American mass spectator sports is still confined by the rules of the game, and many of these sports still retain to a greater or lesser degree the playfulness, humour and character-shaping traits that are so vital to sports as a dimension of modern life. But the increasing emphasis on physical absolutes, the million-fold thrill of the 'bone-crashing' tackle, play up the beast in man, the *Spiesser*'s secret idol.

The concluding chapters of the section dealing with the *Mythos* over *Logos* syndrome are concerned with very specifically German phenomena which relate to other societies only in the most general sense. Though racism is rampant in America, its polyglot background hardly allows for comparison with Glaser's 'gilded race of Germans'. The concepts of 'blood and race' and 'blood and soil' appear in America only amongst the freaks on the fringe of society or else in compartmented associations of national origin, which in their diversity contain their own best antidote.

The chapters 'National Exaltation' and 'The Word "German"' require a rather more detailed commentary. Here Glaser raises two issues which, though again specifically German, have more than just general applicability to the American scene. The romantic fusion of religious and 'nationalistic' pietism found emotional expression in German national exaltation, which intensified when the springtime of the Wars of Liberation did not bring the yearned-for unity. Lacking historical roots and more pragmatic in expression, American nationalism nevertheless created its own myths and knew its own exaltation. Hans Kohn called attention to the ambivalence of America and American nationalism:

> Such are the ambiguities of its birth, which put it in opposition to the feudal remnants in society and politics which have survived in most of Europe until very recently and in some southern European countries until today, and of its present situation, which — very different from the promise of the earlier stages of its history — makes America by policy the protector of 'reactionary' movements in other countries than its own.[21]

The need for the mythological reconstruction of the American past increased in direct proportion to the steadily decreasing importance of the present in the nation's ideals. The result was an ever louder shout for 'greatness' in everything as this greatness faded into material plenty and the meaningless verbiage of an unattainable — and unwanted — equality.

Glaser maintains that German nationalism found its 'crowning expression' in the word 'German', which as adjective and noun became the expression of absolute values. 'Whatever was German remained unequalled, whatever was unequalled was called German' (p.171). Anyone familiar with the vocabulary of American nationalism cannot fail to see the parallel, despite the differences between 'what' was unequalled in each case. An insistence, not only on national uniqueness, but on incomparable greatness is the first rung on the ladder of *Historismus* which leads to the dead end of uncritical national fetishism. Great as American traditions and institutions are, and unlike as they are to those of Germany, they are both the products of, and remain subject to, the cross-currents of world history, and the key to the direction these currents take in each society is the attitude of the recipient. 'Modernism' in its many facets is shaped by those who receive it — and pervert or embrace it, depending on their political and cultural maturity. A 'young' and therefore 'vulnerable' culture, America's hope rests in its relative political maturity. The vaunted 'depth' of German culture proved too shallow to compensate for its political immaturity.

In the third and final part of his book Glaser comes to the tantalizing world of 'repression and complex', the most difficult area to relate from one society to another because of its close affiliation with the realm of the subconscious. Those not trained in the intricacies of social pathology must tread the tempting avenue of allusion with caution. The reader unacquainted with the German myths and idylls Glaser covers should, none the less, probe the psyche of his world to see if there is a hint of symptom there of what became syndromic in Germany. Syndromic for the *Spiesser* was his 'rude, excessive, unsublimated petit-bourgeois sexual world' (p.187), his perversion of tenderness and femininity alternately into saccharine sweetness and repulsive lust. One does not have to be a devotee of the Women's Liberation movement to be aware of the perversion femininity has undergone at the hands of the mass media. This is a world-wide development, but it has assumed frightening proportions in America. The abyss of sexual repression has not diminished because of the so-called sexual revolution. On the contrary, the ostentatious freedom of one level of society — in itself not the answer — has left repression all the more entrenched. The subterranean outlets of sexual repression in America are the proper subject of the specialists' attention. An awareness of their existence and their motivating force in bourgeois behaviour is vital for the social critic. The scope and depth of the aspect of the problem becomes apparent in Winthrop Jordan's examination of American attitudes towards the Negro.[22] The fall-out of repressive attitudes uncovered by Jordan among the colonists because of the 'mixture of Bloods' (Jordan, p.166) was properly prefaced by the assumption that 'presumably all Englishmen would have had similar reactions (allowing for enormous and significant variations among individuals and groups) to the attributes which set the Negro apart if they had perceived these attributes in similar contexts' (Jordan, p.136). 'A logical explanation for the white man's infidelity', the black woman's tempting and passionate 'warmth' also served to shift responsibility for the act from him to her — as he compensated for his fear of 'sexual inadequacy' and 'racking fear and jealousy' of the 'particularly virile, promiscuous and lusty' black man (Jordan, pp.451-2). The forced

emancipationist façade of modern American sexual mores barely covers
the currents of repression underlying it.

If repression and complex revolve to a large extent around the
perverted image of woman perpetuated by man, the picture of the
masculine hero plays a vital part in setting it into relief. Hero worship
in Germany developed through a succession of wars and eventually
manifested itself with glandular intensity. The breathless adulation
of leaders and their memories in Germany can hardly be found in less
sanguine societies. But the persistence of myths such as that of pristine
Patton foiled by communist conspirators from rescuing civilization
(on both sides of the Atlantic) is only one clue to the role the hero
plays in the American philistine's adjustment to the trials of reality.

An important if superficial factor in the German *Spiesser*'s
adjustment to life attracted Glaser's attention under the catch-phrase
Biermystik. The 'white heat' of nationalism 'scorched' even the buds
of democracy in Germany and where unemotional 'cool logic and
pragmatic sobriety' might have laid the foundations for a democratic
state, the incredibly pompous language of German nationalism laid
the foundations for its opposite (p.201). The laboratory of these
excesses was the beer hall; fuelled by alcoholic dreams the *Spiesser*
lost his fear of uncertainty. One of the hallmarks of German society has
been what Dahrendorf called its 'yearning for synthesis'.[23] This
hankering after 'harmonious' solutions while side-stepping the detailed
and painful process of historical dialectic, is far removed from the
pragmatic give-and-take of American politics. However, in the
increasing tendency of American presidents to take short cuts 'to the
hearts of the people' this adoption of the synthetic solution plays a
more and more important role. The circumvention of the political
process and the direct appeal to the masses via the beer-mystique —
colloquialism and all — is the most undemocratic trick of modern
demagoguery. If it was still clever manipulation under an F.D. Roosevelt,
its ghastly righteousness of late has lowered it to the level of its worst
historical antecedents.

The recruiting ground for national heroes and their admirers in
Germany was to be found in the youth movements, but Hitler perverted
them utterly. Glaser charges these organizations with breeding
'mob-romanticism' but fails to draw attention to the poignant idealism
and innocence often associated with these groups. Victims more than
agents, these youths became part of the destructive pattern once they
grew older and had to rely on the twisted memory of lost ideals. More
cannot possibly be said of youth movements anywhere. Once the

vinyards of hope, their graduates are doomed to settle for the vinegar of the *status quo*.

Bedevilled by ever more difficult problems, modern man is particularly afflicted by what Glaser calls the 'tendency to repress' and the 'incapacity to sublimate'. In Germany these symptoms had some weird effects. The many contradictory cultural impulses of the nineteenth century – drawn from the traditions of the Baroque, the Enlightenment and Neo-Classicism – constantly generating new trends, presented the limited intellect with insoluble problems. Escape routes were found in conjuring visions of the make-believe world of the Orient or in the venomous search for scapegoats.

The search for – if not the destruction of – a scapegoat is the centrepiece in the arsenal of the *Spiesser*'s self-defence. It was the feeling of inadequacy in the face of an ever more demanding world, compounded by a lack of comprehension of its *raison d'être*, which made him seek some form of scapegoat. The Jewish minority in Germany was large enough to serve as the 'general garbage dump of resentments and as an outlet for uncompensated feelings of inferiority', and at the same time small enough for discrimination against it not to matter in terms of the national economy (p.220). Glaser's observation that the vacuum of ignorance of Judaism in Germany, caused by centuries of ghetto existence, was readily 'filled with tales of horror and terror' is to the point; moreover, these tales, as anything derogatory relating to the scapegoat anywhere, were relished. A consideration of American history brings to light recurrent instances of scapegoat-hunting with the accompanying myths. These include the recurring nativist, religious racist and political vendettas singling out minorities for contempt and persecution. The minorities singled out as 'garbage dumps' for popular resentments and uncompensated inferiority complexes were usually large enough to serve the purpose and not too large to really matter; their crimes were the products of myth and fabrication and were generated by genuine hardship. The most painful and touching examples are to be found in the black anti-Semitism of recent history.[24]

The apparent gulf that separates the incomprehensible cruelty of public treatment of the Jew in Germany from the land that became a refuge for so many cannot conceal the fact that the differences in private attitude are slim. Almost two centuries of the myth of the Declaration of Independence have hardly dented the bastions of prejudice. The real difference is in public policy. Public policy is in the end something very much like the expression of the people's will. It is

of the essence of the American's ambivalence that he beds himself in the
confort of his prejudices to compensate for his complexes and, at the
same time, appeases his conscience by consenting to a public policy
which safeguards against his own excesses. The *malaise* of the *Spiesser*
is the same everywhere.

In Germany it resulted in Glaser's 'Ghastly Idyll': alongside the
crematoria of the concentration camps and death camps flower beds
were tended by the executioners (see p.238). Höss, the commander at
Auschwitz, was touched when mothers tried to save their children, but
alas, 'he could not afford to show even the slightest emotion', he even
loved 'his gypsies', though gassed they had to be (pp.239-40). In the end
it was all possible because of widespread indifference not so much to
others' deeds — which is unending — but rather to the progressive
destruction of the moral self. Secure in the comfort of his own
impotence, of not having to act, the German *Spiesser* became what
Glaser calls 'the sheep that followed the ass'. Large-scale indifference
to the deterioration of their society has brought Americans to the edge
of crisis. Their churches are 'ossified' like those of Glaser's Germany.
They cannot much longer live on the unearned interest of the founding
fathers' accomplishments, nor will adherence to the myths of old suffice.

Glaser's book deals with Germany. It speaks of an 'unsilent majority'
that shouted mindlessly and without thought raised the man to power
who was to lead it into doom. Why the allusion to America's 'silent
majority'? It is the prerogative of silent majorities everywhere to raise
their voices — just as each individual speaks his mind. Fritz Stern has
shown that German illiberalism at home 'distorted both the style and
substance of German foreign policy',[25] and that the pressures thus
generated eventually caused the cataclysm. America's leaders appeal
to the 'silent majority' to speak: as individual Americans heed this
invitation and join the chorus calling for action at any price, Mr Glaser's
sad tale may induce them to caution.

Notes

1. *Webster's New International Dictionary,* 2nd edn, Springfield, Mass., 1952, p.1841.
2. Adrian Braunbehrens in the *Politische Vierteljahresschrift,* Opladen, 1968, Jol.IX, Heft 2, p.292.
3. Those who strive to overcome the past and in the process 'foul their nest'.
4. D.W. Brogan, Introduction, in Henry Adams, *The Education of Henry Adams,* Boston/Cambridge, Mass., 1918, 1946, 1961, p.xv.
5. Ibid., pp.171-2.

6. Ibid., p.272.
7. Ibid., p.304.
8. Ibid., p.297.
9. Ibid., p.315.
10. Ibid., p.316.
11. Ibid., p.318.
12. R. Hofstadter, *Anti-Intellectualism in American Life,* Alfred A. Knopf, New York, 1963, p.409.
13. Ibid., pp.33-4.
14. Allen Drury, 'Inside the White House, 1971', *Look Magazine,* 12 October 1971, vol.35, no.21, p.51.
15. See James M. Glass, 'Yippies: The Critique of Possessive Individualism', *Political Quarterly,* January/March 1972, vol.43, no.1, pp.60-78.
16. Where Darwin and Darwinism were embraced and honoured 'unusually quickly'. Richard Hofstadter, *Social Darwinism in American Thought,* Beacon Press, Boston, Mass., 1955, p.5.
17. William Graham Sumner, *What Social Classes Owe to Each Other,* Arno Press, New York, January 1972 reprint of 1883 edition.
18. Hofstadter, *Social Darwinism,* p.8.
19. Ibid., p.9.
20. See S.M. Lipset and E. Raab, *The Politics of Unreason. Right-Wing Extremism in America 1790-1970,* Heinemann Educational Books, 1971.
21. Hans Kohn and Daniel Walden, *American Nationalism,* Van Nostrand Reinhold, New York and London, 1970, p.1.
22. Winthrop D. Jordan, *White over Black, American Attitudes Toward the Negro, 1550-1812,* University of North Carolina Press, Baltimore, 1968; ch.IV, 'Fruits of Passion: The Dynamics of Interracial Sex', pp.136-78.
23. Ralf Dahrendorf, *Gesellschaft und Demokratie in Deutschland,* Munich, 1965, p.242.
24. Nat Hentoff, ed., *Black Anti-Semitism and Jewish Racism,* Schocken Books, New York, 1970.
25. Fritz Stern, 'The German Past, the American Present', *Columbia Forum,* New York, winter 1971, pp.24-33.

CULTURE AS FAÇADE

The philistine is not conscious of culture — yet he considers himself the wellspring of the nation's culture.

Culture is façade — and yet it is not deception; behind the façade is nothing; he *is* façade.

His sense of art is permeated by barbarism; war and art, vulgarity and beauty become interchangeable concepts; he is not conscious of this schizophrenia; the split personality is the essence of the philistine.

The Goethe one reveres resembles the soldier king; beauty is admired, but it is actually nakedness; purity is advocated but it is sterile purity; the exalted phrases one speaks are empty; the ideals one strives for are really the *Spiesser*'s idols; the avenue to inwardness is littered with sentimental journalism; the tunes one sings are trash, the revered myth is colportage; and the tenderness of home suffocates in velour.

Culture is farce — the thought and verse one hallows turn into important propaganda for judge and gallows, the philistine notices this and conforms, because he sees now that his own cultural beliefs are being propagated by his peers.

1 MASTER GOETHE

'Culture is ours, they say, because we have the "Classicists"; ours is not just the foundation; no, for the whole edifice is based on it; we are this edifice.' Nietzsche's observation in the *Unzeitgemässe Betrachtungen* takes note of a very appropriate moment in the intellectual development of the nineteenth century: by retreating to the position of 'It is already done', the philistine says, 'No need to search any more.' He 'owned' classical culture and thereby was guaranteed a position of the highest rank in the cultural hierarchy. This feeling of superiority became especially pronounced after the defeat of France in 1870-71, although one secretly feared as a cultural 'rival' what one professed to despise as mere 'civilization'.[1] Nietzsche characterized the misconception that it was German culture which was victorious in this struggle as a 'most destructive delusion, which could turn our victory into a complete defeat: into the defeat and even the extirpation of the German spirit for the sake of the German Empire'.

'Goethe, the master of German Classicism', was one of the 'empty busts of plaster' (to use an expression by Egon Friedell) which the German philistine reverently placed on his mantlepiece: one looked up to him because he was the exemplar; he therefore belonged in the inventory of the exemplary home and family. Moreover, he became the national idol in whose name the people could call themselves a nation of 'poets and philosophers'. Hermann Hesse sketched such a Goethe in his *Steppenwolf:*

> The finely chiselled, strongly expressive face of the spirited and elegantly groomed sage, complete with the famous flashing eye and the hint of solitude and sadness veiled by the courtier's bearing. . .

During the nineteenth century, 'honest' attempts were made to turn Goethe into the 'noble master' and the 'titanic intellectual hero'. This 'ideological' Goethe was deprived of the most important features of his work. His humanism, his belief in the primacy of the idea in relation to reality, his emphasis on civic awareness and most of all his cosmopolitanism were distorted into brute force, racism and folkish nationalism. The essence of classical humanity with its moral and ideal aspirations was hardly accessible to the 'official' interpretation of the

nineteenth century. The Goethe of a 'super-German' Germany was at
once 'elementarily German' and 'Faustian'; Faust was regarded as the
highest symbol of the self and therefore was passionately cherished as
a man eternally striving, dedicated to science and energetic and
pioneering (but conveniently deprived of the Faustian agony of doubt
and guilt for the sake of national revival). One can see traces here of
Spengler's total equation of the Faustian with the Nordic-Germanic.

Distortion was more difficult to accomplish in the case of Goethe's
other works. Iphigenia, the heroine of the play *Iphigenie auf Tauris,*
could hardly be transformed into a spear-carrying Valkyrie, even
though the visual arts managed to turn her into sentimental trash — as
can be seen in Feuerbach's work.[2] To be sure, there was a genuine
longing for Goethean humanism; the *Gartenlaube* expressed this wish
in its sentimental fashion in 1879; 'May Goethe's pure and noble
Iphigenia also unfold her blessings over art and literature in this new
century.' But this wish came, after all, from an old-line liberal, the
founder of the journal, Ernst Keil.[3] The real spirit of the age was better
expressed by Julius Langbehn[4] when he complained that in this play
Goethe had 'worn the cloak of an alien style'; to Langbehn, *Iphigenie*
was the product of an aged man; the heroine acted in a Grecian manner
when 'she would have been better off conducting herself Germanically'.

Stefan George and his circle, especially Gundolf,[5] re-interpreted,
then fitted, the cosmopolitan Goethe for the conservative revolution.
Now he became the amoral hero, a member of an élitist and esoteric
lodge where women were occasionally enjoyed in privacy, and a pioneer
of the future empire of the aristocracy. Goethe's friendship with
Schiller was surrounded with mystique or even homosexualized.

When Hindenburg's Government misused the centennial of Goethe's
death on 16 March 1932 to appeal to Germans all over the world to
proclaim their unity and heritage, it was not the Goethe of Ortega y
Gasset's festival oration, a Goethe pleading from the very heart of man,
whom they proclaimed. The Germany that 'rose from slumber' in 1933
claimed to bring with it an 'immortal Goethe', while in reality, to use
a phrase of Max Kommerell's,[6] German 'youth grew up without Goethe'.
It was characteristic that Rosenberg's 'Legion for German Culture'[7]
held its first meeting during Whitsun 1930 at Weimar, thereby 'linking
itself to the immortal heritage of the great sage'. Hermann Burte's[8]
image of Goethe's human and elementally German nature as 'breathing
Germanness', though physiologically unclear, was ideologically to the
point. In Chapter 10 of *Mein Kampf,* where Hitler examines the causes
of the German collapse in 1918 (amongst which are the 'bolshevization,

prostitution and corruption of art by the Jews') he laments: 'How would Schiller have been inflamed, how would Goethe have turned away in revulsion.' Under the victorious banner of National Socialism the fusion of the German 'spirit' with the struggle for Germany had been realized. What had been 'Let there be truth amongst us' and 'The voice of truth and humanity rings for everyone' now became, in the lofty terminology of National Socialism: 'Whoever pledges himself to Hitler's banner has nothing else to call his own', 'Beware of blackjacks', 'Blood is more than gold', all in the name of race and community.

Notes

1. The 'difference' between the 'superficiality' of French civilization and the 'depth' of German culture was broadly accepted in Germany and stressed in nationalistic writings. The French responded in kind making use of equally broadly based references to 'teutonic' muddle-headedness.
2. Anselm von Feuerbach (1829-80), highly successful German neo-classical painter, famous for his representations of antiquity and portraits of contemporaries.
3. Ernst Keil (1816-78), the liberal founder and first editor of the *Gartenlaube;* he was influenced by the Young Germany movement.
4. Julius Langbehn (1851-1907), was called the 'Rembrandt German' after his book *Rembrandt als Erzieher,* published anonymously in 1890; he stressed the irrational elements of culture over the prevailing realistic and naturalistic trends.
5. Friedrich Gundolf, pen name for Gundelfinger (1880-1931), literary historian and writer; he was also a member of the esoteric circle of writers around Stefan George.
6. Max Kommerell (1902-44), literary historian and writer who was close to Stefan George. He stressed the role of literature as a moral force setting standards of conduct.
7. The 'Legion for German Culture', founded by Hitler's chief ideologue, Alfred Rosenberg (1893-1946), was a proto-Nazi organization promoting folk- and race-oriented cultural programmes and policies.
8. Hermann Burte, pen name of the writer and painter H. Strübe (1879-19–), who denounced the 'cultural decay' of Wilhelminian Germany and advocated in his works the rebirth of the fatherland through a new god-like German man. Cf. his novel *Wittfeber, der ewige Deutsche,* 1912.

2 POTSDAM IS WEIMAR

The revolutionary creators of German democracy after 1918 held a view of German Classicism different from that of the official traditionalists: defeat had also made a revision of aesthetic judgements and prejudices advisable; the misinterpretation of German Classicism was to be rectified. The choice of Weimar as the seat of the National Assembly was an acknowledgement of the spirit of the Enlightenment and undefiled humanitarian classicism. For a few years Weimar again became Weimar — but only for a minority; the reactionary 'flower of German intelligence' longed for the proven coalition of German Classicism and Prussianism — or rather, since these currents of life and thought were not to be amalgamated unchanged, a fusion of 'updated' versions of German Classicism and Prussianism. For the average German the beauty of illusion and chauvinistic toughness had long formed a natural union.

Hitler and Goebbels, who were exceptionally good at tracing 'archetypes' of German consciousness, made arrangements for the opening of the first *Reichstag* of the Third Reich at Potsdam to incorporate the great qualities of Weimar. Patriarchal dignity (embodied in the 'old master' Hindenburg), bourgeois respectability (demonstrated in Hitler's cutaway), and a religio-ethical spirit (reverberating in the ringing of church bells and the proverbial chime of 'loyal and honest forever'[1]) attended the massive parade of national organizations. The great masters were remembered — Kant, Goethe, Schiller and even Dietrich Eckart;[2] every nationalistic German now perceived that Hitler was at home in the 'noble and lofty heritage of the classical German language'.

However, only a few hours later, Hermann Göring almost ruined the façade of cultured phrases behind which Hitler tried to hide the initial measures of National Socialist terror from his philistine and bourgeois followers. 'The *Führer*', he said, 'at Potsdam today ushered in a new era.' 'Weimar has been overcome', he continued, meaning the Weimar of the Republic. But his words also implied the destruction of the 'false' cultural Weimar and the refashioning of the 'genuine Weimar' that had taken place at Potsdam; in both instances 'Weimar' meant the opposite of what the Nazis thought it represented. With reference to these sometimes mutually exclusive and sometimes closely identifiable localities, which were so pregnant with symbolism, the German economist Werner Sombart had, prior to 1918, already advised his contemporaries:

> Militarism is the realization of the heroic intellect in the martial spirit. It is Potsdam and Weimar in the most exalted union. It is 'Faust' and 'Zarathustra', a Beethoven score in the trenches. Are not the 'Eroica' and the 'Egmont Overture' also the truest expressions of militarism?

This display of aesthetic judgement by a prominent man may be excused when one considers that prominent German professors, poets and philosophers were then engaged in 'intellectual service' to the nation. Still, it is worthwhile to linger a moment and consider this view of art because it had had such military overtones for a considerable time past. German Classicism was identified with ostentatious posturing, systematization, orderly arrangement and organization. It was viewed as victory over chaos and anarchy by discipline and drill. (Moulding and coercion would be more to the point.) German Classicism was seen as aesthetic strategy and therefore to be interpreted as a sub-species of the *ars militaris*. Hence the praise of Moltke as the great artist of war and the great warrior among artists: 'War will not lack an air of artistry as long as it is waged under men like Moltke.' Langbehn noted with relief that the nation of poets and philosophers had become the nation of warriors and artists: 'War fused with art — this is a Greek, a Germanic, an Aryan battle cry.' Its relation to Prussianism also made him consider German Classicism as a manifestation of the martial at parade:

> The term 'soldier of the line' derives from the august and symmetrical lines of troops in formation; the work of art becomes classical when it develops its individual character, both in form and in spirit, along such august and symmetrical lines.

The Wilhelminian era thereby assumed the combined heritage of antiquity and German Classicism: Athena of Greece was goddess of war and art, Goethe and Schiller were 'Germanic heroes'. This heritage was passed on by patriotic professors, teachers, writers, publishers and preachers until Langbehn's fantasies on the nature of art and the martial at parade became an immense reality at the annual Nuremberg party rallies. 'With raised banners and closely formed ranks'[3] the marching was now done in the name of German culture too. Goebbels's biographer Wilfried Bade put the following words into the mouth of the party anthem composer Horst Wessel, words which were revealing and expressive of the cultural policies of National Socialism:

> The stormtroopers are marching for Goethe, for Schiller, for Kant, for Bach, for Cologne Cathedral and for the Knight of Bamberg. . .[4] Now we must toil for Goethe with beer-mugs and blackjacks. But once the battle is won, then we will extend our arms and embrace our spiritual heritage.

Notes

1. 'Üb immer Treu und Redlichkeit', a somewhat pompous German song and proverb in praise of loyalty and honesty — to which popular humour adds caustically: 'And should you steal something, share half of it with me.'
2. Dietrich Eckart (1868-1923), journalist and writer, also editor of the weekly *Auf gut Deutsch;* in 1919 he published a poem called 'Feuerjo' which contained the later Nazi battle-cry 'Germany arise'. Eckart was a personal friend of Hitler's.
3. Glaser is here making an allusion to the party anthem 'Die Fahnen hoch, die Reihen fest geschlossen', which was sung after the official 'Deutschlandlied'.
4. A famous medieval statue in Bamberg Cathedral.

3 NAKED AND BEAUTIFUL

Classicism was identified with nudity — this equation (like the identification of Potsdam with Weimar) again had little subtlety but was convincing for the primitive mind: the 'cultured' philistine had encountered it repeatedly at school and on museum visits. While the prudishness and repressed sexuality of the second half of the nineteenth century made 'decent' everyday apparel mandatory, the nakedness of man could now be unashamedly admired in marble and plaster busts, torsos and full figures; the more antique the statue, the fewer veils and leaves were required to cover the most exposed parts. Since actual physical nakedness was something people did not dare to experience any more, classicized ideology and the august sculptures of Hellas appeased troubled consciences. Whereas the mostly nonconformist avant-garde and anti-bourgeois schools of art battled constantly to emancipate Venus and make her into a simple bathing beauty, the taste of the masses, and especially the 'official' government interpretation of art, remained addicted to the nude of mythology. Arnold Böcklin's *Triton and Nereide* (1875),[1] for example, clearly shows the various elements which made nudity acceptable and even venerable: in the woman, well-developed breasts and temptingly transparent veils; in the man, an expectant and longingly raised head framed by blond strands of hair; everything is alienated by the use of myth. Triton's lower half is a fish but executed in a completely naturalistic style. 'What joy it will be when I can dwell amongst men who live in the nude': this pipe-dream of the *Sturm and Drang* poet Heinse, who, incidentally, can be made responsible for many of the post-pubertal fantasies of the nineteenth century, at first remained unfulfilled: to be nude was not the prerogative of men; it was reserved for remote gods and semi-gods, those who dwelled in 'golden ages' and inhabited Olympus or Valhalla as 'Night', 'Day', 'the Sun', 'Dead Warriors', and so on. On the one hand, this restriction constituted an inhibition of the individual's 'aesthetic drive'. On the other hand, it gave rise to an exaltation of the physical which became a part of common culture. This was reflected in such tasteless metaphors as 'sublime body' and 'divine bosom' and from the very beginning exalted the artistic, and later the real, cult of the body to the highest level in the hierarchy of values, as a kind of aesthetic myth. That the average psyche was subject to this mentality is clear from contemporary advertisements, which combined claims for support garments with the likeness of hellenic gods; but it also applied to the esoteric lodges – as in the case of Hans Blüher[2] and Stefan George – where the adulation of the body reached the stage of complete extravagance and tastelessness.

The concept of *kalokagathia* (i.e. the harmony of soul and body, the desired accord between a beautiful soul and a beautiful body), which German Classicism inherited from the Enlightenment and then developed further, was already turning into a cult of the physical in the nineteenth century. Whereas Wieland had insisted that the soul must always shine through the body, physical beauty was now more important. This misconception was fatally strengthened by the views of the gymnastic movement,[3] which crystallized around the Latin phrase *mens sana in corpore sano;* their views infiltrated schools, gymnastic societies, fraternities and festival oratory, penetrating deeply into the minds of students. The use of Juvenal's phrase was a particularly malicious distortion, because he never intended to assert the nonsensical notion that a healthy body posits a healthy soul and vice versa. Rather, he urged parents to beseech the gods upon the birth of a child that *orandum est, ut sit mens sana in corpore sano.* In view of the later developments in the nineteenth and twentieth centuries (National Socialism in particular), it would have been most fitting to stress the *orandum est ut sit:* one ought to beseech the gods that in spite of the body's health a healthy soul and a healthy spirit may find room.

A beautiful body was considered evidence of moral purity: to be as white as alabaster or marble was seen as a sign of spiritual purity. Proper proportions silenced the call for spirit and soul in a person. The 'vain chatter' of the pseudo-mythological art of the *fin de siècle* had many themes; it portrayed blooming meadows and carpets of flowers, nudes reclining near springing waters, demigods striding in hallowed groves, nymphs and naiads hidden by shrubbery and fauns in the forks of trees. At times the titles still suggested themes of 'spirituality' as they toyed with temptation and uncertainty. To give an example of this art, Stuck's[4] portrait, *Sin,* did not really come to grips with the problem of sin; rather, it was aesthetic-erotic playfulness, the alluring art of the boudoir. Stuck wanted 'to create beauty to adorn life'. The aesthetic veneer of the portrait affected the artist himself: he wanted to live the beauty of his art. So it was that Stuck or Lenbach[5] developed special rites for practising their craft which entailed the use of incense and formal clothes in an over-decorated studio environment, which influenced considerably the plushiness of contemporary interior decoration. The accoutrements included velvet, silk, weaponry, jewellry, brocade, lace, Persian carpets and Gobelins: the aesthetic value of these items rose in indirect proportion to their utility. Whoever entered the 'festive hall' or 'cathedral' of art and worshipped at its 'altar' could even become the beneficiary of a 'black mass'; whoever once 'beheld beauty with his eyes' was 'forever in her chains'; even the base and profane appeared beautiful when it was covered by an aesthetic veneer. The decorative art of the time, denounced by Nietzsche, was therefore potentially a most immoral art. It elevated appearances to reality and, by the use of appearances, twisted reality into antipodes, creating 'artful' façades behind which the forces of barbarism could gather strength.

The perversion of the concept of beauty in the visual arts also found expression in literature and music. Lyric poetry, epic poetry and the drama were constructed in keeping with the 'golden mean': mood, plot and language were to be manifestations of the noble and sublime. But they did not really express the noble and sublime; more exactly, they were grand gestures, exuding airs of nobility and exaltation. One of the less offensive practitioners of this art, Stefan George, placed the 'unblemished' and 'immaculate' at the core of his poetry. Wolters[6] considered George's *Algabal*[7] to be governed by the concept of 'majesty and uniqueness'; for he would prefer murder to tolerating the slightest, even unintentional offence to honour. Dressed in 'silk of blue/studded with sapphires and sards/seamed by silvery ornaments/but with bare arms unadorned' — this is the poet's picture of his Late Roman imperator and hero.

He smiled as pale his hand extended
from golden trough the millet seed
when through the column's silence came the Lydian
his brow bowed at the masters feet.
The peaceful doves are fluttering skyward
'I gladly die as my lord stands aghast'
his breast ere now a heavy dagger pierced
as purple riv'lets grace the emerald floor.

The sadistic perpetrator portrayed as the shining knight — aestheticism could hardly be exaggerated any further! These were the poetic allures of the dandy, the *parvenu* who concealed his philistinism with *épater le bourgeois* and who mistook physical beauty for beauty of the spirit,

precious stones for precious character, formal clothes for dignity, and
cigarette smoke for incense.

This 'self-indulgent emptiness' (Bertolt Brecht) appears in the music
of Richard Wagner who, not without reason, felt so deeply attached to
Ludwig II.[8] Be it *Algabal, Schloss Linderhof*[9] or *Tristan,* all are
equally marked by a literally maniacal craving for beauty which was
coupled with the repression of truthfulness. Dishonest because they
were intoxicating or enticing, Wagner's musical means were convincingly
portrayed in Thomas Mann's novella *Tristan.* Retracing the flood of
tones in a rhapsody of words, Mann wrote:

> Descend, carnal night, bring them solace, embrace them with your
> bliss and release them from this world of lies and loneliness. . .and
> Brangäne's sombre song of warning then brought the ascent of the
> strings that transcends all reason. . .

'How lovely' (and not 'how true'): this was the emotional reaction of
the uncultured or over-sophisticated public; music was sensual rather
than ethereal; here, too, the regression of the intellect in favour of
sensuous euphoria held sway.

A basic concept of German Classicism was cancelled out by
aestehticism; one of the most profound definitions of beauty was
drowned in romanticism. For Schiller aestheticism was the path to
freedom, because beauty without truth and truth without freedom
did not seem possible to him. (Schiller's freedom was man's capacity
to deliver himself from the bonds of matter and the force of gravity.)
As beauty made man free, it simultaneously connected the world of
ideas with the sensual world; substance and form entered into perfect
union. As it captured the intellectual for the world of matter and the
senses, it prompted the sensual man to think and conceive of form.
Whenever man naturally possessed this harmony between his two
natures, he was graceful; achievement of this harmony through struggle
reflected his dignity.

Continuing the nineteenth- and twentieth-century misinterpretations
of the classical conception of beauty, the National Socialists decreed
an aestheticism of empty forms. They endowed the 'Greco-National
Socialist' body with a 'grace' which really spelled brutality, and with
a form of dignity which reflected racial arrogance. Anatomy was
trump — 'never was humanity closer to antiquity than today' (Hitler).
Rosenberg's interpretation of the Greek world was in the same vein:
as long as it remained Nordic and Aryan and was not contaminated by

democratic-Semitic influences, beauty was 'the essence of Greek breeding'.[10] Classicism was cancelled out in the name of classicism: man was beautiful not to be true and free, graceful or ennobled, but rather to entice to race-conscious copulation. Monotonous like all pornography, characteristic Nazi art studded its temples with racially perfect specimens of the masculine and feminine species. 'We are not prudish', said Goebbels, and he was right: whereas representative pupils of Stuck, such as Marc[11] and Kandinsky,[12] had at least distinguished themselves by certain technical skills, these were absent now and there remained only biological concoctions adorned by mythological abstruseness. The satirical pen best characterizes these traits: Adolf Ziegler[13] was considered the master of the German *mons veneris:* Arnold Breker's[14] statues of the German male, all sharing the same brutally empty facial expressions, magnified the Nazi Tarzan to ideologically colossal proportions.

It was difficult for the art critic who did not wish to be identified with racism or National Socialism to comment on such art; but a mere inventory could easily be considered by the 'initiated' as a sign of criticism or even resistance. With this in mind, Gert H. Theunissen commented in the *Kölnische Zeitung* on the so-called 'Great German Exhibition of Art' held in Munich in 1938:

> . . .This time it is not Terpsichore[15] but a life-size goddess of art which represents Ziegler's praise of naked beauty. Once more, reality is reflected so exactly that one is tempted to believe this blushing beauty shed the light burden of her robes only a moment ago. Her carefully executed nakedness still breathes the warmth of life and her opalescent flesh holds various allures. . .Sculptures are less well represented than paintings, but here, too, works of unique approach are offered. As last year, Joseph Thorak[16] exhibits the largest number of sculptures. The gigantic bronze of a muscular male holding grapes in his left hand has been complemented by an equally muscular and tense female with bulging hips called 'Hospitality'. A massive nude called 'Coronation' raises a wreath on high as her feet press backwards against the pedestal: here the sculptor wishes to create the impression that the mighty figure hangs suspended. . .

Hitler's artistic dreams had been realized. In *Mein Kampf* he laments Germany's desertion of the Greek model:

It is the marvellous fusion of the most splendid physical beauty with the most brilliant intellect and the noblest soul that makes the Greek ideal of beauty eternal. . .As a rule the spirit dwells, if healthy, only in the healthy body with any degree of permanence.

As art honours the body by creating its image, so discipline must steel it. In other words: a gymnastic Rembrandt coupled with an artistic Hercules. In the autobiographical section of his book, while recounting his arrival in Munich in the spring of 1918, Hitler enthusiastically celebrates the later 'capital of the movement' as a metropolis of German art. 'Whoever does not see Munich', he said, jumbling his negatives, 'does not only not know Germany; he does not know German art if he does not see Munich.' This enthusiasm is easily understandable if one realizes that the nineteenth-century *Goldschnitt* style of painting and literature[17] had had its centre at Munich. It was here that Ludwig I created 'golden Munich', the Athens on the Isar, a classical rhapsody of life transposed into a correspondingly questionable style of architecture. In addition, behind the aesthetic façade of German Classicism, an uproarious atmosphere of rawest folklore pervaded the city. There was also a rich selection of racially, nationalistically and cosmically oriented Bohemian circles and the appropriate pamphlet literature. 'A German city! What a difference from Vienna. I became ill when I merely reflected on that Babel of races.' Hitler, nameless, déclassé and an artistic failure, though still much interested in the ideology of art, could feel relatively comfortable here. Later on the city would garner 'the *Führer's* rewards'. Following 'great models' and the motto that 'monumental edifices are not buildings but rather the ideas of a community expressed in stone' (Rosenberg), Hitler continued the monumental style of building. Interior decoration during the Nazi era was also decisively influenced by the plush atmosphere of nineteenth-century Munich. Initially in the 'Brown House',[18] then at Obersalzberg,[19] and finally in the Berlin Chancery,[20] this led to a mixed style deriving inspiration from the saloon car and the beer-house. The new style was characterized by smoothness, sterile pretension and hypocritical folksiness, and fittingly complemented Sepp Hilz's 'rustic Venus'.[21] It seems therefore rather appropriate that the National Socialist version of 'nudist classicism' found its historic home at Munich.

Notes

1. Arnold Böcklin (1827-1901), Swiss painter of landscapes and historical scenes. He spent most of his working life in Germany and Italy. His paintings strongly reflect the myths of 'positive' bourgeois culture — that is, the evasion of the problematic aspects of life through the superimposing of ideals.
2. Hans Blüher (1888-1955), writer and metaphysician who was influenced by Nietzsche's philosophy of life; he was also an advocate and historian of youth movements such as the *Wandervogel.*
3. The *Turner* movement, founded by *Turnvater* Jahn during the Napoleonic wars (see p.15, n.13).
4. Franz von Stuck (1863-1928), Munich painter and professor of art who stressed the importance of allegorical and mythical themes; he was influenced by Böcklin.
5. Franz von Lenbach (1836-1904), favourite portrait painter of the 'great men' of the age.
6. Friedrich Wolters (1876-1930), writer and historian, member of the Stefan George circle.
7. Cycle of poems by George, published in 1892.
8. Ludwig II (1845-86) [64-86]), eccentric Bavarian king and patron of Richard Wagner.
9. Schloss Linderhof is one of the palaces built by Ludwig II in Upper Bavaria near Garmisch-Partenkirchen. Beautifully located and expensively decorated, buildings like this contributed to Ludwig's large debts and added to the pressures that led to his mental imbalance, the loss of his throne, and his suicide.
10. Rosenberg used the word *Zuchtbegriff,* a term drawn from animal husbandry.
11. Franz Marc (1880-1916), a painter whose style developed from Early Impressionism through Cubism to abstract form. He was influenced by Kandinsky, travelled widely, residing temporarily in Paris, and spent the pre-war years in Upper Bavaria. He died in battle at Verdun. During the National Socialist period his works were banned.
12. Wassily Kandinsky (1866-1944), Russian painter who trained in Munich. From 1914-21 he worked in Russia, and from 1922 he taught at the Bauhaus in Dessau; in 1933 he went to France. Kandinsky was a pioneer of abstract art.
13. Adolf Ziegler, painter, president of the National Chamber of Arts *(Reichskunstkammer);* he initiated the activity against 'decadent art' in 1937 and led the resulting campaign.
14. Arnold Breker (born 1900), sculptor achieving prominence during the National Socialist period because of his heroic-monumental style.
15. The muse of the dance.
16. Joseph Thorak (1889-1952), Munich sculptor and professor of art whose work deteriorated to the level of monumentalism and empty pathos during the National Socialist period.
17. The *Goldschnitt* style emphasized the delicate and decorative elements in art especially through the selection and use of precious materials.
18. *Das braune Haus,* one of the National Socialist party's official buildings in Munich.
19. Obersalzberg, Bavarian mountain and site of Hitler's hideaway, the *Berghof.*
20. The colossal *Reichskanzlei,* designed by Speer, corresponded to Hitler's conception of beauty; later it was the scene of his death.
21. Hilz's 'rustic Venus', a painting which most appropriately reflected the racist National Socialist conceptions of beauty.

4 BEAUTIFUL, CLEAN, CLEAR

The glorification of the body and of well-proportioned nudity was complemented by the rejection of the 'ugly' body and of 'ugliness' in art *per se*. 'Ugly' was everything that did not correspond to the prevailing superficial, optimistic conception of life, its shallow unproblematic nature, and its smooth glibness. To the petit-bourgeois mind, art was a part of living room culture. It was a kind of adorn-your-home art, with portraits over sofa and marital bed as icons of bourgeois complacency and lust. Any challenge to this cow-like aesthetic contentedness by painters or poets who portrayed the 'other' side of life or touched on it in their presentations was taken as an outright personal affront and combated with venomous passion.

'I think we must have the courage to cold-bloodedly prevent the public proliferation in every form of all that makes use of the mask of art', demanded Class, the chairman of the Pan-Germans, in 1912.[1] Calling for 'pure art', he rejected paintings that 'served sick tendencies'. Class considered even the Emperor too weak in this matter and not conservative enough. But aside from the fact that Wilhelm, personally or with his court, was unmatched in his lack of taste, he had often categorically and as a matter of policy rejected 'the art of the gutter':

. . .At the sight of the marvellous remnants of antiquity one is overcome by the same feeling; here also dwells an eternal and unchanging law: the law of beauty and harmony, of aestheticism. . . Under cover of this realization I would like to caution you: up to now the art of sculpture has remained relatively uncontaminated by the so-called modern schools and currents; up to now it has maintained its high and exalted position. . .Art that disregards the laws I cited is no longer art, it is factory work, handicraft, and that is something art should never become. . .Whoever. . .separates himself from the law of beauty and from a sense for aesthetics and harmony which, consciously or not, dwell in every breast. . .sins against the fundamental sources of art. . .To us, the German people, the great ideals have become enduring values, whereas other peoples have more or less lost them. . .The cultivation of ideals is at the same time the highest task of culture. . .It can be accomplished only if aided by art, an art that ennobles rather than descends into the gutter. . .May you always retain these high standards; may my grandchildren and great-grandchildren be accompanied by equal masters.

William II loved Richard Wagner, passionately read Ebers's novels,[2] detested lyrical poetry that was not in the patriotic vein, and most other literature, which he considered useless and immoral. He conceived the design for the painting *Peoples of Europe, Protect your Holiest Treasures,* which portrayed royal castles, Valkyries, Mars and the martial cross, and a feathered Siegfried.[3] He composed the 'Song to Agir'[4] and conducted recitals of Eulenburg's *Rosenlieder.*[5]

Under the protection of government favour, aesthetic conservatism gathered together all those who were able to portray with 'delicate brush' the saturation of the Wilhelminian period: superficial happiness and the contented commonplace, the rude health of peasant and philistine, mythological 'purity and cleanliness'. In regard to style, only Naturalism, i.e. photographic realism, could be considered, a choice which could also be ideologically substantiated: 'True Germanic art is naturalistic; wherever this does not apply it is due to alien influences which forced it from its racially predetermined course' (Chamberlain). In the field of *belles lettres* it was above all the poets of 'German inwardness' who satisfied the demand for purity and lucidity. In this connection school textbooks are especially revealing, because it was here that the seeds of the petit-bourgeois attitude towards literature were sown. Uhland for example was considered a 'Classicist'.[6] The first edition of his *Lieder* (1815) contained an unfortunate misprint in the first sentence which gave *Lieder* as *Leder;* the sentence thus read, 'We are leather. Our father sends us into the wide world.' Actually, this mishap rather appropriately reflected the nature of these songs. Egon Friedell, to whom we owe this anecdote, softened the impact by referring to 'gilded leather wall coverings'. German textbook editors were of the opinion that Uhland's poetry derived 'from the sources of his own national heritage. . .resting fully and completely on national foundations'. They considered him the 'Walther of the modern age';[7] next to him they considered Rückert as 'one of the greatest lyric poets of all time', whose romantic-epigonic work — with its sentimentality, pseudo-contemplativeness and minstrel airs — indeed reflected the *Zeitgeist* very well.[8]

On 12 April 1913 the Prussian Chamber of Deputies discussed the question of modern art, with reproductions from the Cologne Exhibition of that year and several issues of the journal *Sturm* as evidence. When the depraved development of the fine arts was criticized in the course of the debate, and when it was stressed that the aim and purpose of true art should be the exposition of the beautiful and exalted in nature and in life ('Sick art' ought no longer to be supported – 'Bravo!'), none of the 443 deputies demurred.

In his official comment before the German Reichstag on the passage of the Enabling Law on 23 March 1933, Hitler declared that the new German National Socialist art was to serve 'the preservation of the eternal values rooted in the heritage of our people'; 'blood and race are again to become the sources of artistic intuition.' Although the Social Democrats rejected the Enabling Law for other reasons, none of the assembled parliamentarians objected to Hitler's formulation. Both incidents are not only very revealing signs of the political, but also of the aesthetic, immaturity of the German parliamentarians. Even in the role of 'the artist' Hitler was in a good position to guide popular *Kultur* successfully.

From childhood on Hitler had wanted to be a painter: 'One day it became clear to me that I would become a painter. *Kunstmaler.*'[9] It was one of the deepest disappointments of his life that his attempt to enter the Akademie der Bildenden Künste in Vienna failed: his trial sketches had been found unacceptable. This episode of his youth was to be of especial psychological importance: on the one hand, it was partially responsible for the fact that Hitler later, when in the possession of absolute power, became energetically involved in defacing German cities, especially Munich, Nuremberg and Berlin, with the monstrous productions of his repressed artistic imagination (not to mention the fact that every totalitarian régime strives to become immortal through monuments in stone). On the other hand, it obliged the propagandists of the movement, who were aware of the master's weakness in this field, to glorify Hitler as the 'great artist'. In consequence, generations of aesthetic miseducation meant that, from the very start, a majority of people gave more credit to Hitler and National Socialism than to other patriotic currents and movements: because the *Führer* had a 'feeling for art' and was 'open to all beauty' he obviously belonged to the better (i.e. art-loving) part of humanity; he was the 'incarnation of the Muses' *(Baldur von Schirach).*[10] Whether consciously or unconsciously, Hitler liked to make use of such aesthetic distinctions; that is, he presented his unfounded or untenable condemnations of others under the guise of aesthetic judgements. In Chapter 3 of *Mein Kampf,* for example, he launched into an uncontrolled attack on democracy and parliamentarianism, 'exposing' them as the monstrous productions of Evil, as abortions, the ugliest of the ugly; parliamentarians were represented as deformed products of degeneration, and treated to countless words of abuse such as 'debased mob, milksops, crooks, gaolbirds, and octopi'; but the outburst is introduced by a remark which is meant to substantiate Hitler's sense for, and understanding of, art:

> For the first time I entered the halls of the Viennese Parliament, a
> building which has been venerated as often as it has been fought
> over. But for me it was only the glorious structure itself which was
> venerable. A hellenic marvel on German soil!

The adjectives 'exalted', 'glorious' and 'hellenic' characterize the cliché-ridden classicism which surfaced time and again in the utterances of the *Führer*. Prefaced by this demonstration of sensitivity, the subsequent political remarks ('How quickly I became enraged by the miserable spectacle taking place in front of my eyes') took an aura of especial 'honesty' and 'sincerity'. 'We, the close collaborators, know', it was later stated by Gauleiter Kube,[11] that Hitler 'is the most sensitive connoisseur of art who has ever led a great nation. I remember how, shortly before the showdown with the Schleicher ministry,[12] he sought spiritual inspiration at the foot of the Pergamon Altar.'[13] When Rosenberg, on Hitler's birthday on 20 April 1943, presented him with a photographic record of the most precious paintings stolen by his staff all over Europe, he did so in the hope that: 'this encounter with the beautiful things of the art so dear to you will allow a ray of beauty and joy to enter your life which is presently burdened by heaviness and grandeur.'

Rudolf Höss, the Commander of Auschwitz, was in this sense also a connoisseur of art, 'open to beauty'. Just as at an earlier time 'classicism' and war had been connected, now the 'Idyllic and the homicidal' dwelled side by side in the world of the SS élite; Heydrich played Mozart, Himmler loved to listen to classical music. 'Hölderlin amidst the gas ovens and executions' is how one German critic (Strothmann) has phrased it, and the war crimes trials revealed such traits time and again, traits typical of people of National Socialist persuasion. In most cases, there was neither pretence nor trickery behind the appalling aesthetic untruthfulness; rather, it was an expression of 'genuine' feeling, acquired through education and passed on by tradition. Since one was aesthetically 'in the groove' there were no qualms of conscience; the ugliness of murder was covered by a veneer of art appreciation. One could approach the entire extermination process from the aesthetic point of view; ugliness (Jews, the vermin) was now liquidated, eradicated, snuffed out in the service of beauty; once this 'business' was completed, the 'brilliant day' would dawn. Such an attitude had been substantially promoted by the bastardization of all that was realistically human — for all represenations of human suffering and grief, of toil and deprivation, of hardship and undaunted courage were considered ugly: Kollwitz[14] as well as Barlach,[15] Nolde[16] as much as Kokoschka,[17] van Gogh no less than Marc.[18] Since hardly an artist worthy the name was free of 'burdens such as these', a generalization, rare even in the case of totalitarian states, holds true: National Socialist art could call no artist, at best an occasional artistic fellow traveller, its own.

Hubert Lanziger[19] portrayed Hitler as Joan of Arc, storming forward; in such a manner Hitler trampled underfoot everything that was objectionable to his 'pure and clear conception of art'. With the opening of the great German art exhibition at Munich the goal was reached; the separation of generically pure art from degenerate ugly art was made visible to all: the beautiful was displayed in the 'house of beauty' *(Haus der deutschen Kunst)*,[20] while the ugly building *(Hofgartengebäude)*[21] housed the ugly works. 'Around us you see the monstrous products of lunacy, impudence, dilettantism and degeneracy', declared Professor Ziegler, the President of the National Chamber of Arts, as he led Hitler and the National Socialist leadership through the exhibition. In 1931 the art critic Weigand von Miltenberg characterized Hitler as another William II and a 'royal Bavarian artist'. 'Hitler is an artist. However, his is that type of artistic mediocrity which either decays in Schwabing[22] or ends in the reactionary stuffiness of the *Akademie,*[23] a mediocrity which has been cursed by the great from Rembrandt to van Gogh.' Like William II before him but now supported by the power and terror of the totalitarian state, in an opening address Hitler ridiculed the artists who, he said, saw national heroes as decadent cretins and on principle portrayed all meadows in blue, the heavens green and clouds in sulphuric yellow, men who obviously (note the symptomatic slip of the tongue) 'suffered from clear vision [sic]'.[24] Since to be German was to be lucid, art had to be lucidly German and Germanically pure as well. 'Art that fails to win the most enthusiastic and dedicated approval of a good majority of the people is insufferable.' The 900 works in the first exhibition, like those in later exhibitions, were selected along these lines: 40 per cent landscapes, 20 per cent male and female figures in varying states of undress, 10 per cent animals, 7 per cent still-lifes, 7 per cent peasants, etc. Everything was either heroic or idyllic, 'sweet' or racialist; it was all 'beautiful and pure' like the allegorical figure, 'The Third Reich', by Richard Klein, which stands naked and bare on a desolate rock, holding a hammer veiled by a halo and a banner bearing the swastika and the imperial eagle, muscular and pea-brained, vacantly staring into a 'better future'.

Notes

1. The Alldeutscher Verband, founded in 1891, advocated the revitalization of national consciousness through the support of native Germans and German interests abroad and also by pursuing an energetic foreign, naval and colonial policy. Heinrich Class (1868-1953) became chairman of the organization in 1908. He consistently represented a strong nationalist position and opposed the Weimar Republic.
2. Georg Ebers (1837-98) wrote archaeological-historical novels and was a member of Felix Dahn's circle (Dahn: 1834-1912). His most prominent work was *Eine Ägyptische Königstochter* (The Daughter of the Pharoah).
3. The phrase 'Völker Europas, wahret Eure heiligsten Güter' was coined by Wilhelm II; he commissioned the painting.
4. In Nordic mythology Agir was the god of the sea.
5. Philipp Fürst zu Eulenburg und Hertefeld (1847-1921), officer, diplomat, poet, composer and friend and confidant of Wilhelm II, was publicly estranged from the Emperor on the discovery that he was homosexual. The *Rosenlieder* were one of his song cycles.
6. Ludwig Uhland (1787-1862): besides being a poet he was a politician, a professor of German language and literature, and an advocate of national union and democratic rights too. His popular romantic poems and ballads are notable for their use of historical themes and for their lyrical simplicity.
7. An allusion to Walther von der Vogelweide (c.1170-1230), the famous medieval lyricist or *Minnesinger*.
8. Friedrich Rückert (1788-1866), a patriotic lyricist engaged in anti-napoleonic literary campaigns, who was also famous for his scholarly translations of oriental literature.
9. *Kunstmaler* – a painter of pictures; Hitler had to make the distinction from 'house painter'!
10. Baldur von Schirach (b.1907) was Reich Youth Leader from 1933-40; from 1940-45 he was Gauleiter and Reichsstatthalter in Vienna.
11. A minor National Socialist party official.
12. General Kurt von Schleicher (1882-1934) was the Prussian general staff officer; during the Weimar Republic's final years he was the 'grey eminence' in Hindenburg's circle and was briefly Chancellor himself before Hitler's accession. He was murdered by the Nazis during the Röhm purge of 1934.
13. A magnificent Greek altar exhibited in the Berlin Pergamon Museum.
14. Käthe Kollwitz (1867-1945), Berlin painter and graphic artist who is well known for her moving representations of the working-class milieu; her work demonstrates an acute social and political awareness.
15. Ernst Barlach (1870-1938), North German sculptor, graphic artist and writer who explored earthy themes and who successfully united the various aspects

of his art with sharpness of characterization and emotional intensity.

16. Emil Nolde (1867-1956; his real name was Hansen), North German Expressionist painter and graphic artist whose work was banned during the National Socialist period.

17. Oskar Kokoschka (1886-   ), Austrian painter and leading representative of German Expressionism; he continued his work in emigration in Prague and London during the National Socialist years.

18. See note 11 on p.50.

19. Hubert Lanziger was a painter of folkish motifs with National Socialist orientation.

20. Munich exhibition hall.

21. One of the Munich Court buildings – transformed into an art gallery after the 1918 revolution.

22. Munich student and artist quarter.

23. 'Official' art associated with the Munich Academy of Art.

24. 'An Sehvermögen litten', which literally means that they suffered the disability of being able to see, though Hitler of course meant that their vision had suffered impairment.

5 THE PATHOS OF SCHILLER

Empty pathos is the most characteristic trait of the 'official' language
of the nineteenth and twentieth centuries. Its origins are easily traced;
that is to say, its structural harmony with the figures of speech used in
epigonic Romanticism and Classicism is easily demonstrated. More than
all other forms of expression, it was political oratory which claimed the
heritage of Schiller, while actually perverting and abusing it:

> The eyes of the people love the festive splendour which surrounds
> the powerful. But their souls love the lustre and brilliance of
> Schiller's language, the majesty of his expression, his gilded and
> purple robe of dominance in the realm of the spirit [G. Riesser].

Schiller's language was the expression of his passionate efforts towards
the 'Education of Humanity'.[1] His inclination towards idealism was
not a turning away from reality; on the contrary, his view of the world
was characterized by a strict dualism: the conflicting concepts of idea
and existence, hope and anxiety, life and death, freedom and coercion,
joy and suffering, peace and war, form and matter, art and reality
constantly imposed themselves on the poet, became part of, and were
reflected in, his dialectical language. The most distinctive features of
Schiller's work are his precise, even if often colourless metaphors (e.g.
in the *Gedankenlyrik*), his bent towards the deeply problematic (e.g.
in the plays), and his clear and prudent manner of expression (e.g. in
the philosophical writings). This lucid thinker and poet was released
from his nationalistic prison for the appreciation of a wider public
only through the effort of Thomas Mann, who gave a memorial address
on the 150th anniversary of his birth which once again presented him
in his true humanity. But during the nineteenth century Schiller
suffered the misfortune of being singled out as the idol of the
nationalistic bourgeoisie: he became the 'moral mouthpiece' and
champion of national unity. The *Glocke*[2] kept in young ladies' rooms,
Tell[3] enacted in colossal settings, and the poet himself portrayed as
the member of a *Burschenschaft*:[4] these were some aspects of the
misinterpretation. A wretched, courageous man who wrestled with
constant doubt and pessimism to achieve works of real humanity, and
who, in prefacing his *Die Horen*,[5] had said that it was a 'miserable and

petty ideal' to write for *one* nation ('a philosophical spirit cannot
tolerate this limitation'), Schiller was placed on a pedestal as the object
of religious adulation. He was a national Schiller, described in primers
as 'captivating and elevating the pristine spirit of youth', and as
'prophetically erasing the profane from the minds of growing youths,
consuming them with sacred fire and then kindling the light of a higher
life in their breasts'. Once again, the most extreme exaggeration was
provided by National Socialism; now there was 'Schiller the
stormtrooper', 'Schiller the comrade of Hitler'.

During the course of the nineteenth century Schillerian pathos
became progressively emancipated. It was no longer the robe of
thought, it no longer enhanced ideas, experiences and emotions;
instead, left to itself, it became a meaningless, arbitrary flood of words;
form and content were no longer in unsullied irreversible union.
Clichés abounded; boxed in by words and deprived of meaning, man
turned in circles to the tune of empty chatter. The influence of Fichte
also proved to be very destructive. The great political impression he
made through his assertion of national consciousness during the Wars
of Liberation, especially on academic youth and its fraternities, had a
fatal effect on language. Fichte was emulated just like Schiller was —
structurally, hardly any differentiation was made between them.
Fichte's exalted phraseology could be adopted unadulterated; it was
a perversion of language in the first place. Moreover, it was Fichte who,
in his *Addresses to the German Nation (Reden an die deutsche Nation)*,[6]
had claimed that, 'unlike the other Teutonic races, who communicate
in superficial and essentially dead idioms, the German people speak a
language which is a living force rooted in the energies of nature'. Since
the German people alone were in possession of a living language, they
alone were capable of genuine culture — 'the German spirit [is] an eagle
which rears its imposing body forcefully to rise closer to the sun,
delighted by its sight'. The identification of the German language with
primitive language, its depiction as a spiritual idiom weighted with
nebulous pathos (as borne out in form and substance by Fichte), had
serious repercussions. At least for the patriotic and race-conscious
writers, who wanted to appear genuinely German, close to their
heritage and aesthetic (and who were passionately devoted to Fichte),
it meant that they need never descend from a certain (very lofty) level
of exalted speech. The flood of words was not to be abated.

The speeches during Schiller Year, 1859, which celebrated the one
hundredth anniversary of the poet's birth as the 'victory of the German
spirit', marked the first stage in this development.

Any foreigner traversing Germany today would be captivated by the sight of gaily-dressed people promenading in all or most of its cities. As they followed the flag the marvellous words of the *Glocke* would be with them, at times even presented in dramatic form. The joyful but earnest strains, the gripping style, he would have been told by everyone, are the creation of our greatest poet, whose birth a hundred years ago is being celebrated today. . .Oh, if on hallowed days the sacred bells could also ring away all obstacles to the unity of our people, the unity which it craves and needs.

In his memorial address honouring Schiller, 'the towering figure', Jacob Grimm supported the plan for the erection of Schiller memorials everywhere. Under the influence of a rigorous literary Darwinism, he advocated that monies intended to assist poets and their widows in need should be spent on monuments instead: 'Schiller columns. . .to be erected by artists' hands. . .would then grace Marbach[7] and other places and, like perennial bonfires, brighten the land; let us not be deprived of the funds and of the sacred balsam of their work by the all-devouring, ever-hungry pouch of the dole.' Now 'the deepest well of German life' began to spring again in full flow; after a whole people 'had devotedly woven a garland from centennial branches' for its 'chosen son', he had 'risen again':

> He is arisen! His words breathe forth like purest flames from mouth to mouth. His song inspires the young to carry on his struggle, and gives the ancient the wisdom of ages. Where German manhood bold and brave gives birth to mighty deed, he is the blessing of the union. So he lives on in glory, ever unforgotten. Hail to him, hail to us who once possessed him [E. Geibel].[8]

The most interesting memorial address was delivered by Gabriel Riesser; it was particularly interesting because Riesser was Jewish. His speech emphatically demonstrated how truly German the Jewish intellectual felt, even where the negative aspects of language were concerned.[9] It showed how completely he was integrated, a fact which was borne out by the choice of a Rabbi as principal speaker for the anniversary of the battle of Sedan at Nuremberg in 1878. Riesser, it is true, was a liberal spirit who fought against the autocratic police state. His speech is therefore proof that at that time it was possible for a man to think, feel and act democratically, even though he was no longer able to use the logically clear and humanely humble language of the Enlightenment and Classicism, but had to adopt instead the pompous and turgid tones of the petit bourgeoisie.

This discrepancy had already been evident in Uhland's radical-revolutionary demands of 1849 in St Paul's Cathedral, which were presented in totally conservative, tradition-bound, epigonic and romantic language: '. . .It would not be in keeping with the natural growth of the newly-rising German oak, if we would crown its top with a nest of hereditary imperial eagles.' This schizophrenic attitude, so significant in the political anthropology of the Germans, is mainly due to the German liberation movement, whose representatives were never able to reconcile the demands for liberty *and* unity politically or linguistically. Judged by their content, the demands of 'revolutionary' youth after 1813 seemed to be really revolutionary, that is, they stressed the call for civil liberties; a linguistic analysis shows, however, that these attempts were from the very beginning swamped by conservative or reactionary thought. Riesser's Schiller address began with the words:

> Let the echo of the joy of multitudes, which has just subsided in your ears, roar on within your souls; the distinguished composition, dedicated to the glorification of a great man's memory, has never given expression to more exalted and generally festive mood.

The speech contained 5,000 words, of which 150 were grammatical comparatives or superlatives; this means that every thirty-third word was a comparative or superlative. This number does not include the many descriptive superlatives such as 'mighty roar', 'high ringing', 'tremendous genius', etc. To show sufficiently clearly that Schiller was noble, majestic, powerful, glorious and unequalled, the appropriate words were massed into rhetorical peaks; the word 'high' alone appears sixty times, similarly the word 'noble'. Schiller represented for Riesser and his enthusiastic and devoted audience the 'most elevated and ennobled human development [Bildung]',[10] the 'purest development of the natural, the most beautiful blossom, the sweetest fruit; he was the most purely spiritual, possessed the highest powers and the most original and childlike sentiments' (and all this in one sentence).

The metaphors, syntax, and subject matter of the political and cultural oratory of the nationalistic bourgeoisie (which, intellectually, was petit bourgeois) during the nineteenth and twentieth centuries are easily outlined: bombastic imagery, the deadening of thought through mythicizing vagueness, the destruction of the essence of conceptualization so that only empty husks of words remained, a galaxy of false, distorted or superfluous genitives, rhetorical inversions saturated with pompous solemnity, and synonyms galore. From the Wars of Liberation to the days of Hitler hardly any change to the official inventory of language is noticeable — other than an increasing accumulation of, and some variations on, these manifestations.

Hofmannsthal's Lord Chandos expresses this in *The Letter of Lord Chandos* when he says: '. . .abstract words, which are necessary for the expression of any judgement, decomposed on my tongue like mouldy mushrooms'.[11] A sentence from Hitler's *Mein Kampf* can also be cited here to illustrate the decay of the language; but his remarks, which were addressed to the opponents of National Socialism, should be considered in reference to Hitler himself and his linguistic precursors in the nineteenth and twentieth centuries. (Karl Kraus observed in 1933 that the 'National Socialist dictatorship dominates everything today except the language'.)[12] These were Hitler's words: 'With an enormous display of words without clear substance or comprehensible meaning sentences are stammered together which are supposed to be as witty as they are senseless.'

The following pages of this book are intended to give impressionistic evidence from which the structural monotony mentioned previously can be seen with all its variations. Chronological order has purposely not been observed because there is no particular line of development but only unchanging word forests (mostly primeval): sources are listed at the end of each quotation, though the structure of the text is more important than the individual author.

Sources are available in great numbers. As far as quality is concerned, the following extracts have been chosen not as selected examples but as typical manifestations. Furthermore, the quotations point to the continuously recurring sociological origins of this language: the literature of academic fraternities and youth movements, popular publications, nationalistic histories, textbooks, monarchistic and governmental announcements, patriotic lyrics and so-called 'quality' literature.

Extensive evidence is being presented at this point because it may also serve to illustrate later chapters of this book; conversely, quotations appearing in other parts of the book serve to complement the material presented here.

I

This little town on the Inn, hallowed by German martyrdom, Bavarian by blood, Austrian politically, was the home of my parents during the late eighties of the last century; my father a dutiful official, my mother a devoted housekeeper, caring for us children with steadfast love and dedication. [A. Hitler, *Mein Kampf,* p.2.]

For the feast today I shall first kill another noble deer with my new bow! Wieland, you shall take pleasure in that. [R. Wagner, *Auswahl seiner Schriften,* p.193.]

For you, Helferich, who gains for us the healing draught from aromatic herbs, for you I forged this delicate vessel of gold, so that you may keep it safely there. [Wagner, ibid.]

The German, in youth often awkward and reserved, is a man of honesty and trust: he has marrow in his bones, his head is full of ideals and his heart is in the right place; the German housewife is the jewel of womankind the world over, the young German girl is like a flower, so gracious, beautiful and pure — the German home is a dwelling filled with discipline and solemnity, yet at the same time an abode of cosiness and intimacy. [H.A. Daniel, *Handbuch der Geographie,* pp.44-7.]

The gentleman who was usually so lively suffered a stroke, which ended his earthly wanderings in the most painless manner, plunging all of us into deepest grief. [Hitler, *Mein Kampf,* p.15f.]

II

And then he too touched her with his lips. And they went to join the others. And Helge Nuntius had experienced his first encounter with love. [R. Herzog, *Gesammelte Werke,* p.136.]

And she will direct her eyes to see. And will place her face to meet another. And lead her hands before princely poverty, and lead her feet over soft, sallow straw. And after wandering far afield will be received with balsam and mountain crystal. And will eclipse the very dust that clouds her garments. And will sort and make order from confusion, and will transform the staff, warm from her hands, into a fruit-bearing tree, a guardian shading the cradle of the world.

[R.M. Rilke, *Briefe und Tagebücher aus der Frühzeit. 1899-1902.*
p.353.]

Beautiful was Susette, the virtuous housewife, as noble in spirit as in
figure, and the fulfilment of all longing: the radiant god had found the
goddess. [W. Schäfer, *Die dreizehn Bücher der deutschen Seele,*
p.252f.]

A diadem of stars he wove into the goddess's hair, and chastely
hidden was the marvel of her limbs. [Schäfer, ibid., p.48.]

No shadow darkened the earthly path, safe in the august temple
the blazing flame gave light to Venus' altar. [Schäfer, ibid.]

You have made love, enjoyed love in your life. Sensual love. And
brutal images, or such that you once thought brutal, arise again. But
also sights so marvellously sweet. . .Which were as sacred as any
genuine moment of truth. Where it came over you like a harsh glare,
and yet it was radiant light, the light that forges souls and welds the
ore of the ego out of the dross. [W. Boelsche, *Das Liebesleben in
der Natur,* p.7.]

III

Storm, storm, storm, storm, storm, storm!
So echo the bells from tower to tower! [Eckart, 'Deutschland
erwache'.]

Bells must ring homage to this book. . .All German bells shall ring,
the bells in Mainz Cathedral and Berlin's *Gedächtniskirche,*[13] and
all the bells down the Rhine to Cologne, not forgetting the silvery
children's chime at Wiesbaden, which normally rings only on
Christmas Eve, yes, the children's chime especially. . .The invalid
lives, so does the thief and so does the whore, and worms that eat
each other live, the German needs room around him, the sun above
him and freedom within himself to grow to beauty and goodness.
[H. Grimm, *Volk ohne Raum,* p.9f.]

Splendid works of thoughtful devotion by our ancestors, who were
better than we are, once flourished in these prosperous regions; the
cathedrals of Freiburg, Strassburg, Speyer, Oppenheim, Mainz and
Frankfurt still reach for the sky with their towers or their ruins.
[Ph.J. Siebenpfeiffer, quoted in H. Pross, *Die Zerstörung der*

deutschen Politik: Dokumente 1871-1933, p.224.]

Come, hatred! Brave, vivacious wind in the sails of the soul, fan, blow, burn, yes, thunder and destroy if you can! You are my fortune and my pride, my guardian and my strength. Come, love! Breath of the gods and soul of the world, you are my shield and comfort in adversity and death. Sacred twosome, come both, be my comrades for life, and be today the strength of my heart, so that I may interpret and make known to the people all that is and ought to be. [Arndt, quoted in G. Kaiser, *Pietismus und Patriotismus in Literarischen Deutschland,* p.220.]

Firm as a rock I hold the conviction that one day yet the hour will come when the millions who curse us now will stand behind us and greet with us the German *Reich,* created by us all, regained through struggle, bitterly fought for, the land of greatness and honour, of power and glory and justice. Amen! [Hitler, *Sportpalast* speech of 10 Feb. 1933.]

The man from Freiburg, with his wife and child, acted piously towards Wilhelm, like the merciful samaritan, and after prolonged suffering Wilhelm regained his health and moved on towards Thun, from whence he came across the sea to his maid. [H. Clauren, *Mimili,* Berlin: p.69, quoted in Killy, *Deutscher Kitsch,* p.80.]

In this Europe I gave the centre to you, so that you would dwell therein, you were to be the heart and from this heart infuse the blood of living life into all other limbs of the great body. And because you were meant to be the heart, you were dear to me as my own heart and will be cherished by me forever. [Arndt, *Fantasien für ein Kühftiges Deutschland,* quoted in E. Weymar, *Das Selbstverständnis der Deutschen,* p.44.]

As the goddess of adversity took me into her arms and often threatened to break me, the will became resistance, and in the end the will was victor. [Hitler, *Mein Kampf,* p.20.]

Land of justice, land of light,
land of swords and land of poets,
land of free men,
and of comrades,

land of eagles and of lions,
land, death soon will stake his claim —
guard your rear, Germania!. . .
May the lord in mercy guard you,
dearest petal of the cosmos' flower,
peoples' bastion, star of honour,
send your ray from sea to sea,
let your word be near and far,
and your sword, Germania. [Strachwitz, 'Germania'.]

As the idealized virgin Germania led the people to guard the Rhine,[14] as, armed with shield and sword, in pictures and songs she led to battle, so she greets the returning heroes today. An august mistress, on her head the imperial diadem, in her hand the laurel and oaken wreath, she rewards great deeds, and welcomes the heroes at the frontier marches, at the gates of cities, and at the victory celebrations before royal castles. May Germania. . .also do her modest share in glorifying the victorious homecoming, and may God, who shed his blessing over our army departing, also bless its return. [*Die Gartenlaube,* Vol.1871, p.440.]

I saw the Rhine like that for the first time as we travelled along its silent waters towards the West to guard it, the greatest of all German rivers, from the greed of our ancient enemy. When the mild rays of the first sun broke through the tender veil of the morning mist and revealed the *Niederwald*[15] memorial to us, the *Wacht am Rhein*[16] roared from the endless transport train into the morning sky, and my breast felt like bursting. [Hitler, *Mein Kampf,* p.180.]

IV

As far as the eye can see from this exalted point stretches the glorious Rhine valley, that envied garden on which nature has poured forth the fullness of her blessings; but the German fatherland lies desolate. German hands have created orchards, vineyards, and gardens of breadfruit trees, lush meadows and parks bursting with exuberant green; but the soil of the fatherland lies waste. [Siebenpfeiffer, quoted in Pross, p.223.]

He looks past her, through the windows into the distance, where the blue mountains darken; into the forest, where the heart of nature beats in eternal becoming and decaying. 'We will live. Will live on.'

More even he cannot say. [Weinheber, *Sämtliche Werke*, p.903.]

And they listened to their blood as it sang in the silence. They rested close to each other, their breath and heartbeat one. Something surrounds them and yet comes from within them. This they feel in the changing tides of their passion urging them ever closer together. And it seemed to them as if it was still the same day as she sang to him and they became conscious of the marvel of their love. It was as if nothing of the pain of longing and anxiety for each other had intervened. Then they trembled softly, awed by the breath of eternal creation which ordained them to use the miraculous power of creating new life for the endless procreation of their blood, from the first dawn to the end of all being. [Zöberlein, *Der Befehl des Gewissens*, p.607f.]

There were many deeply moving, separate incidents which touched all those present. In the springtime. . .hundreds of people in the fullness of life went to their deaths under the flowering fruit trees of the estate, most of them unaware of their fate. This picture of becoming and decay is still before my eyes. [R. Höss, *Kommandant in Auschwitz*, in M. Broszat (ed.), p.129.]

V

But then we are greeted by the joyful song of healthy youth and joining those around the fire we feel steeped in the spirit that was the distant longing of our own youth. The sacred inner fire is still guarded almost like a secret, but 'already the flames are licking the sky'. [Stählin, *Der neue Lebensstil-Ideale deutscher Jugend*, p.31.]

Whoever knows the soul of youth will be able to understand that it is she who most joyfully receives this call to battle. [Hitler, *Mein Kampf*, p.10.]

A young man's life is dedicated to the purest service of the spirit of truth; thus it shall surge over the future of our people. Behold youth! The youthful pledge remains sacred to the man. [Fries, quoted in Pross, p.107.]

May all men of energetic will and independent thought join with the spirit of youth in secret union. May they honour as their lord and master the three-fold greatest spirit, the spirit of truth, which dwells as avenger and saviour amongst the people and guards against injustice with its court of vehme,[17] so that the spiritual in the people's lives does not expire. [Fries, ibid.]

Not only did he have to guide his German viking vessel of doom along its way with a forceful hand. He had to wrestle too with all the mental habits of another day. [E. Bölsche, *Was muss der deutsche Mensch von Naturwissenschaft und Religion fordern*, p.4.]

A fire had been kindled, which one day must forge the sword to win back freedom for the German Siegfried, and life for the German nation. [Hitler, *Mein Kampf*, p.406.]

VI

As for probably every other German, now for me too the most unforgettable and greatest time of my earthly life began. [Hitler, *Mein Kampf*, p.179.]

Oh youth! The early dreams of your life taught you to love and practise the joyful war-dance! Warriors! Those, however, who received this consecration, are urged by the twisting flames to feel the sacred earnestness of German community, German unity and oneness; they are exhorted to devote their united power to our people as a hortatory sign. [Fries, quoted in Pross, p.107.]

Preserve the Prussian proficiency of old, show yourselves as Christians by joyfully enduring your sufferings, may honour and glory follow your banners and arms, and set an example to the world in manly discipline and virtue. As you know, you are destined to fight a clever, brave, well-armed and cruel enemy. Once you encounter him, remember: no pardon will be given, no prisoners will be taken. Just as the Huns under King Attila made a name for themselves a thousand years ago which in tradition and in fairy tales still points to their ominous might, so must you reinforce the name of Germany in China for a thousand years to come, so that no Chinese dares ever again to even look askance at a German. Maintain manly discipline, may God's blessing be with you, the prayers of an entire people; my wishes are with you, each one of you. Open a path for culture once and forever! Now you may go. Adieu, comrades! [Wilhelm II, 'Hun speech', Bremerhaven, 27 July 1900.]

Out of the distance the sounds of a song reached our ears and came closer and closer, leaping from one company to the next; and then, as the hand of death was busily reaching into our ranks, the song came to us and we passed it on again: Germany, Germany above all, above all in the world. [Hitler, *Mein Kampf,* p.180f.]

Like millions of others, my heart too was overflowing with pride and joy, releasing me at last from this paralysing feeling. I had so often sung 'Germany above all', I had cried *Heil* at the top of my voice so often, that it seemed almost a belated act of grace, being permitted to appear as a witness at the court of the eternal judge only now, to see the truthfulness of these sentiments made manifest. [Hitler, ibid., p.179.]

His first question to the wounded closest to him had been whether the enemy was beaten. When the answer was an enraptured 'Yes', he asked, 'Where did he flee to?' To which an unfortunate who had lost both legs responded, 'To Paris.' Only then did he notice, grateful to the eternal Lord, that he still had both his legs; before him was Paris, behind him Germany and the field-hospitals, to the left Switzerland. His right hand paralysed by the fall, a bullet in his chest, a gash in his head, Mimili in his heart. [Clauren, *Mimili,* p.68.]

To fall? To die? To lie somewhere fatally wounded? 'And should a bullet hit me, I cannot wander home.' And then out of the very depths, resounding like an organ and somewhat uneasily: 'No more blessed death is there than to fall in the face of the enemy.' [W. Beumelburg, *Sperrfeuer um Deutschland.*]

Seven years ago today these fields witnessed the fatherland's most glorious victory, and the thousands who were sacrificed to the victory passed joyfully on to the fathers, for they died in the conviction that their blood was shed for sacred things, for the future of the fatherland above their graves. [Hase, quoted in *Weltgeschichte im Aufviss,* p.55.]

One day it will be said of the young men who fell, as can be read on the obelisk: They, too, died for the liberation of the fatherland. . . The eternal will judge us. . .who as Germans wanted the best for our people and fatherland, who wanted to fight and die. [Hitler, speech of 24 March 1924.]

When the death notices came in from the Western Front fathers and brothers exclaimed: Where there is much sadness there is also much honour; and mothers, wives and sisters were also consoled in their suffering by the realization that one leaf in the expanding wreath of German glory belonged to their little home. [H.V. Treitschke, 'Zum Gedächtnis des grossen Krieges'.]

We all fell for your glory,
be our wreath, Oh Germany!
My brother's tilling of the soil,
a fit remembrance of my toil;
My mother caring for her womb
cares for a flower on my tomb,
The boy so slim, the girl so slight
are my reward in mortal night.
Above my grave our land blooms on;
a heroes' grove, young, beautiful and strong. [W. Flex, 'Die Daukesschuld'.]

Wherever a German has fallen for his fatherland in the call of duty and lies at rest, and wherever the German eagle has sunk its fangs into the land: that land is German and German it will remain. [Wilhelm II, speech of 2 March 1898.]

But when the morning comes with colours bright,
I never count the men lost in the fight,
I only relish life and bless this martial fray,
proclaim it holy,
and believe again in man's triumphant day. [L. Ganghofer, *Eiserne Zither – Kriegslieder,* p.79.]

This was the German infantryman during the war. . .No gratitude can be great enough. An image: the highest peak of the Alps, carved into a face under a heavy steel helmet, calmly and earnestly surveying the German lands, along the Rhine to the open sea. The day will come. [E. Jünger, *In Stahlgewittern.*]

Millenia may pass by, but one will never be able to mention or speak of heroism without paying homage to the German army of the World War. Out of the mist of the past the iron front of grey helmets will then become visible, unwavering and unyielding, a symbol of eternity. But as long as there are Germans, they will remember that these were once sons of their people. [Hitler, *Mein Kampf*, p.182.]

VII

If, after centuries, [success] were to greet a certain person after all, perhaps a hint of the coming fame will irradiate his latter days. It is true that these great ones are only the marathon runners of history; today's laurel wreath touches only the forehead of the dying hero. [Hitler, ibid., p.232.]

And amongst them I will also consider that man who, as one of the best, dedicated his life to the awakening of his and our people with his poetry and his thought, and in the end his deeds: Dietrich Eckart. [Hitler, ibid., p.781.]

Struck by this first really pithy folksong in centuries, which has given wings to the present-day nationalist fervour, I had to visit him, the composer of the song which time and again will remind coming generations of their fathers' deeds, deeds which satisfied yearnings long nourished by the noblest nation. [*Die Gartenlaube,* Vol.1871, p.543.]

Schiller columns. . .fashioned by artistic hands. . .would then grace Marbach and other places. . .let us not be deprived of the necessary funds and of the sacred balsam [of this work] by the all-devouring, ever-hungry pouch of the dole. [J. Grimm, quoted by K.M. Michel in *Frankfurter Hefte,* p.888f.]

Bismarck was his name, Bismarck! And he filled the world with his name so that in centuries hence his heroic saga would still resound as Germany's ode of joy and celebration! One man was gone. Bismarck! Bismarck! And had to die, as all men die. The church clock in a near-by village chimed eleven. And the clock ticked on. [Herzog, *Hanseaten,* p.330.]

Standing on hallowed ground, hallowed by the footsteps of one of the mightiest of my ancestors, as even his enemies. . .called him while still alive, I grasp the goblet full of German wine, offered me by the city. [Wilhelm II, speech, Bielefeld, 19 July 1897.]

This day is blessed by the spirit of him who reposes at

Charlottenburg,[18] and by the spirit of him who lies in the
Friedenskirche.[19] [Wilhelm II, speech, Berlin, 18 Jan. 1896.]

The Emperor's insignia of former imperial glory, kept at Vienna,
seem to maintain their marvellous spell as the pledge of an eternal
community. [Hitler, *Mein Kampf,* p.11.]

The German Emperor has drawn his sword: the German people
march. May all good spirits be with them, may God himself, the
eternal arbiter of battles, bless them on their bloodstained path and
in their strenuous task! The devout prayers, the passionate wishes
of those who stay at home are with the brave men marching out.
[Verlautbarung des Alldeutschen Verbandes, quoted in A. Kruck,
Geschichte des Alldeutschen Verbandes, 1890-1939, p.70.]

First the beloved and revered royal couple in deep mourning, their
devoted labour and concern, and the plight of the fatherland. And
then immediately the joyous chase to the Rhine, across the Rhine;
and the king's expression becomes more and more cheerful, and his
army more and more exultant in victory, until the thousandfold
'Hurray!' upon entering Berlin and to God the Lord we sing praise.
[*Centralblatt für die besamte Unterrichtsverwaltung in Preussen,*
1863, p.595f., quoted in Weymar, p.152.]

The national anthem rang out tumultuously in the valley, the sacred
words: 'Rest secure, dear fatherland', intoned by a thousand voices,
resounded jubilantly down from the oak forest, more powerful in
their effect than ever before.[20] Then the Emperor walked up to
Moltke and, looking at him firmly but engagingly, offered the loyal
companion-in-arms his right hand; and his imperial greeting expressed
the gratitude of all who had co-operated, whether they were still
alive, or whether they had fallen in the struggle for the aim so
passionately gained. [F. Heyl in *Die Gartenlaube,* Vol.1883, p.551f.]

Today, Field Marshal, fate permits you to be guardian over our
people's recent rising. This, your marvellous life, is for us all a symbol
of the indestructible vitality of the German nation. German youth
therefore thanks you today. . .May this vitality also transmit itself to
the newly-opened representative body of our people. But may fate
also bestow on us the courage and determination which we sense
around us in this room, sacred to every German, as men who, fighting

for our country's freedom and greatness, stand at the foot of its greatest King's bier. [Hitler, speech, Potsdam, 21 March 1933.]

The quotations are loosely aranged around the central aspects of pathos in nationalistic language; these are simultaneously the central aspects of petit-bourgeois thought and sentiment, as will be extensively demonstrated in the following chapter. It will be sufficient here, therefore, to outline a few contours only.

Section I deals with the philistine's way of life from birth to burial, with his 'earthly wanderings'. The years of youth, beautiful years'; he leads a pastoral life, enjoys a sentimental marriage and presides over a sentimental household.

Section II demonstrates the 'sublime years of love', as 'he' blushingly traces 'her' steps and brings his goddess home to the shrine of sweet and heartfelt romance.

Section III emphasizes that above everything else church bells ring, that God dwells in the German fortresses of the Church; 'fervent devotion' shapes the metaphors and the rhythm of petit-bourgeois language; whether it be workday or holiday: one always has a German confession of faith at the ready! Germany — land of eagles and lions, guarded by the virgin Germania!

Section IV complements this Christo-Germanic religiosity with its cosmic counterpart: the philistine dwells in and is at one with the ebb and flow of nature; he feels it in the simmering of his bloodstream and knows of primeval causes.

Section V demonstrates his capacity for enthusiasm. If the fire is burning, 'the flame ablaze', then he is already 'brimming over', particularly if he is young; but he 'remains true' to emotions like this.

Section VI details the direction of the upsurge: war is the catchword! Up, to the joyful dance of swords! The expanding wreath of German glory is being woven.

Section VII deals with glory — with martial glory, of course, but also with poetic, musical, political and monarchical glory. All the ancients were pithy characters, especially the ancestors of the Emperor; the philistine cowers submissively 'at the foot of his greatest King's bier'.

The language of nationalistic pathos lacks imagination: analysis reveals only a handful of fundamental traits; these traits appear with such frequency and in such concentration that even otherwise acceptable formulations seem tasteless and shoddy; the stereotyped phrases are taken from a relatively small domain of language.

The central concept of the vocabulary is the word 'German'. This area of vocabulary also includes 'the most German of all rivers, the Rhine', often used as a superlative to the word 'German'. Germanness always 'radiates light'; the vocabulary built around the words 'light' and 'fire' represents enthusiasm, bravery, and the mood of a new beginning. The German is devoted to ideals and sacred values, to sublimity and grandeur. Within his scale of values important phraseological roles are played by magnanimity, loyalty, chasteness, virtue and purity. In him, toughness and tenderness come together in 'delightful harmony'; like a lion or an eagle, he leaps heroically into action, sword in hand; at the same time he is sensitive, mild, unspoiled, sincere, sweet and attentive to all the small things in life. He believes devoutly in God or the gods; much is sacred and eternal to him; his actions are sanctified; blessings hover above him, in temples, cathedrals and before altars — but he also approaches nature humbly. As he is today, so were his ancestors since primeval times. This is particularly evident from the definite bias towards using an antiquated mode of language.

Sentence structure is often made to fit the mode of the passage in the most exaggerated manner; slowly and broadly flowing sections of idyllic or idealizing character alternate with turbulent, restless sentences, constructions stressing the superlative, and repetitious and exclamatory sentences; there are many sentences implying desire and longing by the use of the subjunctive, and some alliteration is used.

Sentences using a present participle construction convey an air of solemnity. The climax of pathos is achieved through the use of series of 'ands' through the use of heaped-up genitives which precede the noun they qualify or through inversions in which the verb is sometimes predicative, sometimes adverbial addition, or else it prefaces the dative object, the accusative object, and at times even the subject.

If one were to fit all these characteristics into a sample sentence, such as might grace a style primer for patriotic orators, it would look something like this: 'May the young of Germany be noble and gracious always, thoughtful and proud, and at the same time remain conscious of the most holy regions of the German land whose marks and provinces were once settled by the devout and valiant race who were our ancestors.'

It is hardly difficult to disentangle this language, which ultimately stems from the Neo-Classical and Romantic periods. But to explain the fact that such superficial, trashy language was accepted not only by the public at large but by the 'cultured' classes in particular, is a rather more complicated undertaking. The lag in the development of 'taste' may be due partly to the fact that both the Enlightenment and the Revolution 'passed Germany by'; absolutist thinking therefore remained comparatively untouched, and the subservience common to everyday life became apparent in submissive mental attitudes and credulous belief in authority: one didn't dare to criticize the language used by such persons in authority as kings, princes, pastors, judges, professors, teachers, poets and philosophers. One could hardly do so, lacking any critical standards in the first place. German schools, in spite of their constant and monotonous emphasis on the 'music of the mother tongue', really valued linguistic education and criticism very little; at times they limited themselves to phobic feelings towards foreign words.[21] The discrepancy between word and concept, which was the root of the evil (one said 'free' and meant 'nationalist', one demanded 'culture' and gave 'the huns' as an example), could have been recognized if logic, clear-headedness and reason had been made the primary principles, that is to say, if one had declared a basic intellectual attitude and had adapted it so that it could be used educationally; but it was precisely this enlightened attitude which was decried by the petit-bourgeois as western decadence.

So it comes about that Germany's intellectual and historical record in the nineteenth and twentieth centuries confirms a Confucian saying:

If the language is not correct, then what it says is not what it meant to say; if what is said is not what is meant, no works will be accomplished; if no works are accomplished, morality and art do not flourish; if morality and art do not flourish, then there is no justice. If there is no justice, then the nation does not know which way to turn. Therefore, arbitrariness with words should not be tolerated. That is all that matters.

Notes

1. *Briefe über die ästhetische Erziehung des Menschen*, 1795.
2. 'Das Lied von der Glocke' (1799), an extremely popular ballad.
3. *Wilhelm Tell* (1804), Schiller's five-act dramatization of tthe mythical Swiss hero.
4. *Burschenschaften* were German student associations of nationalist persuasion.
5. *Die Horen*, named after the goddesses of the seasons, was the most important literary journal of the classical period of German literature. It appeared from 1795-7 and was edited by Schiller.
6. Fichte's intensely patriotic appeals to the German nation to resist the French (1807-8); they were intentionally polemical and do not reflect Fichte's profound philosophical achievements.
7. Schiller's birthplace in Baden-Württemberg.

8. Emanuel Geibel (1815-84), politically a nationalist and conservative, became the 'official' lyricist of German unification under Prussian auspices and received an annual pension from the Prussian King after 1843.

9. Gabriel Riesser (1806-63), liberal politician and journalist who, himself a Jew, fought for the emancipation of and equal rights for Jews.

10. The word 'Bildung' reflects formal education as well as taste, cultural milieu and character traits.

11. Hugo von Hofmannsthal (1874-1929), a gifted and sensitive Austrian poet who became an original and leading exponent of German Impressionism and Symbolism; his librettos to Richard Strauss's operas contributed to their success. Hofmannsthal was an early contributor to George's journal, *Blätter für die Kunst.*

12. Karl Kraus (1874-1936), Viennese editor, journalist and pacifist; he was also a gifted satirist, reformer and critic of culture.

13. The Emperor Wilhelm Memorial Church was destroyed in the Second World War, but the ruins were incorporated into a modern memorial.

14. To be sure as a German river, both banks German rather than merely the border!

15. Colossal monument commemorating the victories of 1870-71 between Rüdesheim and Assmannshansen on the right bank of the Rhine.

16. Popular song celebrating the Rhine as the bastion of Germany's guard against the enemy in the West.

17. The *Vehmegericht* was a secret court of laymen in late medieval Germany which provided for order in chaotic times. It was especially common in Westphalia.

18. The Berlin palace of the Prussian kings.

19. A Potsdam church constructed in the mid-nineteenth century; the burial place of Friedrich Wilhelm IV and Emperor Friedrich III.

20. From the 'Wacht am Rhein'.

21. *Fremdwörter*. The campaign against them became a mania under Hitler.

6 *SPIESSER* ROMANTICISM

Carl Schmitt once commented that 'all Romanticism is in the service of other, unromantic energies. It holds itself aloof from the laws of definition and determination, which means it becomes all the more malleable in the service of alien forces and authority.' This was of course not a characterization of Romanticism itself, but it described the result of its perversion. Romanticism was made to 'do service': selected elements, torn out of context, served 'alien forces'. Apolitical conduct, as exemplified by the escape from reality or the vision of a pure and beautiful inner world, was concealed by applying the label 'Romantic', thus leaving the road clear for the 'revisionists'; without being committed to it themsleves, they could make use of such culture as a façade behind which they could carry on their hectic and fateful political activity. While they propagated slogans like 'politics ruins character' and 'true culture is introspective culture', they themselves were distinguished only by their absolute want of character as well as any kind of culture.

The essential traits of Romanticism — its liking for the medium of the fairy tale, its partiality towards the unconscious, the imaginary, the weird, mysterious, childlike and ingenious, its longing for the infinite and its wistfulness — these traits can be fully appreciated only from the point of view of the 'paradoxical' and the 'universal' — both central elements of Romantic aestheticism. Romanticism has to be understood as an attempt to reconcile the contradictory, to grasp and embrace the totality of the human soul, of mundane and celestial reality; it is an attempt to reconcile feeling and *esprit,* heart and intellect, sentimentality and irony, day and night, reality and surreality, piety and nihilism, national literature and world literature. By isolating individual traits however, the equilibrium of this dialectical view of the world was completely destroyed; sentiment, subjectivism and irrationalism became overworked.

This ideologizing process was caused to a large degree by German philology: its 'fall from grace' did not just begin with the Third Reich. A few words from Thomas Mann may serve here as characterization, even though they properly relate to the Nazi era, the era in which epigonic Romanticism reached its zenith: he said one could speak of a 'philological ideology', a 'Germanistic Romanticism' and a 'devotion

77

to nordic values', which had their origin in the academic sphere and
which were impressed upon the German people by the use of an idiom
of mystic propriety and pompous tastelessness with words such as
'racial', 'folksy', 'fraternal' and 'heroic', adding an element of fanatical
cultural barbarism to the movement.

During the nineteenth and twentieth centuries, many men chose
the profession of university professor or high school teacher, not
because of an inner need or because of any artistic or intellectual
distinction, but simply on grounds of tradition or family origin. Any
rapport with language and poetry should demand acute intellectual
awareness and standards; since this capacity for critical judgement was
often absent, there was a widespread tendency to escape into
non-committal vagueness which did not require any particular thought;
rather, it merely involved the piling up of pompous phrases, which
were readily available as part of the 'cultural tradition'. This philological
jargon filled many volumes and was most aptly unmasked by
Tucholsky's[1] observation: 'You pierce it with the needle of reason and
all that remains is a little heap of bad grammar!'

The principal themes of Romanticism now that it had been
trivialized were to be found in the poetry of moonlight strolls, sylvan
solitude, and 'nightingale madness' (Heine). Some of these themes will
be discussed in more detail later. In the context of the original
Romantic movement, even in Eichendorff,[2] they must be seen
contrasted with knowledge of the demoniac world spirit and the
nihilistic imperilment of mankind. The joys of 'happy wandering' and
communing with nature in forests or on mountain peaks were
considered as alternatives to technology and urbanization and were
elevated to the level of cult worship (in Hitler's youth movement for
example) as representing an existence both foreign to and far from
reality. A provincialized pastoral kind of literature developed: it had
nothing of the spirit of realism found in Keller[3] or Gotthelf,[4] but it
had a lot of the mustiness of velour instead. It celebrated fruit, earth
and beast in mythical services and glorified the proud, defiant,
blond-haired eternally German heroes and maidens who ennobled their
race by copulating. All this was expressed in a language which
overflowed with hoary comparisons and metaphors, but which could
not hide the petit-bourgeois mentality revealed by grammatical and
syntactical slips. 'The Romantic vision was idea and eternity', observed
the prince of Nazi poets, Hanns Johst.[5] Under cover of Romanticism
a muddled idealism was being declaimed; here, too, mythologizing
chatter replaced the struggle towards a precise understanding of values.

With logic, morality was lost too: undefined 'values' and 'ideals', undefined 'grandeur' and 'exaltedness' can easily serve to conceal brutality, vulgarity and the longing to destroy. 'The sword then is more sacred tnan the pen' (Johst), the German oak more important than the man, fecundity nobler than the child; there was no lack of this brand of idealism in the Third Reich. Nietzsche had already observed in 1878: 'Where you see the ideal, I see the human, oh so human.' Robert Musil hit the mark when he noted that the demand for ideals governed education 'like a police authority controlling all expressions of life'. The literature of the nineteenth century, as far as it deserved to be considered serious writing — realism, naturalism, modernity *per se* — was almost completely banned from textbooks.

In the realm of political education the *Gemeinschaft*[6] was the romantic ideal — and to this very day that conception has blocked the acceptance of a reasonable concept of society in Germany. The concept of society *(Gesellschaft)* entails the realization that people within the framework of a state may well be opposed to one another, that pluralism is humanly just, that the state must harmonize this natural give-and-take and arrange it into manageable forms; in other words, it entails parliamentarianism, the role of the opposition, democracy as such. The concept *Gemeinschaft* flows from the idealizing, unrealistic notion that a people is a monolithic unit, bound together by blood and fate, 'the aboriginal creation of mysterious life'. It was the brute distortion of human individuality in favour of a romantic delusion. *Gemeinschaft* was considered good, 'society' evil; *Gemeinschaft* was organic, 'society' artificial; *Gemeinschaft* was God's work, 'Society' the work of men. Political education amounted to instilling into the young factually untenable and unnatural conceptions which could not stand up to reality, and which only prompted a further escape (idealism had already been the starting point) into an exaggerated idealism.

A people's community *[Volksgemeinschaft]* ! Youth trembles in deepest awareness when this word resounds, because it expresses the fusion of the most beautiful past with the fertile future, transcending the decadent bourgeois epoch. It is the holy will of youth which matures the ego and consummates it in the 'we'. For youth knows that the world of its fathers was destroyed by particularism after it had been progressively externalized and hardened by the liberal credo. [J. Lesser]

Only within the community can the people and the individual fulfil

themselves and intensify life. As far as this 'world of its fathers' was
concerned, epigonic romanticism had at the ready a number of clichés,
which gave an impressive and colourful picture of the 'German *Michel*'.[7]
the venerable ancestors, especially those of the Germanic and medieval
periods, were loyal, brave men (knights and nobles of Bamberg[8]) with
chaste women in the style of Dürer's secularized madonnas. Or they
were pious monks who built cathedrals with devoted passion, but cared
more for the Emperor than for God. Sometimes they were even dumb
fools like Parsifal; but almost always they were singers, *Minnesänger*[9]
or *Meistersänger*.[10] A glance at the picture sections of school textbooks,
history books, magazines for the young (especially *Jugendlust*[11]),
magazines for family and home, and even cigarette coupon catalogues
or the advertising circulars of the governmental milk distributing agency,
bear these observations out. This world of escapism and dreams was
quickly traversed: it consisted of the following areas: 'The age of proud
knighthood', 'The noble band of singers', 'German family life',
'Bourgeois society', and 'With God for king and fatherland'. In
caricature the German *Michel* appeared as a dreamer: he dreamt of the
German Middle Ages, of imperial grandeur and imperial greatness, of
Minnesänger, of many collections of funds for cloisters and barracks,
for Valhalla and for the completion of Cologne Cathedral. Ancient
German ideals accompanied one on the path to 'solitude'. To be
'lonesome' was the pendant of being part of the people's community
(Volksgemeinschaft). It was the other extreme of epigonic romantic
eccentricity; they

> follow him into the unknown as confidential companions, from
> the crowd they whisper comfort and counsel, appear as candles of
> the night in times of danger, and dwell in heart and mind, causing
> him to remember that he must always find the measure of life in
> harmony with himself and his people. [F.L. Jahn]

During the nineteenth and twentieth centuries the romanticism of the
German *Spiesser* underwent several transformations until, for the 'new
German man', the 'hieroglyphs of nature' (Philip Otto Runge[12]) had
become stuffed animals and the German *Erzgebirge,*[13] Romantic
paradox and universality had become *Rübezahl,*[14] and the 'blue
flower'[15] had become a gentian.[16] 'I sat recently in my cramped
study. . .amongst old books and stuffed animals, in our Erzgebirge,
where Rübezahl's German Romanticism hums between ice-age glaciers
and the scent of the gentian's blue flower lingers on' (E. Bölsche).

Notes

1. Cf. pp 200.
2. Joseph von Eichendorff (1788-1857), one of the masters of Romantic poetry.
3. Gottfried Keller (1819-90), Swiss-German poet and novelist; he is a prominent representative of realism in literature and of progressive political ideas too.
4. Jeremias Gotthelf (pen name for Albert Bitzius, 1797-1854), Swiss-German writer whose work is committed to giving a realistic portrayal of the peasant environment of his home.
5. Hanns Johst (b.1890), Expressionist dramatist who became president of the Reichsschrifttumskammer (National Chamber of Literature) in 1935.
6. Roughly translatable as 'community', but it has emotional, historical and 'blood' associations not usually implied in the English term.
7. 'Der deutsche Michel', the proverbial good-natured simpleton and victim of connivance.
8. An allusion to the famous medieval sculpture of a knight in Bamberg Cathedral.
9. Troubadours in medieval Germany.
10. Medieval masters of the crafts, poets and singers; they are celebrated in Wagner's opera.
11. A popular journal; the title translates as 'The Joy of Youth'.
12. Philipp Otto Runge (1777-1810), the initiator of German Romanticism in painting, he was influential as regards both his artistic and his theoretical work.
13. A German mountain range bordering on Bohemia which figures prominently in song and in tale.
14. Rübezahl is a figure from German mythology who guarded the mountain treasures in the Riesengebirge — a mountain range also bordering on Bohemia.
15. The 'blaue Blume' is a key symbol of Romantic poetry and its yearning for the eternal; it was first prominent in Novalis's *Heinrich von Ofterdingen* (1802).
16. The gentian is a very common Alpine flower which is often referred to in mountain folklore and song. It grows to considerable size and age and its roots are used in the distillation of a popular Schnapps.

7 IN THE ARBOUR

People of the Biedermeier epoch did not try to face reality, to form it or to resist it.[1] The difficult political, economic and social circumstances (the suppression of liberty, the social unrest during the progressing industrial revolution, the poverty of the people) stunted the spirit of the people; a general wavering of the will to act was noticeable. It is symptomatic that in Spitzweg's work long walls or thick bushes often block the path to the outside and guard against world and time.[2] Biedermeier man was an introverted type; he escaped into his inner self, as is evidenced by his efforts to preserve for himself an ultimate refuge of quiet and happiness in a chaotic world, or by his undisguised resignation. Action, passion, dedication and activity *per se* were shunned because he was convinced that everything was in vain anyway. This 'escape into the inner self' put man in danger of wasting away in philistine narrowness; it also promoted petit-bourgeois mentality and a 'German escapism, an anxiety-ridden kind of German philistinism, and a German brand of utopianism' (Friedrich List). The term Biedermeier was intended as a parody of philistine mentality; but it was coined only at the end of the epoch. At its core this period is genuinely inward-looking; it was sustained by an attitude to life drawn from the depths of melancholy, which can be criticized for political and economic impotence but not for dishonesty, optimistic superficiality or lack of reflection. The Biedermeier period was marked by genuine idealism which, however, in such an idyllic form was 'uncertain and dangerous'.

In his observations on idylls *(Über naive und sentimentalische Dichtung)*, Schiller pointed out that 'false' idyllic idealism is 'terrible' in its effects. Schiller saw the genuine idealist as leaving the world of nature and experience and withdrawing into another realm because he cannot find in reality 'what reason after all compels him to seek: the unchanging and the absolutely necessary'. The dreamer, on the other hand, observed Schiller, leaves the world of nature arbitrarily, 'to indulge in the selfishness of lust and the moods of fancy without inhibition'. 'He does not base his freedom on the independence from physical bondage, but on the absence of moral norms. The dreamer therefore denies not only human character — he denies all character, he is completely without law, he is therefore nothing and serves no purpose.' This, Schller noted, leads to an 'unending plunge into a bottomless abyss', it must 'end in complete destruction', because 'respectable' human traits are not fulfilled but perverted.

When this is seen in the context of nineteenth-century development, it means that the idyll lost its ethical-moral justification, that it was completely 'without law' and, in its 'denial of moral norms', became a 'ghastly idyll' (which will be discussed more extensively in another context). The escape into the self was now no longer a retreat from danger, an existentially felt imperilment, not even an excuse; it had become a principle of life — 'a nothing, and it served no purpose'. The dream was not a longing for the eternal, but a 'playing at dreams', no upward striving, but immersion in the delights of aesthetic or aesthetico-physiological enjoyment. Deep emotions and beautiful moods could now be attached to anything and everything without commitment: nature, the fatherland, war, God and religion, even crime, because, as non-committal traits which were assumed according to the mood of the moment, they did not ultimately matter to man. This existential innocence was passed on to the National Socialists as the heritage of the 'official' nineteenth century: 'inwardness', next to 'struggle', was one of the leading phrases of the Third Reich's cultural policy. Publicistic sense told Ernst Keil[3] around the middle of the nineteenth century that the time had come to satisfy the German bourgeoisie's need for inwardness with a journal which could also be read by the daughters of the house and at the same time would promote mores, manners, honour and the happiness of society. As a liberal of the year 1848 and a prisoner of the restoration, he initially kept the contents of his journal *(Die Gartenlaube)* free from conservative and socially regressive thoughts. However, the basic view of the journal, which — certainly unconsciously — used an empty and therefore false inwardness as a cultural façade, was essentially petit bourgeois and reactionary. So it was only a question of time before the characteristic nationalistic contents were added; and, true enough, soon the oft-portrayed Germania was at its masthead: a monstrous maid, robed in a Persian carpet with German imperial ornaments on it, wearing health sandals and bearing assorted weaponry, cast-iron laurel garnishing her forehead, and with a raised arm setting a crown on her flowing hair (it is interesting to note that her head was proportionally the smallest part of her body).

'The Lord's greetings be with you, dear people in German lands', so began the preface to the first issue, addressed to 'all friends and readers'.

When you sit surrounded by your loved ones through the long winter evenings at the comforting stove, or in the springtime, when pink and white apple-blossoms flutter from the trees and you and your friends recline in the shady arbour, then read this journal. It shall be a paper for the home and for the family, a source of information for the grown-ups and the little ones, for everyone who has a warmly beating heart and still enjoys the good and the noble. . .But above all it shall be pervaded by a hint of poetry as if it were the scent of a blossoming flower, and you shall be comfortable in our arbour, where you will find good German well-being that speaks to the heart. So try us out and God be with you!

It is true that this journal, with its mixture of 'Alpine dairymaids and archdukes lying in state, intrepid hearts and sensitive nymphs, of cultural history and Germanic myths. . .of dripping sweetness and mild stupidity' (Wachtel), was an extreme example of German inwardness. Structurally, other forms of inward 'mood' did not lag behind the family journal; they were even more dangerous because they could satisfy aesthetically higher standards and sometimes even represented 'advanced' literature. Carossa's[4] case can be mentioned in this connection. Carossa was no National Socialist. In a sense he could even be considered as a representative of intellectual resistance or 'inner migration'; prompted by his will to live 'inwardly', not to engage himself, to remain isolated from adversity and to rely on a world 'of values', his conduct is so much more revealing. His account of the First World War (*Führung und Geleit*) contains the characteristic sentences: '. . .As my patron I chose that Flemish peasant who calmly tilled his soil as the battle of Waterloo raged around him. I rarely had time to read in those days.' Carossa believed that he was at one with Goethe when he cultivated his own personality. On his mountain top overlooking Passau he led the life of a 'sage'. To the admiring pilgrim 'the matron of the house presented milk, nuts, crisply-baked bread and fresh butter from the farm' (Rothe). Whatever offered itself in the way of 'prudent experience' was rendered carefully in 'handicrafted' sentences: 'But how must the lover of the animal world feel when, on the sunny heights of Oberzell, he encounters the emerald lizard, reminding him of southern journeys.' Whether lizard or Hitler's fiftieth birthday (1939) — the style remained the same:

This birthday is one of those which Rilke called the 'emphatic' ones: the fiftieth. A mere congratualtion was unfortunately ruled out from

the very beginning as unsatisfactory; it was intended to be combined
with a clear confession to the Führer. . .I compiled citations from
some of my books. . .Whoever read them carefully must have seen
in them a courteous but direct appeal to the man whose decisions,
after all, governed our future. The good wishes at the end, therefore,
were also meant very sincerely. . .I sent my letter and soon forgot
about it.

What is embarrassing is not the birthday greeting to Hitler, which can
be understood in the context of the time, but the *post facto* stylizing
of the occurrence by the poet, how he captures in amenable plasticized
form what should have been characterized by a hard formulation,
revealing the tragic situation. Only a poet of German inwardness could
have displayed such tasteful tastelessness!

On the occasion of the festive final meeting of the Fifth German
Workshop of the Office of Literary Affairs *(Amt für Schrifttumspflege)*,
in 1938, Carossa presented his address 'Solitude and Community'
(Einsamkeit und Gemeinschaft); an anthology celebrating Hitler's
birthday in 1941 contained a hymn to Hitler by Carossa; during the
same year at Weimar he was chosen as the president of a 'European
writers' league'. Again: what terrible schizophrenia! Here is a German
writer whose whole being does not contain one shred of National
Socialism, who instead feels obliged to the 'old master Goethe', and
who yet let himself be used as a façade for the National Socialist state.
'No, my friends, we do not fear an alienation from Goethe, neither in
our German world, nor in the other!' Carossa said in his Goethe address
in 1938. Reality looked different: only a few miles from Weimar,
Buchenwald concentration camp had been erected — 'a sentimentally
cultivated worship of the past and the uninhibited, brutal will to power
thus created the new, typical fusion of Weimar and Buchenwald'
(Kogon).

Notes

1. The term Biedermeier refers to the cultural milieu of the years between 1815
   and 1848. Literally translated, *bieder* means honest, gullible or naïve; the
   very common surname Meier stands for everyman here.
2. Carl Spitzweg (1808-85), a prominent Biedermeier painter.
3. See note 3, p.40.
4. Hans Carossa (1878-1956), popular German novelist whose neo-Romantic
   style displays elements of an emulation of Goethe.

8 OF TRASHY TUNES AND COLPORTAGE

Where songs were sung 'one gladly stayed',[1] because the *Lied* was an expression of inwardness; it echoed the German soul. When the writers of the *Sturm und Drang* (Storm and Stress) period[2] and the Romantics declared folksongs to be the genuine pearls of poetry and artificially and artfully imitated the naïve genre of folklore, this was a distortion of the 'simple life', but it was so without political or philosophical undertones. The contrived folksong − in the sense of Schiller's definition − was sentimental and even as Goethe's *Heideröslein* never great poetry; rather, it was the natural abreaction of the human compulsion to sing, which is physiologically and psychologically completely justifiable. Now, whoever (in the terms of the popular song) 'was sent out by God into the wide world' so that he could 'sing his song' at the same time 'rode against France' and 'hugged and kissed his maid' because she happened to live 'on the banks of the German Rhine' or proved for other reasons to be a truly *German* girl. In epigonic Romanticism, beginning with the Wars of Liberation, the *Lied* was given an ideological interpretation: that of Germanness. A wide and muddy flood of *kitsch* heralded what was to be the joy of the German cultural philistine for one-and-a-half centuries: the sentimentality of his anthologies of domestic bliss and 'lyrical devotion', the empty cult of the fatherland and the chauvinism of fraternity songs, the twisted emotional world of his songbooks and school primers. It was an inexhaustible arsenal for ancient German heroes, smiling German girls with blonde braids, silver-flowing meadow brooks, the barrel-hall gaiety of old Heidelberg, moon-struck idylls, the 'Rhine-conscious' hatred of Frenchmen, and the rosy dawn of a brave Prussian morrow on horseback. All this emanated from societies and fraternities, from drinking bouts and flag-raising ceremonies, from classrooms and the texts of songs. Eventually it was aligned with and fitted to National Socialist doctrine. The *Reichstag* debate concerning the Enabling Law[3] was characteristically opened with a recitation by Göring, who delivered the Eckart[4] poem 'Germany Arise' in a brutally bawling voice. The House rose in respect. So it happened that political nadir and lyrical nadir coincided; but to the petit-bourgeois consciousness of many parliamentarians the poem at least may have appeared perfectly in order.

'The sacred language of our ancestors calls us: Up, you singers! and protect the German word!' The young poet who converted this demand into miserably poor poetry was personally an honest, brave and sympathetic man. Of Theodor Körner one of his editors writes that 'the finest leaf in his wreath of glory was his death', with which he sealed what he 'had written for his fatherland'. But this was not poetic fulfilment; it was poetic tragedy: Körner, who certainly would have developed poetically had he lived, was now fixed in a genre of post-pubescent lyricism of wine, love, the sword and German oak trees — all objects of patriotic rather than aesthetic reverence. Possibly he was already plagued by doubts in his youth 'whether he, who stood only at the beginning of his career, would be found worthy by the strict judges of aesthetic criticism to take a seat at the heroic banquet of immortality'. His advisers, publishers and interpreters did not share this doubt: his hero's death made up for all artistic shortcomings and inabilities. His example can therefore be seen as representative for many poets of the nineteenth and twentieth centuries.

The superficiality of the Biedermeier epigones was of a different kind. The place of lyre and sword was now taken by the embroidery frame and the lute. The great yellow moon no longer passed in romantic majesty over the silvery world, but twinkled down into the arbour of jasmine. The postillion bugling in the mild summer night no longer evoked longing and yearning for distant things. In the age of the petit-bourgeois parvenu the bugle's call courted the hand of the nobleman's daughter instead (Scheffel). Wherever one turned, one heard birds chirping, saw blossoming forget-me-nots, violets and young maidens who always blushed at the correct moment; after 'reading a manuscript of verses' Mörike[5] observed:

The sweet stuff without spunk and gut
has weakened all of my entrails!
It smelled, and I'll be damned if not,
of camomiles and roses frail.
I felt quite sick and drab and dull,
and looking for relief I ran
into the garden there to pull
a hearty radish, and began
to eat it 'til it ended,
and thus was fresh and mended.

The representative lyrical poetry of the Wilhelminian epoch was

concerned with 'security'; it was burdened with social and political
repressive complexes: 'inwardness buttressed by might' (Thomas Mann).
On the one hand, one dwelled on the nationalistic pathos of the poetry
celebrating the Wars of Liberation; on the other hand, one inclined
towards the sentimental idyll of epigonic Biedermeier lyricism. The
fusion of these two elements was not new in itself, but it had not been
apparent to this extent in the preceding decades. Holy anger or exalted
pride, or unrequited love together with the beauty of nature and
Wanderlust, presented in harsh or lilting melodies: even today these
elements have not completely faded from the programmes and texts
of singing societies. (See the popular songs: 'Far away at Sedan', 'The
Watch on the Rhine', 'The Trumpet of Vionville', 'The Chargers of
Gravelotte'.) Generations of singers were nurtured by the events of
1813-15 and 1870-71; the songs of 1914, 1933 or 1939 were only the
past warmed up.

The lute is silent, the shining swords are ringing.
Come forth my sword and join the happy tune! (Körner)

German people, most magnificent of all,
your oaks prevail but you have fallen. (Körner)

God is with us and we are with him!
The Lord alone be honoured!. . .
He himself has beckoned in our hearts:
People of Germany, arise! (Körner)

Sacred fatherland,
in hazard,
your sons stand
as your guard,
as perils threaten,
sacred fatherland,
see weapons beckon
in every hand. (Schröder)

Germany — sacred word, full of eternity,
transcending the ages, blessed be.
Hallowed are your lakes, hallowed your groves,
and the wreath of your silent heights,
down to the emerald sea. (Möller)

Witness the rosy dawn in the East,
The signal of freedom and sunlight.
We stand together in life and in death
may happen whatever is right. (Padun)

Now let the banners fly into the glowing dawn,
which leads us to new victories or consumes us in death. (Baumann)

As far as the trashiness of the contents and the low level of artistic
form is concerned, this form of lyric was during the past century and
a half truly 'ageless'. Even the rhymes (which are noticeable in these
examples only occasionally) speak for themselves: purple flow and
warming glow, fire and sire, dark night and fire bright, glowing sunrise
and heroic demise, glorious shine and sacred shrine, banners flying —
heroes vying, called by pride — measured stride, timelessness and
loveliness, sunlight bright and man's delight, candlelight and heart's
delight, cosy and rosy, silence and cadence, lilt and tilt, forlorn and
born, brave and behave, star and far, dark and hark, thief and belief.
Consequently, it was no longer difficult to fill up these lines with
standardized patriotic thoughts; the manufacturers of German song
could look back on a long tradition.

Even Stefan George, who did not use rhyme and whose artistic
niveau was entirely different, belonged to those who dwelled on the
poetry of 'security'. Like the young Rilke, who did not, however,
elevate the mistakes of his youthful lyric to the poetic principle of
his life, George tended to handicraft the human and even more so the
inhuman into lyrical concoctions with an attitude of sublime
indifference.

So I descend the marble steps,
a headless corpse rests in the centre,
my dearest brother's blood seeps down,
silently I gather up the purple train.

This 'aristocratic' pose clashes only outwardly with the piously
moronic chauvinistic idyll (as in the patriotic soldier song): in both
cases petit-bourgeois inhumanity, a mixture of sofa romanticism and
brutal brawling, is given expression, here in select, there in folksy
language.

Richard Wagner and Ludwig Ganghofer can be mentioned in this
context. Wagner often enough created music 'of the utmost geniality'

which transcended everything existing before him 'with its manifold rhythms, imaginative richness of sound and originality of instrumentation'. But extremely conventional passages very much lacking in imagination can also be found in his work. The Pilgrims' Chorus and Wolfram's songs in *Tannhäuser,* for example, are 'marked by a fatal resemblance to the musical heirs of Romanticism such as the "minor masters" of German male choral groups' (Mayer); similar passages occur in other operas; frequently it is precisely Germanness, German *Minne,* [6] German sensitivity, German popular character which are offered in shopworn music; music, however, which understandably pleased the petit-bourgeois mentality more than any other; the àlien, the abnormal, the un-German-seductive (as in the world of Venus) is musically much more perfect, even the work of genius. But viewed as a total work of art (and that is what he strove for) — music, poetry, settings, ideological attitude and aesthetic expression as a whole — Wagner's work is 'the trash of dreams', 'cheap mythology', 'which doesn't even contain ideological truth any more'.

The mixture of colportage and myth in Wagner's work was pointed out by Ernst Bloch: 'Karl May[7] and Richard Wagner shake hands.' Like the trashy popular tunes of epigonic romantic or Biedermeier lyricism, primitive emotions in Wagner's works are concealed by a veneer: dissatisfaction with the petit-bourgeois economic situation becomes the myth of the *Rhinegold,* philistine eroticism becomes Tristan's suffering, nebulous groping for the 'sublime' appears as the search for the Holy Grail.[8] The highest standards were set: the very depths of the human and celestial worlds were to be plumbed — but nothing was thought through consistently; the striving for truth becomes a pose. Wagner the poet, philospher, mythologist and theologian was in reality only a clever routinist, a Saxon Smart Alick who — at least in view of contemporary taste — knew how to use cardboard backdrops and theatrical machinery to such advantage that one might imagine oneself on horseback in a German forest or swimming in the Rhine. And he knew how to make the music sound as if it represented something 'exalted'. Wagner can be 'rescued' from himself and his public, which worshipped and still worships at Bayreuth, only if his works are de-mythologized and transformed — against his will but consonant with their true content — into what they really are, grandiose colportage: 'The forest's feathered friends chirping their picture-postcard tune, Siegfried traversing the wilderness of Kurdistan, carnival music resounding at Valhalla's gates, the cheap movie-house poster intruding on the stage with glaring scenes and

ominous destinies — the friend of the *Nibelungs* notes what is intended
but is not put out' (Bloch). Now it becomes clear why Ludwig II
sensed a congenial spirit in Wagner (Neuschwanstein and Linderhof
were architectural colportage!), why Hitler was so enthusiastic about
Wagner: both shared the petit-bourgeois joy in sensationalism and the
pleasure in backstairs romanticism. Even if slightly distorted (in a
medieval and architectural sense in the case of Ludwig, racially and
ideologically in Hitler's case), it could be experienced to the full by
great King and great *Führer* alike. The tendency to the maudlin in both
of them, as well as in their idol Wagner, is unmistakable. In Vienna
alone, Hitler is supposed to have attended *Tristan* between thirty and
forty times and to have seen Lehar's *Merry Widow* six times within six
months; in 1933-4 he re-read all of Karl May's books; then he had
arrived at the point where he could make colportage the principle of
pragmatic politics: 'sublimation' was no longer necessary.

Hitler's list of artistic pleasures somehow omits Ganghofer. His
work too was mythological in content: the religion and hymnal of the
forest.

> Oh susurrous, verdant bliss! You eloquent book of becoming and
> decay! You impenetrable mystery, you, the image of smiling lucidity,
> the well of all things that are healthy! Dwelling place of all beautiful
> and satisfied dreams! And every death in you is life renewed!

If 'silence in the forest' sounded a little chatty, the ideological basis was
brief and clear: beneath the canopy of the alpine forest, German people
(mountaineering types) find themselves and find the one they love
('And now she threw her arms around his neck, strong and hot, and
clung to his lips as if she drank new life from his kiss'); in the alpine
forest one becomes hard and capable of action: 'If one could only
exist as the forest: rejecting the weak and the low and only tolerating
what is strong and healthy. . .to rise so proudly beyond the shadows of
the depths and to seek the light, the sublime regions! If one only could!'

Ganghofer did: during the First World War he 'found himself
completely'; colportage had become reality; what the writer, sometimes
painfully, sometimes with greater facility, had wrested from his fantasy,
now offered itself to the war correspondent in real life: the girl, the
selective process of nature, the sun on the mountain tops, the eternal
melody, the lusty shout — no longer were they fiction, 'they were a
reality: Germany'. 'The beautiful girl's gaze is quite right. Beauty is a
sort of conquest. So truly gay and without care like this beautiful young

creature our German homeland shall be too.'

'In spite of the almost intolerable hardship, this war is a mineral
spring for our people.' The voice of the crown prince rose.
'Everything that is good and capable of living is being strengthened
by it, the weak are being revitalized, the helplessly sick are being
blown away.'

When this evening I wandered home amidst roaring rainstorms to
my cramped cottage through the dark night I saw the brilliance of
our German sun, sublime and beautiful.

Everywhere one can see the ancient trees growing, and the rustling
in the air becomes an unending melody in the style of Richard
Wagner.

In my soul was a passionate cry: 'Fly, fly on, you German brother
up there'. . .He disappeared into the brilliance of the sun, which
always was too bright for my eyes. I had to whisper two words:
'German flight!' From these syllables and their images, proud and
hopeful thoughts grew in my mind.

Now Ganghofer too plucks the 'iron lyre' mightily: the German song
wells up in him, a fountain of health, as it did of old in 1813 and 1870:
'O sacred war! Creative power!'. . .'A slender boy, his blood so young,
the bullet met him, met him well./The helper, nurse and doctor stand,/
to witness a German death.' Whoever read these 'soft and yet hearty
lines, these poetic and yet realistic verses', had to feel that here love of
the fatherland and holy anger 'had created verses flowing from the
depths of the soul'; he had to feel that here the spirit of the German
song rang forth again — 'if he was a German', he could 'find his soul
again' here *(Augsburger Zeitung).*

Notes

1. Popular saying: 'Where there is song one gladly stays — bad men do not sing.'
2. A creative early period of the Classical age, corresponding in time to Goethe's
   and Schiller's youth; its most characteristic expression is to be found in their
   youthful works.
3. The 1933 Law granting Hitler four years of what amounted to dictatorial
   power, periodically renewed.

4. See note 2, p.43.
5. Eduard Mörike (1804-75), one of the truly great German lyrical poets whose
   life and work reflected the tensions of the conflicting forces in nineteenth-
   century life.
6. Courtly love in medieval Germany.
7. Karl May (1842-1912), enormously successful German writer of adventure
   stories with North American and Near Eastern locales.
8. A wide, deep dish which was the object of a mystic medieval cult. The saga
   of the Grail draws on Christian and Germanic traditions and figures
   prominently in some European literatures, including German literature and
   Wagner's musical dramas.

9 SENTIMENT AT HOME

Biedermeier life was carried on mainly in the home. It is not surprising, therefore, that during this epoch a particular emphasis was placed on interior decoration, especially of the living-room. Painters portray interiors time and again, and poets give us detailed descriptions. When Adalbert Stifter in his *Studien* lets his hero dream of a home, he fills it with furniture which is 'rare, massive, simple, sharply edged, and lustrous'.[1] The living-rooms do not give an impression of ostentatious splendour — no wallpaper, but bright whitewash and painted cornices; the wooden chairs often have curved legs and with their broadly indented backs offer comfortable seats. Lots of pictures decorate the walls; the sewing table is the permanent preserve of the housewife; the sofa is worn from much use; the bureau serves to hold an extensive private correspondence; the china closet contains a number of memorabilia. As the focal point of family life, the living-room is furnished pragmatically and sensibly.

The respectable parlour in the 'velvet era' *(Plüschära)* was ornamental, the room to show off — it was overstuffed, overloaded, overfurnished. 'Inwardness' became demonstrative: it was ostentatiously turned outward. 'Here is our peaceful, homely comfort' — and everyone shall see it! Tiny window panes and heavy curtains over the windows, and yet the urge to show off: a cult of prestige! This explains the preference for glossy things: silk, satin, patent leather, gold frames, gilded stucco, tortoise shell, ivory, mother-of-pearl, and assorted meaningless decorations. It was a world of substitutes — a world of pretence — with painted tin posing as marble, plaster of Paris as alabaster, and papier maché as rosewood. The exotic palm tree in the bay window was made of paper, the appetizing arrangement of fruits consisted of wax or soap; sofa, easy-chairs and curtains suffocated with frills and velours (Friedell). The garden was drawn into this world of illusions as well.

> The sloping garden was liberally decorated with dwarves, mushrooms, and assorted cleverly imitated ceramic animal figures; a ball of mirror-glass rested on a pedestal, reflecting the face of the beholder in various funny ways. Even an Aeolian harp, several grottoes and a fountain were there, which threw artful jets of water in the air as

silver fishes tumbled in its basin [Thomas Mann] .

The garden dwarf was no longer only playfully ornamental, but filled an ideological need: here prevailed loyalty and sincerity, diligence and idyllic bliss! The artificiality of this living-room 'culture' was greatly promoted by a wide divergence between form and 'content'. People's homes were dolls' houses or 'parlour dream-worlds', often copied from artists' studios and designed for people who had often become hardened and who well appreciated the realities of the founding years of Bismarck's *Reich* and of the age of imperialism. The exclusion of technology from the home up to the turn of the century, even though people were literally obsessed by the idea of progress, is another revealing symptom of bourgeois and petit-bourgeois romanticism. Inside the house the photographs were placed on an easel and one crept off into Old German shadowy alcoves and Wagnerian love-grottoes; the safe was hidden behind the gobelin curtain. The outside world was far away, 'not even the passing clouds could be made out through the profusion of greenish light' (C. Gurlitt). Plaster of Paris imitations of the *Venus de Milo* and medieval madonnas were the deities of the house. But outside another deity prevailed:

Do you see the little white church amongst the raven-black cypresses over there? That is the bygone age, still reaching down into our days. The small yellowish tower with the tiny cupola holds a bell, green with age: it rings with that love which is not of this world. But look more carefully. The cross, reaching from the cupola into the boundless miraculous blue, extends into a long, suspicious point. A lightning conductor! The two-fold insurance of the modern day: above the mystic cross the metallic rod, taming the rays of heaven with the insights of physics, of science. . .The old and tarnished bell may call, but when the black storm cloud rises like a bird of prey and menaces with her glowing fangs. . .the light conductor is stronger − it is the cross of *our* day. . .' [Bölsche] .

The National Socialists adopted the style of the velvet era with few alterations. Göring's Karinhall[2] with its reflections of peasant and hunting lodge styles ('Two equine heads adorn the gable, mythology guards the parlour' [Bloch]), Hitler's 'Brown House', his Chancery (a mixture of plushness and classicism) and his villa at the Obersalzberg (with touches of Bavarian folksiness) set the tone. So we find Göring thinking and meditating at Karinhall in a genuine German hermitage, an imitation of Saint Jerome's, with even a young lioness crouching at his feet. Or we see Hitler as he 'planned for Germany's greatness and future' and 'wrestled with himself' seated facing the 'eternal mountain world', surrounded by chintz curtains, peasant furniture and secularized religious pictures, or else amidst the brocade world of Berlin. In its pretended authenticity and inwardness (that is, in its aesthetic as well as architectural perversion), this milieu resembled the world of the *fin-de-siecle* philistine, who some mornings returned from the bordello to an architectonically 'most sacred' grotto of marital bliss. It also evokes recollection of those concentration camp guards who, 'after the day's labours and pains', returned to their homes, a ring of idyllic dwellings surrounding the camp. 'My wife had a paradise of flowers', Rudolf Höss writes of his villa at Auschwitz. 'In the garden the children always had assorted animals which were brought by the prisoners. . .Or they splashed in the garden pool. Yet their greatest joy was when Daddy could join them. But Daddy only had little time for these joys of childhood', because he had to gas Jews. 'My wife time and again urged me: Don't always think of your duty, think of your family too.' It is true that Höss does not provide a description of the interior of his house, but the life-style of many other National Socialist philistines of varying stature is well known: it was 'snug and serene' and always polished; in the living-room there were many knick-knacks and a potted lime tree, a representative bookshelf including Goethe, Binding[3] and party pamphlets; glass frames held yellowing photographs and more recent ones (from the days of conscription and reserve duty), 'Loyal and honest forever',[4] and hound the Jews!

Notes

1. See note 4, p.15.
2. Göring's pompous residence near Berlin, which was named after his first wife.
3. Rudolf G. Binding (1867-1938), lyricist and storywriter who was influenced by D'Annunzio and wrote lyrical love stories, though he did use martial themes too.
4. See note 1, p.43.

The demands of reason deprive the petit bourgeois of his philistine
contentedness; escaping from enlightenment he seeks his support in
Mythos; but the *Mythos* to which he clings is false: confused rambling
takes the place of religion. Trusting in the sublime, he descends to the
vulgar; from nationalism the path leads to bestiality; brutality,
initially a rhetorical gesture, becomes reality in the end.

The intellectual becomes an anti-symbol; the 'evil West' gives
birth to democratic decadence. Professors pose as heroes: humanism
is misrepresented as mundane barter, socialism as the corruption of
the people. To be conservative and German really means to be
reactionary; leadership becomes a label for élitist rowdyism; man
breaks out of the confinement of humanism and degenerates into a
beast of prey. The petit-bourgeois misses every opportunity of leaving
the wrong path. *Logos* capitulates before the *Mythos* of race, blood
and nation; the word 'German' gilds everything.

Yet the breakthrough of the instinctive does not even create 'noble
beasts'. The philistine's cherished dream — the Third Reich — was an
emporium of 'vulgar demons'.

1 REPULSIVE INTELLECTUALS

Immanuel Kant's definition of the Enlightenment pointed to the great possibility of human self-realization:

> Enlightenment is man's emancipation from his self-inflicted nonage. Nonage is the incapacity to use one's reason without guidance by another. This immaturity is self-inflicted if its cause lies not in a lack of intelligence, but in a lack of will or courage to use it without the guidance of another. *Sapere aude!* 'Dare to use your own reason' is, therefore, the axiom of the Enlightenment.

Before the celebration of Kant's two-hundredth birthday in 1924, the Minister of *Kultur* was visited by a delegation of student fraternities from Königsberg University, who still adhered to the practice of duelling; the delegates declared that if the main speaker at the celebration should think of making reference to Kant's work *On Eternal Peace,* quiet could not be guaranteed; they hinted that disturbances would be initiated.

The 'public use of reason', demanded by Kant, had never been sufficiently recognized as a guiding principle in Germany. In a way, the German people was unable to make real contact with its own intellectual tradition; even the greatest democratic reforms of the nineteenth century, the work of Freiherr von Stein, remained moored in theory. Germany was and remained a 'belated nation' (Plessner); the 'joyful age of the Enlightenment' (Dilthey) did not receive 'official' response here. Whereas in other countries, especially the USA, France and England, the Enlightenment inspired successful efforts to make man into a rational and political being *(animal rationale* and *animal politicum),* in Germany there was a flight, to use Goethe's words, into 'passion, intoxication and lunacy'. This was represented as the objection of sensitivity to the coldness of reason: as if, correctly understood, the Enlightenment negated the importance of the irrational and the emotional; as if Kant had written only a *Critique of Pure Reason* and not also a *Critique of Practical Reason.* (After all, German Classicism and Romanticism had already contained the corrections called for by the trivia of false Enlightenment.) The Enlightenment demanded of course that the emotions should not be emancipated, that

intellect and emotion remain mutually (!) bound, that in the realms of
public life, the state and society, man, as a political animal, should be a
thinking being governed solely by reason; from these spheres emotion
had to be rigorously excluded. But particularly in these areas *Logos*
was replaced by *Mythos* — 'a *Mythos* of life, which created a new type
of man' (Rosenberg); this was not a genuine *Mythos,* but a spiritual
confusion under that name and distinguished by only one reliable
criterion, that illogicality and anti-rationality prevailed.

'Certainly, the time will come when man will do the good because
it is the good' — but it did not come. And even Lessing, who like
Schiller was convinced that man could be educated to perception,
insight and reasonableness, was rejected and ridiculed along with the
Enlightenment. The voice of the rationalist meant little to the
nineteenth and twentieth centuries: ever since the appearance of
epigonic Romantic writings such as Arndt's, the German character had
been identified with emotion, and intellect had been regarded with
contempt as its antipode. 'Intellectual' became the fashionable
curse-word of the anti-rationalists, used to ridicule man's attempts to
emancipate himself. The highpoint of anti-rationalism came during the
Weimar Republic: the murky waters seeping from all sorts of private
myths and groups united to form a mighty stream; the intellect was
the 'adversary of the soul': this was the characteristic formulation in
Ludwig Klages'[1] teachings. Wilhelm Stapel[2] observed that man's soul
withered once he immersed himself in the world of the intellect;
rationalism was sweated by the highly strung whereas *Mythos*
blossomed from the blood (Hussong). The Third Reich 'finally took
care of the intellectuals'; for the sake of racial convenience they were
simply equated with the Jews: 'repulsive intellectuals with long hair,
horn-rimmed glasses and a five o'clock shadow' (Leers). The former
Bavarian Minister of Culture Hans Schemm informed Munich professors
that from now on it was not important whether something 'is true, but
whether it is in keeping with the direction of the National Socialist
revolution'. That National Socialism 'did not lean towards abstract,
dry thought' was well exemplified by Hans Schemm. Though he claimed
to have read 'Praxiteles and Sanskrit, the sacred book of the Indians' in
his youth *(sic!* an authentic phrase from one of his speeches), he was
sceptical of art and science, especially of their so-called 'objectivity':
'After all, what is reason', he asked. His answer was: 'Logic, calculation,
speculation, banks, stock markets, interest, dividends, capitalism,
careers, fraud, usury, Marxism, Bolshevism, crooks and villains.' With a
convincing 'definition' like this Schemm was a loyal servant of his

master: according to Hitler (in *Mein Kampf*) man should never fall for
the lunatic idea that he had graduated to become master of nature; man
could never free himself from his instincts. (In the jargon of non-
commissioned officers this meant: leave the thinking to horses — they
have larger heads!) The 'Jewish cult of the intellect' destroyed a people;
and running parallel to this political, ethical and moral contagion of
the people was the physical poisoning of its body. Hitler therefore
went on to concern himself with the danger of syphilis, which was a
greater threat to the National Socialists than intellectualism: the pure
German state must 'not look for the infusion of mere knowledge, but
should pay attention primarily to the raising of totally healthy bodies'.
A people of scholars, 'if these are physically degenerate, weak-willed
and cowardly pacifists', would not conquer the heavens; a rotten body
was made not in the least aesthetically more pleasing by a brilliant
intellect; boxing was still the best exercise. Since the National Socialist
was convinced that he who thinks doubts, he had to feel loathing for
the thinker and sympathy with the brawler. Karl Follen, one of the
Black Knights of Giessen at the beginning of the nineteenth century,[3]
expressed the same sentiment even if in a much more sublimated way
than Hitler: 'I prefer a good sporting song to all your Fouqués and
Goethes'; and the names of the two poets were supposed to stand here
for Romanticism and Classicism.

Notes

1. Ludwig Klages (1872-1956), philosopher and psychologist who was
   preoccupied with the 'methaphysics of immanent life forces'.
2. Wilhelm Stapel (1882-1954), conservative editor and journalist.
3. Karl Follen (1795-1840), poet and politician and a radical leader of the
   student movement. He was forced to flee to the USA where he died in an
   accident. The Black Knights of Giessen were a group of radical liberals in
   Hesse during the post-Napoleonic period.

2 WESTERN DECADENCE

Writing during what he called the 'Medieval Age of 1932', the left-wing writer L. Bauer complained of a 'dullness and stupidity in the air'; 'it is advisable to read Voltaire. It is even more advisable to live Voltaire!' That was indeed a naïve wish; to prescribe France as therapy was impossible for two reasons, which in the end were based on the same objection. From the earliest times France had been Germany's arch-enemy, but especially since Napoleon's invasion (French chauvinism was of course completely on a par with German chauvinism), in addition the French were 'by nature dependent on reason, full of deluded vanity and pig-headed craftiness' (Arndt); they did not possess the depth of the German soul; Germany's foreign neighbours lacked, for example, 'morality, discipline and respect, especially for marriage' (Funke); 'an honourable relationship between a man and a woman' was impossible in France. Speculative thinking, profundity, inwardness, earnestness, reverence, domesticity, idealism and constancy were Germanic; exact science, superficiality, extraneousness, irresponsibility, frivolity, mass society, sociability, materialism and fickleness were French (Daniel); the German language was noble, whereas French was 'trivial, alien chatter, mere blabbering and twaddling'. Leadership was German, parliamentary democracy French. In Langbehn's *Rembrandt als Erzieher*,[1] Paris is seen as the city where 'the good blood has dried up. No wonder, then, that a man like Zola is drawn to this capital of Celto-romanism, this city of the *demi-monde* and of democracy; here, moral and political disease complement each other.' There was no reason to envy the French the ideas of 1789. These were 'flesh of their flesh and bone of their bone. We have a maginficent substitute for them anyway: the ideas of the Wars of Liberation' (Wahl). The Enlightenment had been the concern of the West, observed Moeller van den Bruck;[2] even after the war, a spiritual Western Front ought to be maintained against the poisonous fumes drifting over from France.

Culture prevailed on the German side, civilization on the side of France. With this impressive formulation Thomas Mann, in his *Betrachtungen eines Unpolitischen* (1918), summed up one century of hatred of France. His altercation with the worldly spirit of France was simultaneously an altercation with his literary brother Heinrich, who had been 'infested' by Western ideas.[3] Thomas Mann saw the

Frenchified literature of civilization as always preoccupied with humanitarianism; he considered that this led to a cheapening of the world and life. For Thomas Mann it was the artist's task to preserve life's heavy and earnest accents. The literature of Western-oriented civilization aimed at politicizing and intellectualizing; the culture-conscious German, however — and this had indeed been the attitude of the petit-bourgeois for decades — knew that politics do not make man more human. Overlooking the truly civic-minded attempts at reform, such as the work of Freiherr von Stein and the men of the Paulskirche,[4] the unpolitical philistine ('politics ruins the character') with his pseudo-aesthetic polish ('only poets leave lasting accomplishments') was made into an ideal. Simultaneously with a repression of a good deal of the German literary tradition, the artist was turned into a mystagogue yearning for death, an intoxicated and dreamy sensualist: the German Tristan versus the French Voltaire. Or else he became the intrepid knight-at-arms despising peace: the Siegfried-like figure of Thomas Mann facing the pacifist decadent Romain Rolland!

> I found it superficial, maniacal and childish to attempt a cure of the world from the position of armed peace; I do not believe that life ever can be peaceful, nor do I believe that our beloved humanity would appear appreciably more attractive living in eternal peace than under the sword. It seemed to me that as long as humankind does not stroll about in white robes, waving palm branches and exchanging literary kisses of brotherhood, now and then there will be war on earth; as long as men have blood in their veins, and not soothing oil, they will want to shed it now and then. Thus, I could not call myself a pacifist.

In spite of these martial tones, Mann's conception of the artist did not match the philistine's in everything: he was too much the Bohemian, too little at home in the bourgeois parlour. The philistine saw in the artist above all a man divorced from the intellect, basically 'positive' and motivated in everything by his good-hearted German soul. He created nothing with his intellect, but everything with his backbone: artists were men who functioned as 'emanations of the people', who 'reached for the stars and brought back eternal values, and provided the organism of the people with spiritual bread' (Shcemm). It turned out that particularly third- and fourth-rate writers were the most successful caterers to the nationalistic instinct — but the 'great' ones served too, after their greatness had been successfully interpreted away.

On the other side of the fence were the 'thinking' intellectual writers, contaminated by Jewish spirit or Jewish blood, who in 1933 were driven into emigration immediately and whose books were proscribed or burned.

Heinrich Heine was the incarnation of all the evils: he was an intellectual, he was left-wing, in short, he stood as an anti-symbol. The struggle against these evils reflected the limitations of the critics. This poet was universalistic; he was ironical; though he was sensitive, he also had intellect; he was liberal, opposed to the *Spiesser,* and he lived in France. Such types, who were frequently identified with the sceptical and ironical Mephistopheles, always had to appear to the enthusiastic Faustian German soul as alien, that is, French.

The hatred for Heine was especially intense because he was not only a total alien, but with his warm sensitivity and often almost trashy sentimentality spoke straight to the petit-bourgeois heart; also, he was not at all a convinced democrat, which made him even more sympathetic; yet he was still an enemy because he refused to make this warm sensitivity and sentimentality absolute, because he did not submit himself to the ocean of feelings but instead made sobriety his principle and in addition was a fighting representative of enlightened humanity. 'Heine is torn by a peculiar discord. It is almost as if part of the Germanic spirit within him strives to reach loftier heights – only to have the Jew suddenly pull him down again by the legs into the morass, where he wallows with pleasure and ridicules all ideals' (Fritsch). For the many editors and interpreters of 'noble poetry' who let themselves 'be woven by the tender and invisible fingers of art into a magic cloth', for whom the reading of a poem became a 'sacred hour at home' or who 'experienced poetry with elemental abandon' (sometimes, of course, the poetry had 'such a delicate elfin body' that it did not respond on request to the reader's caresses, the chaste creature!), for all these people, to whom lyric was like 'the ring of a distant bell' ('which on its extended journey soaks up the melody and essence of nature, not telling us from whence it comes, and whether it is the bronze bell that speaks or the mouth of the world, tasting the sweetness and the power of the verses'), for all of them Heine's poems had to fall utterly flat and, with their alienating and disillusioning effects, at best appear as 'elegant French pleasantries' (Gregori). The fame of a man like Heine, observed Heinrich von Treitschke, 'was only possible in a generation which had, over alien dreams of brotherhood, irresponsibly forgotten the ancient conflict between Aryan and Semitic feeling'.[5] In his *History of German Literature,* which is one of the worst and most stupid emanations of the national anti-Semitic movement, Adolf Bartels said: 'Heine is Jewish. More than any other art form, lyric is the expression of a people's character and soul. It is therefore impossible that he could be the greatest German lyricist together with or next to Goethe.'

> While the rhymes of Eichendorff have an air of restraint and scope, Heine's rhymes are pointed, sharp, almost hoarse. . .Listen to the enervation in the phrase 'ich weiss nicht, was soll es bedeuten' [the first line of the *Lorelei* song] and the words will immediately prompt a shrugging of the shoulders and an extension of the palms in a typical Jewish gesture [Stapel].

For the National Socialists, Heine was an alien with 'shallow roots' who, 'falling a victim to sentimentality, experienced emotions of joy and pain only superficially' (Arp). The editor of the *NS-Büchmann,* 'the German people's treasury of quotations', apologized for 'Heinrich Heine's continued presence in the chapter "Selections by German Writers", adding, 'this does not mean that the editor considers him part of German literature'.

The nineteenth century was marked by a craving for monuments; but when in 1892 the erection of a monument to Heine was proposed, no German municipal administration accepted the offer; even Düsseldorf, Heine's home town, refused. Later on, however, a rather undistinguished memorial plaque was put up in Frankfurt, 'the city contaminated by Jews'. The struggle over the monument, which went on for decades, showed on the one hand the impotence of Heine's admirers, on the other hand the power of his philistine enemies, who did not 'want to see their most sacred feelings trampled underfoot by Jewish aliens'. A Heine memorial was considered a 'challenge to Christian and monarchical', later to 'national and Aryan Germany'; whenever plans were made to realize such a project, the 'pro-German' public was mobilized against it. When it became known in 1926 that Heine's grave in Montmartre was to be decorated, *Der Stürmer*[6] referred to the 'Jewish pig in Montmartre': 'The German Republic reimburses the preservation of a grave in which a rascal of the first order is rotting.' The controversy over Heine therefore provides revealing insight into the soul of the philistine, who attacked everything rich in intellect, especially if it was 'foreign', with downright rabid hatred.

Notes

1. See note 4, p.40.
2. Arthur Moeller van den Bruck (1876-1925), conservative writer; author of *Das dritte Reich* amongst other works.
3. Heinrich Mann (1871-1950), novelist and biting critic of German society.
4. The Paulskirche in Frankfurt was the site of the Constitutional Convention in 1848-9.
5. Heinrich von Treitschke (1834-96), gifted and prolific writer, historian and professor whose writings and lectures at Berlin University had a strong nationalistic bent with racial overtones; they enjoyed great popularity.
6. *Der Stürmer* was a virulent National Socialist weekly, published from 1923 on by Julius Streicher (1885-1946), a former teacher and propagator of anti-Semitism; he was *Gauleiter* of the Nazi party in Franconia from 1924-40 and condemned to death at the Nuremberg war crimes trials.

3 PROFESSORS AND HEROES

The National Assembly of 1848 in the Paulskirche was called the 'Parliament of Professors'; liberalism was alive, especially in the educated levels of society; sociologically and economically it could find roots only in a democracy of distinguished men. But a dangerous ossification was already becoming apparent: the younger generation, influenced by the students' associations and the gymnastics movement, stood aside, they placed German unity before German liberty. The ideas of Freiherr von Stein, who had wanted to replace a 'dead sense of duty' and 'slave-mentality' with civic awareness, were still circulating; a scant, even if fairly influential section of academics was still quite conscious of Kant's teachings on the state of laws, of Hegel's philosophy of the state as the realization of the moral idea, and Humboldt's discourses on the limitations of the state's functions; but after the failures of 1848 many of these middle-class people made a compromise with power. National liberalism distanced itself from the 'shallow Enlightenment'. Prussia, as the 'precursor of national unity', now became the prototype in its domestic conservatism too; in the end even 'the old liberalism', the 'last bastion', capitulated before the 'compulsion of Bismarck's *Realpolitik*'.

Bismarck declared in a speech before the Prussian Chamber of Deputies *(Landtag)*: 'I seek the honour of Prussia in the principle that Prussia, above all other considerations, should remain aloof from any shameful connection with democracy.' In a speech before the budget commission of the Prussian *Landtag* on 30 December 1862, he asserted: 'Germany does not look to Prussia's liberalism, it looks to Prussia's power. . .Prussia must gather and retain its energies for the opportune moment, which has already been missed several times. . .The great questions of the day are not solved by speeches or decisions of majorities. . .but by blood and iron.'

The constitution of the North German Confederation (and its almost identical successor in the Second Reich) was fittingly characterized by the American historian John Motley as: 'a case of Charlemagne with American institutions' — in which the 'American institutions' only constituted the fashionably tailored outer garment. Moreover, the parliamentarians were not willing to work intensively for an extension of their rights. In 1848 a proudly democratic tone had still prevailed;

106

but the opening address of the North German Reichstag[1] already
showed a readiness to submit to a masterful will. 'Ever most serene and
all-powerful King! Ever most gracious King and Lord!. . .In deepest
respect we attend on Your Royal Majesty, yours in loyal service and
obedience — the Reichstag of the North German Confederation.' That
was not the language of a people resolved to participate in government!
When the Empire was proclaimed on 18 January 1871 in the Hall of
Mirrors at Versailles, the celebration revealed clearly the spirit of mind
which had preceded the foundation of the Reich and which would
pervade it in the future. The King first of all inspected the guard of
honour of a grenadier regiment and had its flag, which had been badly
torn in the first battle of the war, carried into the hall, where an altar
had been erected. A soldier choir sang the sixty-sixth Psalm. The
principal oration was given by the Court preacher Rogge, brother-in-law
of the War Minister Roon: it was a punitive homily addressed to Louis
XIV. Then everyone sang 'Now Praise We All The Lord' and 'Be Hailed
In The Wreath of Victory'; only the military was represented — the
German people being symbolically represented by privates from various
regional regiments, who had been ordered to attend. The same Eduard
Simson who, twenty-three years earlier on 3 April 1848 had offered the
crown to Friedrich Wilhelm IV in the Knights' Hall of the Berlin Palace
as the representative of a free, democratically elected Parliament
(rejected by the King because it was associated with the 'filthy stench
of revolution'), had come to Versailles (oh, irony of fate!) as the leader
of a bourgeois 'imperial deputation'. Now he too had become a national
claqueur. Yet as a civilian he had to wait in the antechamber. In the
order of the day of 18 January 1871 the virtues of the Prussian man
which were to be especially relied on in the pan-German state were
listed as honour, comradeship, bravery and obedience. The bourgeois
word 'liberty' was missing.

   According to a remark by Benedetto Croce, it was especially due to
German professors that after 1871 German philistines walked around
with 'the so-called Sedan smile' playing on their lips, 'this sense of
superiority over other peoples, this contempt for the decadent or
already degenerated Latin races, for moral corruption and the misery
of parliamentary squabbles'. Croce observed that German Academe,
after the failure of the 1848 Revolution, which had been a product of
the Enlightenment, had at first retired into the 'quiet life of scholarship';
'Germany had an abundance of scholars and professors who were
mostly very limited, naïve, and childishly gullible in their judgement of
practical and public affairs, which corresponded to their mentality and

way of life.' To them 'inwardness' and learned meditation were not innate, but imposed from the outside; therefore their activism was not extinguished, but only repressed. They strove eagerly to climb 'upwards' in the social hierarchy, whose top places were filled by the officer corps. This striving for 'recognition' manifested itself in servility, vanity, intrigues, and especially in a sometimes very rude militarism and chauvinism of the pen, in an intense hatred of Western democracy and Western parliamentarianism. Their arrogance, which had its roots in their own anaemia (based on repressed inferiority complexes), took this form: we Germans fear God and nothing else in the world! It was astonishing what aggressive impulses burst out of otherwise well-behaved and ordinary professors and school teachers in the face of official approval and encouragement. Whoever remained aloof from this *furor teutonicus* was attacked and slandered. Theodor Mommsen complained about this isolation in his *Political Testament;* it may also have been the reason why he did not continue his *Roman History.* Although he was initially open-minded towards Bismarck, he realized in the long run that this man had broken the nation's backbone ('Dear adolescent fatherland!'). Of Mommsen's oppositional attitude Julius Langbehn said:

> Among the German scholars of the nineteenth century is one who shows a quite surprising resemblance to Erasmus: Mommsen. Just as the one was opposed to Luther, the other is hostile to Bismarck; a certain half-ironical interest in intellectual and moral currents that are alien to the core of the German people characterizes both; but as then, so today the German people, as far as it has genuine feelings, will stand with the true representatives of its nature.

The humanitarian restraint of the German professors was loosened further by the First World War; the break with the tradition of the Enlightenment was quite complete, the 'ideas of 1914' were thrown against those of 1789. The metaphysics of Germanness, the cult of Fichte (1914 was a Fichte year), communal romanticism and the conception of 'war as being of the essence of things' characterize the 'and yet' philosophy.[2]

The defeat of 1918 did not bring a decline of the reactionary professorial spirit; it was now further nourished by the embittered realization that the weak, degenerate Western powers had shown themselves superior; compensation was found in the 'stab-in-the-back legend.'[3]

A review of the development which led from hostility towards
democracy during the Weimar period to the triumph of National
Socialism demonstrates how terribly the representatives of higher
education erred when they joined the opponents of democracy
under the illusion of an obligation to remain loyal to traditional
patterns of thought [Litt].

Berlin University was the centre of the crusades, concealed beneath
the robes of science, against democracy. When L.L. Schücking was to
be called to Berlin,[4] an investigation first had to determine whether he
had once 'given a speech in a public square of Breslau with the title
"No More War"'; since this was true, he was not called. Reinhold
Seeberg, the leading theologian of the University, opened the official
memorial service in 1919 for the students killed in the war with the
words: 'Invictis victi victuri'.[5] Substantial sectors of the University
applauded Hitler's appointment as Chancellor with great enthusiasm;
they did this not because, living in an ivory tower, they did not know
what was going on, but rather because the realization of their yearnings
was now at hand. The Third Reich was expected to bring the final
victory over 'Westernism' and liberalism. But the latter did not have
to be fought any longer: it was becoming extinct 'like a flame that
silently dies' (Bracher).

Philosophers who dealt with the essence of being in the academic
realm forgot the most rudimentary rules of decency in the world of
actual being; Heidegger, for example, disavowed his teacher Husserl
immediately after Hitler's takeover, because he was Jewish. Heidegger
understood the signs of the age: 'the splendour and magnificence of
the awakening'; the acquisition of knowledge fell into the same
category as military and labour service — this was the tenor of his
speech when he assumed the *Rektorat* (rector's office) on 27 May 1933.
One observer commented that 'at the conclusion of the address one did
not know whether one should reach for a Greek philosophical text or
march with the storm troopers' (Löwith). Paul Hühnerfeld has pointed
out that ultimately German fascism and Heidegger's thought were
nourished by the same roots, that they differed in level, not in kind;
romanticism joined forces with nationalism and intolerance against
those whose thinking ran differently. 'We want the sacred and the
heroic. We want boldness and spirit; that is the Teutonic style, the
German style. . .Therefore salute the new German literature. Hail to the
most supreme leader! Hail Germany!' This ideological-literary serenade —
a speech at the book-burning ceremony in Bonn on 10 May 1933! —

was the work of the German philologist and aesthete Hans Naumann. He and Ernst Bertram, both close to the Stefan George circle, considered the 'springtime storm of the German movement ravishingly beautiful'. In reviewing the history of the German university in the nineteenth and twentieth centuries, one must speak less of its capitulation in 1933 than of its fulfilment.

Notes

1. Lower house in Parliament.
2. The *'Dennoch'-Philosophie,* the attitude to life that makes the seemingly unattainable possible and no obstacle insurmountable.
3. The popular legend that the German army was never defeated militarily in the First World War but 'stabbed in the back' by socialist traitors at home.
4. Levin Ludwig Schücking was a scholar and professor of English literature at Leipzig and Erlangen.
5. 'Those who have been conquered will conquer the victors.'

4 HEROES, HAWKERS AND DEMOCRATS

The philosophy of liberalism rested on the conviction that man is an independently thinking, responsibly acting and therefore mature being, or that he can be educated to this end. A democratic constitution guaranteeing the inalienable rights of the citizen, ministerial responsibility to Parliament (parliamentary control of the government) and the division of power was supposed to aid the realization of this idea. However, German liberalism with its constitutional-monarchist and later national-liberal wings soon diluted the democratic-parliamentary concept in favour of an estate-oriented conservatism. With his acknowledgement of the 'sacredness of kingship' Freiherr von Stein subscribed to a patriarchal kind of liberalism; he wanted reform from above and concessions to be granted to the immature populace out of 'fatherly understanding'. Although Hugo Preuss, the principal writer of the Weimar Constitution, had links with Stein, his 1918 draft of the document marks a radical turnabout; in the process he even vetoed the élitism and privilege-consciousness of academic liberal thought. The constitution was now interpreted as the gift of a mature people to itself. The citizen was considered sovereign; national consciousness would have to replace submissiveness as the cohesive bond of the body politic.

This did of course house the liberal conception under an appropriate democratic roof, but it over-taxed the German people simultaneously: the actual practice of democracy and parliamentarianism had even fewer roots in Germany than the ideas of liberalism; it may, incidentally, be considered symbolical in this connection that the German Reichstag building was financed by the French reparations of 1871. George Lukàcs has observed that the Second Reich only harboured 'dying last Mohicans of German democracy'. One need hardly add that previously, with the exception of 1848, the openings to practise democracy were even more remote. William II despised parliamentarianism and democracy throughout his life. Of the deputies he said: 'The sooner such scoundrels are kicked out, the better! The German parliamentarian and politician can't help but become a pig in time!' The protestant churches strengthened the alliance of 'Bethlehem and Potsdam'; their affinity to democracy, influenced by Luther's conception of secular authority, had — at least until 1945 — never been very strong. More will be said elsewhere about this and about the role of the Catholic Church, which, despite its inherent conservatism, was pushed into the democratic-liberal camp during the *Kulturkampf*[1] of the Bismarck years.

The German, according to Lagarde,[2] is by nature aristocratic. In contrast to the Celtic egalitarian he is against 'un-German democracy', which gives the power to rule not to the 'noble' and 'superior', but to the 'inferior' (E.J. Jung). Indeed, criticism was not unjustified since it was the bourgeois and petit-bourgeois 'balloting imbeciles' (as Hitler called them) who opened the road to power for the 'inferior' National Socialists. Of course this development was due not to the system of parliamentarianism, but to the political stupidity of the voters. And, on the other side of the coin, it was particularly this petit-bourgeois stupidity which spoke up in favour of élitist ideas, in accordance with the motto: the masses are 'the others'. Nietzsche's aristocratic attitude and his anti-democratic stance are understandable in so far as his revulsion came from the realization that the petit bourgeoisie was effecting the rapid decay of culture and the beginning of a barbarian age. He saw that the moment was nigh when a *terrible simplificateur* (Burckhardt's term) would overpower the depraved petit-bourgeois masses and lead them from their 'democratic stable' into a nationalist prison. The 'unpolitical' Thomas Mann thought that Western democracy would deprive Germany of its best and deepest attribute: its problematic nature; Germany would become 'boring, obvious, stupid and un-German'. Stefan George's anti-democratic aristocratism and aestheticism were not unrelated: art and culture, supposedly the creations of a few singular individuals, would be destroyed by the apathetic masses; banal 'mediocrity' must not be allowed to rule. In his time poem he cautioned:

> I your conscience · I the voice
> to penetrate your callous cursing anger:
> Only the low prevail · the noble perished:
> faith now is gone and love is withered.

Ernst Jünger serves to illustrate the military component of anti-democratism: he considered democracy vapid, devoid of toughness and without healthy brutality, it lacked a warlike metaphysic and a soldier mythology. 'The day that witnesses the collapse of the parliamentary state through our hands and our proclamation of a national dictatorship will be the most festive day of all for us.'

According to Moeller van den Bruck, youth recognizes 'the enemy in
liberal man'; youth confidently awaits the realization of an anti-
democratic Third Reich that will rise out of the steely bath of war:
'We told ourselves then that this war had been our education. Today
we ask ourselves in doubt: was that really true? In bitterness we hope
that it was!' Jünger believed that the conservative German transcends
all party political conflict and turns, beyond liberal political thought
which has ruined Germany and Europe,

> everywhere to man in the German and to the German in man. He
> trusts that there are still a lot of people in Germany whose reason
> was not only not corrupted by the Enlightenment but who retained
> the clarity of understanding. People with genuine, plain, and simple
> insight, with strong, masculine and elemental passions and the will
> to live by them.

The heroic man, the man of will, was pitted against the 'hawker', the
prototype of the democrat. During the First World War the sociologist
Sombart differentiated between 'English hawkers' and 'German heroes'.
'Everything that relates to military matters has precedence with us. We
are a people of warriors...Warriors deserve the highest honours the
state can give...the heroic way of life achieves its greatest consecration
in the heroic death.' Ernst Jünger spoke of 'warriors and shopkeepers':
'The war is our father — he sired us in the glowing womb of the trenches
as a new generation, and we acknowledge our origin with pride. Our
values therefore shall be heroic, the values of warriors and not those of
shopkeepers who would like to measure the world with a yardstick.'
Spengler declared that the German Republic was not a body politic,
not a 'mighty vision', 'nothing arousing', but a business enterprise.

The heroic had for a long time occupied the top position in the
German philistine's pyramid of values, and the most varied symbolic
figures were brought into play in the representation of the heroic. The
state based itself on the glory of its 'great men'; greatness was
associated with war more than anything else; the state was the temple
of glory, the Pantheon; for decades these clichés found expression
again and again in poetical, philosophical, artistic or architectural
works. Glorification of the heroic, in opposition to foreign flabbiness,
was in accord with a devaluation of mercantility, of the 'shopkeeper
mentality', which took pains to achieve in peaceable competition the
best possible profit (and not honour), and which bargained its way
instead of striking hard and aggressively. For example, Hitler's

antipathy to commerce and industry should be understood not only as the socio-pathological reaction of the frustrated failure, of the anti-social type pushing his way upwards from wretchedness; more especially it arose from decades of practice in bragging by the petit bourgeoisie.

> During the wildness of my younger years nothing troubled me as much as the fact that I was born in a time which would obviously erect its temples only to shopkeepers and bureaucrats any more. The waves of history seemed to have abated to the point where the future really seemed to belong to the peaceful competition of peoples, that is, casual mutual cheating with the exclusion of forceful methods of resistance.

In the search for the vanished heroic age Hitler's rhetorically larded platitudes refer above all to the age of the Wars of Liberation, when 'in time of war a man was still worth his salt', and 'God let iron grow';[3] Arndt's martial songs and the rhapsodic Germanizing sentimentality of Jahn and Fichte are his stylistic models:

> Why could one not have been born a hundred years earlier? Around the time of the wars of Liberation, for instance, when a man, even if he was not a businessman, was still really worth something! I had often thought vexedly about the belatedness of my earthly wanderings and considered the time of 'peace and order' ahead of me as an undeserved meanness of fate. After all, even as a boy I had not been a pacifist, and all educational efforts in this direction came to nought.

The new Reich, pronounced Rosenberg, would not repeat the mistake made by the Greeks; at that time 'Greek democracy triumphed over the yearnings of the heroic man of race (the Aryan Greek)'; 'money, and with it the sub-human, triumphed over blood'; 'aimlessly the Hellene begins to occupy himself with trade, politics and philosophy, recanting today what he praised yesterday; slaves from all parts of the world shout for "freedom", the equality of men and women is proclaimed.' The 'Objectives' of the Third Reich could be read *e contrario* out of this: economic ruin, political dilettantism, intellectual barrenness, the establishment of a modern slavery and the cheapening of women were dominant features: the struggle against enlightenment and democracy was 'successful'. The content and form of Hitler's ideas is apparent if

one takes the arguments advanced by representatives of anti-democratic
currents and reduces them to the level of the tavern milieu[4] of a slightly
inebriated petit bourgeois who distinguishes himself amongst his
companions by a certain rhetorical manner.

Since the Jew was responsible for everything evil he was also
responsible for parliamentarianism:

> Jewish Marxism rejects the aristocratic principle of nature and
> replaced the eternal prerogative of vitality and strength with the
> mass of numbers and its dead weight. Thus it denies the value of
> the individual in man, contests the importance of national heritage
> *[Volkstum]* and race, and thereby deprives man of the prerequisites
> of his existence and culture. . .This kind of democracy has therefore
> become the tool of that race which, by its inmost nature, must shun
> the light of day now and in all future. Only the Jew can praise an
> institution which is as filthy and untrue as he is himself.

Hitler takes issue with the 'parliament vermin' and the 'general
depravity of the gang who imagine themselves to be called to participate
in "politics" ' particularly in the third chapter of *Mein Kampf.* Goebbels
called abuse 'the excrement of the soul'; Hitler knew that, in order to
convince the *Spiesser,* rancour or, better yet, vulgarity is most
advantageously substituted for argumentation. So he 'thumps on the
table': within the span of sixteen pages, the most important part of
the third chapter, he calls the parliamentarians and that section of the
press sympathizing with them, among other things: old uncles, herd of
sheep, numbskulls, deformed gang, inferior persons, gnome-like leather
merchants *(sic!),* simpletons, stupid incompetents, political vagabonds,
miserable characters, milksops, brazen creatures, parliamentary
profiteers, inferior powers, intellectual robber barons, criminal
accomplices, riff-raff of the press, pack of beggars, rascals, scribblers,
mob, pack, incapable buffoons, puffed-up dilettantes, intellectual
demi-monde of the worst kind, subservient nothings, scum, profiteers
avoiding the light of day. . .Hitler found similar expressions for
parliamentary activity.

Hitler attempted to present his prejudices against democracy as
scientific findings by frequently referring to his extensive study of the
parliamentary-democratic situation ('. . .thinking for weeks. . .
whenever I had the opportunity I returned again and again. . .a year
of this calm observation. . .during the course of a number of years. . .').
The concrete results of this so-called lengthy period of observation and

reflection are meagre enough (corresponding to Hitler's intellectual coefficient); the intellectual void is recognizable even in the style: Hitler repeats his words and his ideas like a record needle stuck in the groove ('the first doubts struck me. . .a whole number of questions struck me at the time'). Hitler does not make much use of the sometimes clever arguments advanced during the Weimar Republic against a democracy that was already debased anyway; his most important argument is the decades-old cliché that democracy and parliamentarianism are manifestations of the decadence of the western world.

> The democracy of the modern West is the precursor of Marxism, which without it would not be thinkable. It acts as a culture-medium for this worldwide epidemic, and the disease grows from it. In parliamentarianism, its outward form of expression, it created for itself a 'mockery made of dung and fire' ['Spottfigur aus Dreck und Feuer'] whose 'fire' appears to me to have regrettably burnt out just now.

A quotation from Goethe's *Faust,* Part I ('Spottgeburt *von* Dreck und Feuer') is wedged into Hitler's rhetorical discharge like a gallstone. It is part of Hitler's cunning use of metaphors to mislead the naïve reader through an image of unproven validity.

In his book on National Socialist education, Ernst Krieck summed up the 'ideological revolution' of National Socialism in phrases like these: blood has now prevailed over formal reason, race over pragmatic rational thinking, organic totality over individualistic disintegration, state over society, the people over the individual and the masses; German education shall continue to develop along these lines: it shall be anti-humanitarian, anti-democratic, anti-Western. In the detailed definition of educational aims like these help was provided by the indiscriminate use of the words 'blood' and 'heritage'. This process was characterized not only by an absence of reason and the ability to think logically, but by the propagation of these deficiencies as positive attributes. It was to be supposed that the racially alike saw in all this exactly what they were supposed to see, namely anti-democraticism. There was blood-heritage, blood-education, blood-obligation, blood-knowledge, education towards blood, etc.

> The foundation of all cultural growth is the hereditary gene or core of being, which manifests itself in hereditary appearance; its value is

represented by the hereditary value of honour, which is also alive in primeaval consciousness [Arp].

In *Mein Kampf* Hitler declared the development of intellectual abilities, of abilities which above all deface the democrat, to be of secondary importance. The body was the deciding factor, pre-military and military education were more important. Especial attention should be given to the teaching of history, because it was here that an anti-democratic, race-conscious world view could be implanted in the hearts of young people. It was the task of the 'ethnic state' to take care 'that at last a world history will be written which raises the racial question to a dominant position'. The subject matter had to be rigorously shaped in such a way that on leaving school the young person 'would not be a semi-pacifist, a democrat or anything else, but totally German'. An education of this kind was only the logical continuation of tendencies which had been very powerful, if somewhat under-the-counter, during the Weimar Republic, and more public, if weaker, during the Wilhelminian era. Hitler had himself received the 'correct' instruction in history in his youth:

> Even today I recall with some emotion the grey man who sometimes made us forget the present in the rich glow of his portrayal, miraculously transported us back into vanished ages, and from the misty veils of millennia fashioned dry historical remembrance into living reality. There we sat then, often excited to fiery passion, sometimes even moved to tears.

Even though Hitler does not give any details about the subject matter of the history lessons, his own person is the strongest guarantor that an ethnical-national brand of enthusiasm, and not democratic-libertarian enthusiasm, was concerned here. The spirit of the German history book in the nineteenth and twentieth centuries was — in the mainstream — correspondingly anti-democratic and anti-liberal.

Oscar Jäger, one of the liberal pedagogues who turned particularly against the national-historical constriction of teaching under Wilhelm II, remarked that when the history teacher reads somewhere or chances to hear at assemblies and banquets 'of all the great accomplishments brought about in the world by our history teaching and our teaching generally, and that it was the schoolmaster who conquered at Sadowa, then he was moved to beat his breast and exclaim: "God have mercy on me, a sinner."'

But it must also be noted that Hitler considered only a few teachers capable of giving the kind of lesson that he had experienced, and that even Wilhelm II's famous critique of the grammar schools pointed out that they were not by any manner of means only the training grounds of the national spirit they were elsewhere purported to be. ('Whoever has attended a *Gymnasium* and looked behind the scenes knows what is missing. . .more than anything else a nationalist orientation is missing.') But this absence of nationalist commitment did not imply *engagement* in libertarian-democratic affairs by a long chalk; it was precisely under the influence of dull philological formalism (and the classical philologist was the key figure in a *Gymnasium* — responsible above all for the teaching of history and German!) that history was 'exercized'. For many students — and not the worst — history was thereby exorcized.

> The content of history. . .One is on the march, one enters an alliance, one united his troops, one reinforces something, one moves forward, one captures, one retreats, one seizes a camp, one resigns, one receives something, one opens something brilliantly, one is taken prisoner, one reimburses another, one threatens another, one marches towards the Rhine. . .one is forced back, one is condemned to death, one commits suicide. . .the whole is without doubt a history of the mentally sick [Benn].

Looking back on his school years, Ludwig Marcuse wrote:

> The humanistic *Gymnasium* will die without a chance of rescue if, as in the days before the war, it again makes common cause with an anti-humanitarian order of society; because it was due neither to Plato, nor to Thucydides, nor to Tacitus that we received only the rubble of culture. Nor was it our teachers' fault, who for the most part were highly educated men, even if they did lack the pedagogical Eros. . .It was due to the tragic alliance of Athens and Agadir[5] that the great cultures which were intended to be communicated to us came to us in the form of instructional lessons in which, quite by chance, the description of a cannon-frame was replaced by the description of Odysseus' shield. The humanistic *Gymnasium* is dead if it decorates a withered order of society only with withered myths; dead, if it cultivates a little group of blown-up, pretentious 'temple guards', so that they can gild trash with 'Homeric sun'.

That's how far the classical concept of culture had come, a concept
that had originally sought the perfection of the human personality and
a 'culture of the soul' in its association with the humanities. In any
case, it is true that Humboldt's ideas on education, which were
supposed to be uninfluenced by society and unpolitical, already
contained the seeds of decay, in other words, of anti-democratic
development. In the world of education it is especially the path taken
by political pedagogy in Germany that demonstrates how the ground
for Hitler's ascent to power was prepared. There was the nationalization
of political education in the monarchistic state, the empty patriotic
pathos associated with it, preparation for the organizational form of
army life and the drill of basic training. The Pan-German League[6] was
foremost in propagating the 'militaristic school': many teachers,
professors and other representatives of academic life belonged to it.
In 1906, 36 per cent of all local leaders of the League were educators,
of whom 57 per cent were university professors; among the founders
of the League were E. Haeckel, K. Lamprecht, and M. Weber. The
critical opponents, like Friedrich Wilhelm Foerster and Kerschensteiner,[7]
could not assert themselves, not even when a new pedagogical trend
received official support in the Weimar Republic. These positive
overtures were blocked by the wide wall of pseudo-classical, nationalist
and ethnic educational ideology which had been erected decades before,
a wall which could hardly be breached. The National Socialist school of
education took over from here; it succeeded

> in recommending itself to the German people as the fulfilment of
> an old yearning for national and social unity and renewed inward
> community, and in claiming responsibility for a genuine, profound,
> intellectual and political renewal in the sense of a 'conservative
> revolution'; this especially since Christianity, the Church and the
> new humanitarian cultural religion could no longer go on parading
> as genuine realities of life. Only when one realizes how intimately
> connected German education was with these historically derivable
> yearnings and expectations can one understand the sigh of release
> and relief with which more than a few German teachers and a large
> section of the academic community itself greeted the takeover of
> power by the National Socialists [Hornung].

Notes

1. *Kulturkampf* was a term coined during Bismarck's struggle with the Catholic Church in the 1870s.
2. Paul Anton de Lagarde (originally Bötticher; 1827-91), Professor of Oriental Languages at Göttingen. He was an active critic of German political and cultural life and advocated national regeneration through religious and politically conservative restorative programmes.
3. 'Gott Eisen wachsen liess': part of an often quoted phrase from a popular nineteenth-century military song, 'the God who let iron grow knew no slaves'.
4. Actually *Stammtisch,* an untranslateable term referring to the weekly round table groups devoted to card games and small talk in neighbourhood taverns; they are popular and proverbial all over the country.
5. Agadir was the site of the show of force by the German navy during the Moroccan crisis of 1911.
6. For the Pan-German League (Alldeutscher Verband) see note 1, p.56.
7. Friedrich Wilhelm Foerster (1869-1966) was a prominent pacifist writer and pedagogue; George Kerschensteiner (1854-1932) was a well-known pedagogue in Munich and also an educational reformer.

5   SOCIALIST TRAITORS

'Denn der Große frißt den Kleinen/und der Größte frißt den Großen/
also löst inder Natur sich/einfach die soziale Frage.' 'For the big one
eats the small one/and the biggest eats the big/this is nature's simple
lesson/how to solve the social question.' This quatrain from the
Trompeter von Säckingen[1] reflects, even if ironically, the Social
Darwinism of the second half of the nineteenth century. The socialist's
'dozy dreams of humanitarianism' stood in opposition to the 'sober
realization' that natural selection and eradication were necessary. The
erosion of the differences between man and animal effected by
Darwin's teaching of evolution in the realm of biology was distorted
in Germany above all by Ernst Haeckel. Haeckel achieved this inasmuch
as he incorporated the special position of the human intellect in this
biological process and thereby raised the battle cry of atheistic
'biologism' against Church and Christianity. At first, of course, moral
categories were still linked together with scientific findings; natural
selection was considered a tool of nature to let the morally superior
emerge as the strongest in the struggle of life: the interplay of nature
appeared as a cunning device of morality (Hegel and Darwin united!).
When such a theory was seen to be untenable from the scientific point
of view, another 'perversion' was devised: those who emerged from the
struggle for existence as the stronger ones were now considered superior
because of their biological strength; the principles of morality were
sacrificed to faith in hereditary biological health. The racial
anthropologists, who usually lacked a sound scientific training, carried
these trains of thought even further by creating a biological value scale
of races, in which the Germanic peoples appeared first on the list.

Most propertied bourgeois rationalized the social problems caused
by industrialization by considering want as guilt, as biological guilt, as
a misery willed by nature; these people had simply not measured up
to the standards of natural selection; imperfection of this kind deserved
to perish. Those elements of society secure by birth and tradition were
thus able to repress their bad conscience; as Social Darwinists they
were anti-socialists and anti-Marxists. What made Marx so dangerous
was the radical humanity of his thought which in other respects, it is
true, had also suffered from a biologistical ailment (e.g. the downfall
of the bourgeoisie as an inevitable natural phenomenon!). The

brutalization of political life by Social Darwinism conflicted consciously or unconsciously with the conception of state and society that prevailed during the Enlightenment and the age of Classicism. The reign of *Logos* was replaced by that of *Bios*. 'This', Schiller said,

> is exactly what makes man human, that he does not remain what mere nature made him, but has the capacity to undo with his reason the moves that she anticipated him making. Man can thus turn an act of necessity into an act of free will and elevate physical to moral necessity.

Blind, irrational instinct, he held, could only create an 'emergency' state; the 'state' was itself 'the origin and justification of any attempt by a newly mature people to transform their natural state into a moral state'. Social Darwinism's conception of the state led man back from a moral to a 'sensuous' state of being once more; the 'societal shaping forces of classical, Christian and enlightened-humanitarian social ethics are being demolished, a process which has during the past hundred years increased rapidly in speed' (Zwarzlik). The importance of Social Darwinism *per se* in the destruction of the humanitarian conception should, naturally, not be over-estimated; it was only a partial component of the 'revolt' of instinct and impulse at this time. Whatever there was left of humanitarian sentiments, manifesting themselves in the alleviation of social distress, was considered a subsidy to essentially 'inferior' persons. Marx's struggle against patronizing socialism and for a classless society struck at the root of the evil; patronizing socialism did not permit a democratic order. In the wrestling for social equality it was particularly the Social Democrats who became the *avant-garde* of democracy; the anti-democratic forces were united accordingly by the fight against the Social Democrats — both in the Second and in the Third Reich.

The 'sinister powers of the depths', the Social Democrats, stormed against everything 'sacred to human thought and feeling', working themselves up to a 'merciless life-and-death struggle' — this is taken not from Hitler, but the *Gartenlaube*. Youth had to be given the conviction that the teachings of Social Democracy not only contradicted divine law and Christian morality, but that they were impracticable and equally disastrous in their consequences for the individual and the mass: these words were proclaimed not by Hitler, but by Wilhelm II at an educational conference in 1890. Hitler wrote in *Mein Kampf:* 'The SPD rejected everything: the nation, the

fatherland. . .the authority of law. . .school. . .religion. . .morality.
There was absolutely nothing that was not dragged into the mire of a
horrible abyss.'

As an underground force, Social Democracy prevented the worker
from leading an orderly life; he rotted in the cities. 'It is to be feared
that the adult worker will spend his leisure hours in the tavern, that he
will participate more than before in political assemblies', that 'growing
children, especially teenage boys and girls, were roaming around away
from home and becoming morally corrupt and degenerate.' This is not
Hitler's 'Lessons of the Vienna Years' but Wilhelm II's reflections on
the worker question. In *Mein Kampf* Hitler gives an account of a
worker contaminated by socialism in Vienna: 'Every Saturday now he
is drunk and his wife, moved by the instinct of self-preservation for her
children and herself, must tussle for the few pennies that she has to
force out of him — usually on the way from factory to pub. If he finally
comes home in person on Sunday or Monday night, drunk and brutal,
and always shot of his last *Heller* and *Pfennig,* then God have mercy on
the scenes that frequently take place next.'

Social Democratic propaganda availed itself of crazy schemes for
world reform, 'whose appeal rests on the fact that the understanding
of the broad mass of the people is sufficiently limited and undeveloped
so that, spurred on by their own greed, they can always be taken in by
the rhetoric of adroit and ambitious leaders'. In *Mein Kampf* Hitler
speaks of the 'repulsively humane morality of the Social Democratic
press with its equivocal phrases of freedom and beauty and dignity,
its misleading jumble of words which labour to convey seeming deepest
wisdom'; as tools it had 'slander and a monumental capacity for
virtuoso lying'. The former is meant for stupid dunces of the middle
ranks and, of course, the higher ranks of the intelligentsia; the latter is for
the masses.'

The catastrophic influence of the nation's poisoners, the Social
Democratic agitators, had to be eliminated — 'mit unbarmherziger
Sichel die hochwogenden Saaten der Friedensstörer und Unruhestifter
niederstrecken'. This is not Hitler's extermination programme but the
Gartenlaube's acclamation of the Socialist Laws.[2] In *Mein Kampf*
Hitler demanded 'the deepest feeling of social responsibility for the
creation of better foundations for our growth, combined with the
brutal resolve to break incorrigible deviationists'.

The Social Democrats were first and foremost 'fellows owning to no
country' — this is not a phrase from one of Hitler's inflammatory
speeches but from one of Wilhelm II's. *Mein Kampf* expressed the same

sentiment in this manner: 'Just as the hyena cannot abandon the carcass, so the Marxist cannot refrain from betraying the fatherland.' A comparison of the texts indicates the consistency with which the socialist movement was described as a national danger. At the same time there was a desire to combat the 'delusion' of world brotherhood and humanity with 'something positive'. National Socialism corresponded ideologically to Bismarck's attempt to make socialism superfluous by way of social reform. In its aims National Socialism was equivalent to a complete inversion of socialist ideas: the concept of humanity became nationalism and chauvinism, the striving for social and economic equality was turned into the myth of ethnic community, the hope for material improvement became patriotic-military asceticism, efforts to shorten the workday were turned into governmentally organized spare-time activities; in National Socialist jargon this was called (in the form of 'lofty aphorisms'): 'Germany above all else!', 'Commonwealth over self-interest!', 'Cannons instead of butter!', 'Strength through joy!'. Showing very clearly that National Socialism was concerned with nationalism and not socialism, Dr Robert Ley[3] said that Hitler spoke not of 'wage and price politics, but of soul, race, blood, soil and fatherland'. Hitler argued in *Mein Kampf* that National Socialism was anti-parliamentarian, aristocratic, nationalistic, millitant, fanatical and ethnocentric. The Pan-Germans too had already found that the 'much and often abused concepts "national" and "social" are only truly consummated, fulfilled, amalgamated and Germanized in the ethnocentric conception of the state'. 'German Socialism', according to Moeller van den Bruck, meant 'grass-roots contact, hierarchical structure, organization'; in this form, he believed, it would take the place of liberalism. Socialism, according to Oswald Spengler, was an exclusively German matter; 'the others cannot experience it'.

National Socialism was rooted in the Christian-social and conservative movements of the late nineteenth century: in this connection Adolf-Stöcker[4] and Friedrich Naumann[5] in Prussia, and Georg von Schönerer,[6] Karl Lueger,[7] Walter Riehl and Rudolf Jung[8] in Austria stand out especially. The DNSAP in Austria (Deutsche Nationalsozialistische Arbeiterpartei), later called DAP, with its recognition of an armed free peasantry, a co-operative artisan class and its firm stance against materialism, 'mammonism', internationalism, Marxism and democracy had a powerful influence on the Bavarian DAP;[9] the fusion of the two parties was effected at Salzburg in 1920 and the National Socialist German Workers' Party came into being. Friedrich Meinecke has called attention to the fascination which must have been exerted by a movement capable of uniting the two great ideas ideas of the nineteenth century, the nationalism of the bourgeoisie and the socialism of the workers. But such a combination could not be termed a synthesis because these ideas represented completely contradictory, irreconcillable elements. (The antonymous concepts nationalism/internationalism, class-state/democracy, Social Darwinism/ social humanism, etc. have already been alluded to several times.) The merger was successful, however, when the ideas of socialism were perverted and brought within the petit-bourgeois field of vision; besides, the National Socialist German Workers' Party never was a workers' party but, like all national-social movements, it was sociologically and anthropologically a party for the petit bourgeoisie. Socialism became nationalism and this was superimposed on the old nationalism, which had been fed by other sources: therefore national-social was a simple pleonasm, and National Socialist German Workers' Party a double pleonasm.

Notes

1. A play by Joseph Viktor Scheffel (1826-86); it had its first performance in 1854.
2. These were laws introduced by Bismarck on 21 October 1878 which severely limited the political activities of the Social Democratic Party; they were periodically renewed until October 1890.
3. Robert Ley (1890-1945) was a prominent National Socialist party leader, also Reichsorganisationsleiter (chief of national party organization) and head of the Deutsche Arbeitsfront, the party's joint organization for workers and employers which took the place of unions and employers' associations.
4. Adolf Stöcker (1835-1909) was a prominent protestant clergyman with strong anti-Semitic tendencies. He was the official court preacher at Berlin from 1874-89 and was also co-founder of the Evangelical-Social Congress.
5. Friedrich Naumann (1860-1919) was a protestant clergyman, writer and politician and also a genuine advocate of social reform based on Christian principles and within the framework of a strong nationalistic state. Naumann figured prominently in the conception of the Weimar Constitution.
6. Georg von Schönerer (1842-1921) was an Austrian nobleman and politician of German nationalist persuasion; fervently anti-clerical, anti-liberal and anti-Semitic, his ideas influenced Hitler in his youth.
7. Karl Lueger (1844-1910) was an Austrian politician and anti-Semitic mayor of Vienna; he was popular on account of the social measures he introduced in communal affairs.
8. Walter Riehl and Rudolf Jung were both Christian-Socialist Austrian politicians of the thirties.
9. The Bavarian German Workers' Party was founded in 1918; Hitler joined it a year later and became the leader of the new NSDAP (National Socialist German Workers' Party) in 1921 after the fusion with other parties had taken place in 1920.

6 GERMAN CONSERVATISM

The German is conservative — this was Richard Wagner's opinion; at the least we can say that, during the nineteenth and twentieth centuries, it was not possible for the Germans to assume any posture other than that of conservatism. Neither liberals nor socialists could expect to come to power; so people generally accepted the established order. A pronounced tendency towards servility and submissiveness could be observed in petit-bourgeois behaviour: it was hoped thereby to 'break through' to the top of society. After the foundation of the Reich, the political and social snobbery of the small territorial capitals (whoever was supplier to the court was at the top of the mercantile hierarchy, the court poet, painter or preacher belonged to the flower of the intelligentsia) developed into an all-German snobbery. More than anyone it was Wilhelm II who took care that sycophancy, narrow-mindedness and a marked weakness of the will predominated amongst the 'pillars of society' and their assistants — especially the bureaucracy. The character of Johannes Kessler, Wilhelm II's court preacher and the tutor of his children, illustrates this attitude. He rose from a poor family background; with his extreme nationalism he represented official German protestantism, with his servility he represented a large sector of the petit-bourgeois academic community; his education was extremely superficial and was couched in the usual phraseology; his view of history ('loyal to Kaiser and fatherland') was marked by the theory that 'men make history'; as a student he 'sat at the feet of the great 'Treitschke'. As the tutor of princes he admired the deep religious inclinations of the Hohenzollern family; he published his sermons under the titles: 'With God to Victory', 'Fearless and Loyal', 'Cross and Sword'. Architectionically as well as in 'other respects' he looked on the Garnisonkirche[1] at Potsdam as his 'favourite house of God' ('The brilliant sun and the eagle flying up to the sun, with *nec soli credit* inscribed on pulpit and organ. . .'). As field chaplain he did not philosophize but 'came to grips with the issues' ('How terrible was the war! But then again, how these tragic sites elevate the heart'). The Wartburg[2] was to him the focal point uniting German nature, German legend, German poetry, German history and German religion; he had no sense of humour but relished the 'pertinent wit' of his Emperor. Luther was his model because he was the most German of Germans, the most pious of the pious; 'Christianity and humour had concluded a union of the heart in this Christian warrior.' Kessler was a man of 'pulsating life' who in 'restless activity worshipped the truly exalted', a man who, in spite of the title of his autobiography, *Ich schwöre mir ewige Jugend* (I Pledge myself to Eternal Youth), 'sensed the workings of the eternal iron laws of nature' — that is, he grew old.

To call such a man conservative is appropriate in Germany since this concept had for a long time, from Arndt and Jahn through Lueger, Schönerer and Stöcker up until the German Christians,[3] been no more than an apostolically antiquated accumulation of petit-bourgeois elements; belief in the empire towered monumentally above this. Since in this world everything is provisional, God alone eternal, it was apposite to connect the verb 'to conserve' with this 'imperishable' idea: 'Christian and anti-Christian being are therefore the two essential and elemental opposites', as Hermann Wagener[4] said in his *Staats- und Gesellschaftslexikon*, 'and nobody shall be called conservative who does not more than anything want to conserve Christianity.'

The Romantics rediscovered the Christian Middle Ages aesthetically; epigonic Romanticism discovered them ideologically; a (conservative) predilection for the Christian knight developed. People imagined themselves back in a vanished world, a blissful Christian ethnic organism of the people, even though the people themselves had played a very small role during the Middle Ages. The Enlightenment was ostracized because it had rejected the historical irrationalism — to which homage was now paid — as man's self-imposed nonage. In his lectures on the art of politics, given in 1809, Adam Heinrich Müller[5] pointed out that the martial spirit was the essence of freedom, pervading every nerve of the state: 'this is the iron that must pulse in every drop of its blood.' The state was 'at one and the same time the temple of justice and a fortress'. The definition of freedom and justice was replaced by metaphor; myth took the place of reflection; irrational and mysterious forces were permeating the state; each individual was a link in the chain of generations: 'The state is the exalted community of a long line of past, present, and future generations.' 'Cross and sword' were held to be redeeming powers, conjured up by the conservatives for the sake of nation and people. God gave prestige and power to the ruling body — the throne and the altar were in fullest harmony; the ruler was king by the grace and the laws of God. Before the first United *Landtag*[6] of 1847, Friedrich Wilhelm IV exclaimed:

> I am compelled to make the solemn declaration that no power on earth shall ever succeed in making me alter the natural relationship between prince and people — which makes us especially powerful in our country on account of its inherent honesty — into a conventional one. Not now and not ever will I permit a written document, like a second providence, to come between our Lord in heaven and this land and rule us with its paragraphs, taking the place of the sacred loyalty of old.

Since the ruler was closely connected to the highest being, to God or providence, he used the words God and providence with corresponding frequency. For the petit-bourgeois the emperor was like a God, and God like an emperor; the National Socialists were later to intensify the leader cult to the most solemn sacredness. Even a man like Hugo von Hofmannsthal[7] engaged himself in the 'service of things to be conserved' and, in the face of 'general decay', using stilted figures of speech, he spoke of a 'conservative revolution', of 'a legion of seekers' who toiled for faith and tradition. That was very disingenuous, for the conservative forces were never seekers — rather, they were 'havers': they had God, people, fatherland, race and blood; and why should the desired restoration be called revolution? Hofmannsthal's speech, addressed to Munich students in 1927, was dangerous because it helped to elevate conservatism intellectually. That Hofmannsthal praised tradition and traditionalism is understandable as regards him personally: as a man lacking in poetic originality — as a secondhand poet of sorts — he was dependent on creative loans from this tradition. In the realm of literature this could be called 'preservation of the inalienable values of the Western synthesis of antiquity and Christianity'; in the realm of politics it amounted to the anachronistic glorification of class conscious or absolutist forms of government. 'Conservative Revolution' meant the 'eternal return of the same', which was in turn a reaffirmation of the old German faith in Barbarossa.[8] The medieval conception of the Third Reich was revived by Moeller van den Bruck: 'The conservative thinks of the Third Reich. He knows that, just as the medieval Reich of our ancient emperors lived on in the Bismarckian Reich, so the Second Reich will endure in the Third.' It was to be a Thousand-Year Reich!

The reality of the Thousand-Year Reich was proclaimed by Hitler on the occasion of the 1934 Reichsparteitag:[9] 'The German way of life is thereby determined for the next millenium.' That was too optimistic by 988 years, but conservatism would not be conservatism if it allowed itself to be diverted from its essential vocation, the ideology of the unreal, by rational calculation. After 1945 it seemed that 'cult-like, monumental needs' had been satisfied; now *Logos,* even if belatedly, was to shape the state. But the conservative 'shudders in the face of such a (mythological) vacuum'! He thrives on 'eternal values', he feels 'in every fibre that this cult-like, this monumental need will again assert itself' (Mohler). Is Germany awakening[10] again?

Notes

1. Famous church of the Hohenzollerns erected 1730-35, during the reign of Friedrich Wilhelm I.
2. The Thuringian site of Luther's anonymous retreat after his ban by the *Reichstag* of Worms in 1521.
3. The *Deutsche Christen* were members of several German national Christian movements aspiring to Christian unity under nationalist auspices. Here we have a reference to the most virulent manifestation of the movement associated with National Socialism.
4. Hermann Wagener (1815-89) was a Prussian publicist and conservative politician and an early editor of the *Kreuzzeitung.* He was later to advocate social reforms within the conservative social order.
5. Adam Heinrich Müller (1779-1829) was a romantic-conservative writer and political theorist. Born in Berlin he was converted to Catholicism in 1805 and entered the services of the Austrian state in 1813. His *Elemente der Staatskunst* became the main work of romantic conservatism.
6. Joint meeting of the provincial estates of Prussia.
7. See note 11, pp.75-6.
8. Barbarossa, Friedrich I, was German Emperor from 1152-90, and glorified as prince of peace and courtly ideas; eventually he became the symbol of national hopes for a regeneration of the empire and nation.
9. Annual party congress of the National Socialist Party at Nuremberg.
10. Nazi battle cry: 'Germany Arise!'

7 LEADERSHIP

The conservative substituted the 'structured society', led by an 'élite', for democratic 'egalitarianism'. In his eyes, the élite was not only the group in power, but the group called to be in power. The aristocratic-monarchial order, with its patronizing and patriarchal attitude, which even extended into family life, was firmly rooted in the nineteenth century. The aristocracy, as for example in the Prussian state, was so strongly connected with the most important positions in the military, the government and the bureaucracy that it seemed impossible to imperil it. In caricature the stiff Prussian *Junker* was shown with whip, top hat, moustache and spurs; his motto was: 'Regress with God for King and Prussia! Down with the constitution! Eliminate property tax! Oysters and chilled champagne, even in the summer! Bring back corporal punishment!' The political philosophy of Müller, Stahl or — towards the end of the century — Langbehn gave theoretical reinforcement to the élitist assumptions of the aristocracy.

> A people consists of bourgeois, peasants, artists, nobles, princes; it is a colourful mass, ordered by certain laws; if these laws are not heeded, the body politic will be diseased; if they are ignored completely, it dies and falls victim to despotism or anarchy. Social Democracy therefore constitutes a regression to the herd-principle of the earliest form of human life; it is unstructured, infertile and inanimate human mass [Langbehn].

The neo-conservatism of the 1920s referred back to this view of the world. Moeller van den Bruck wanted to replace the parties with a corporatist class system; leadership, naturally, should be left to the élite, which would emerge from the impending 'conservative revolution'. Leadership was therefore no longer up to a traditional group such as the nobility; only deed and action identified those called to lead. This meant opposition not only to the egalitarian principle of democracy, but also to the nineteenth-century principle of legitimacy. The successful fighter establishes the norms; decision takes the place of succession; law and power resemble a soccer-trophy: the strongest wins it. Such modern Machiavellianism was now mythologically camouflaged: one did not become a leader because one was rowdy; rather, leadership

130

fell to the person in whom the irrational life forces of race and blood culminated. This was political theology and, simultaneously, it stimulated the petit-bourgeois lust for power: 'everyman', so to speak, carried the marshal's baton in his genes.

The 'dominating nature' was characterized by beauty, *eros* and the blood of race. Stefan George said that a 'ray of Hellas had fallen' on the young generation destined to rule. Life, then, was no longer base — it was to be seen as 'glowing'; one searched for harmony in the physical and the spiritual, and went through life with one's head held high. An ideology based on domination and service, on league and empire was hardening into shape in George, and it was even more pronounced in his pupils — Friedrich Wolters for example. With its forced language and a maximum of petit-bourgeois pathos, this ideology was in the final analysis only the sublimation of misdirected sexual energy: the *eros* of the man's man, directed at heroes.

This was even more apparent in Hans Blüher's 'philosophy',[1] which interpreted all leadership and greatness as the product of the 'union of men' and its eroticism.

> Mankind's political state depends neither on his intellect, nor on his economics. . .there is a more deeply anchored fate which forced mankind into the situation in which it actually finds itself now. . . Wherever nature brought forth a truly state-building organism, it could do so only by breaking through the sovereignty of family life with its heterosexual striving.

Blüher saw in the love for each other of splendid and beautiful young men of Germanic race the birth of bravery in the struggle for a national ideal, romantic spirit, piousness and a yearning for sacred living; 'in the hours of greatest tension there exists a union which is without purpose and yet of the deepest human relevance. Three creeds spring from the experience of the union of men. The creed of the human state. The creed of the union. The creed of the nobility.'

The National Socialists took over the idea of a masculine-fraternal élite and the idea of leadership:

> State and people have nowhere been the result of a common concept of man and woman; rather, they were the result of the union of men purposely directing itself to some particular aim. The family sometimes proved to be the stronger, sometimes the weaker support of political and ethnic structures. Often it was purposely

put into the service of the same. But it never was the cause nor the most important support of a state, that is to say, of a social community with political power [Rosenberg].

Rosenberg considered the man as creative, the woman as lyrical; this fact had to be remembered when the 'breeding of a coming generation of German-conscious people' was undertaken. Within the masculine fraternity of the SA homosexuality was openly practised, but not romanticized: the brutal mentality of the storm trooper was not at home in the deifying sentimentality of George, nor in the erotic pompousness of Blüher. Their 'and-why-not' morality made the deduction of the claim for leadership from more 'concrete' motives appear more appropriate. After the murder of Röhm and leading SA personalities homosexuality no longer played an important role. As a new male fraternity the SS assumed the mantle of the SA: race, blood and the capacity of systematic, cold-blooded cruelty were the chief criteria for leadership selection and élitism. However, in a certain sense the sodomite romanticism continued to assert itself. The virtually manic search for beautiful male figures perpetrated by Heinrich Himmler, for example, could not just be explained by the delusions of the breeder; it was also compensation for a repressed physical inferiority complex, which especially in people with homosexual tendencies gives rise to neuroses.

The SS was defined as a 'league of German men of nordic characteristics selected in accordance with specific criteria' (Himmler). It was characterized by 'strong and faithful ties' to the great blood lines of the people. 'The awareness that the fulfilment of the deepest German yearning is found in the service of the people' demanded a 'fusion of the strongest internal unity in closed ranks' (d'Alquen). In his speech on the 'Nature and Tasks of SS and Police' in January of 1937, Himmler pontificated: 'Guided by unalterable laws as a national socialist military order of Nordic men and a sworn community of its clans, here we have taken our place and march into a distant future and wish and hope that we not only be the heirs who did better, but moreover the ancestors of future generations necessary for the eternal life of the Germanic German people.' Himmler hereby connected elements of youthful ideology from the wars of liberation to the Third Reich: student fraternities, gymnastic societies, *Wandervogel*[2] groups, Free Korps,[3] ethnic action groups. So the aristocratic airs of duelling societies and the mysticism of the beer hall, the euphoria of the campfire and the idyll of the mercenary soldier were united. It was the ideology of conspiratorial gangs, the romanticism of heroic heathendom; brutality and psychopathy triumphed; grotesque mediocrity dreaming of excellence prevailed. Shibboleths served as guides in the education or rather type-casting, of the young leaders in medieval-type castles.[4] 'Their faces were cold with hard lines, their eyes were unapproachable' (Stumpfe). These shibboleths had been the yearning of generations of young men's leagues 'a warlike youth flowering in the fulness of physical vigor and quickness' (W. Menzel).

The leadership and élitist mythos was so successful because it filled the petit bourgeois' metaphysical vacuum created by the destruction of faith in the nineteenth century. A secularizing messianism appeared: the 'leader' was yearned for as the nordic saviour; the 'new man' confessed to the 'God who lifts the arms', 'to the winter solstice God renewing life, leading the nation from the grave, revitalizing it and freeing it of care. To the God who raises it and ennobles it. Who makes Germany to the cultural hoard of a new humanity' (Bengmann). The message 'which came from somewhere' raised the self of the petit bourgeois to an idol, an idol of over-dimensional mediocrity, thereby releasing them from their own selves. This caused a maximum of psychological satisfaction: as one worshipped the leader, one worshipped the self, the personal (petit-bourgeois) super-ego — 'The true statesman combines in himself a paternal attitude, warlike spirit and charisma. . .The true statesman thus is ruler, warrior and priest at the same time' (Stapel). 'The leader is radical; he is what he is with all his being, and he does what he has to do. The leader is responsible; that is to say, as the incarnation of God's will he executes it. God give us leaders and bring us to true allegiance' (K. Becke). 'So let us return to the ancestors' mores:/from the midst of the people he comes to the fore,/leader of empire as we have conceived/him in the hearts of the people received' (Vesper).

'Tomorrow has now become today', declared Julius Petersen in 1933, 'The end-of-the-world mood has been transformed into a mood of renewal; the ultimate aim enters the perspective of the present. In the depth of the people all powers of the ancient yearnings are alive, and the dreams that comforted the past are. . .drawn anew to the light of day. . .The seeds of the New Reich have taken root. The yearned-for and prophesied leader has come.' Hitler thus became 'the romantic' enthroned: a hero reflecting the romantic longing for the revival of German history, German art, German literature and German saga pervaded by Barbarossa, Luther, Hutten, the Knight of Bamberg, Faust, Siegfried and Parcival. This was a serious misunderstanding: Hitler was only a mean dwarf who had quickly brewed together a leadership and hero mythos from all the remnants of a century's *Spiesser*-ideology caught in his petit-bourgeois ganglia. In *Mein Kampf* he demanded a 'Germanic leader-democracy' with 'free election of the leader, including his obligation to assume full responsibility for all his actions and omissions'; incompetents and weaklings will not 'dare' to assume responsibility — Hitler's irrational logic of decisions gaily tumbles on: should a weak 'fellow' once steal in (*einschleichen,* i.e. creep in), he would be found and confronted with the shout (apparently derived from the imitation of Schiller's pathos): 'Get thyself away, thou cowardly rascal! Retract thy foot, thou soilest the steps; the portal to the pantheon of history is not for schemers but for heroes.' What is leader-democracy? Who chooses freely? To whom does the leader pledge his obligation to the assumption of responsibility? To whom does he owe responsibility for his actions? Why are incompetents rejected? How does one know whether the right one entered or a schemer stole his way into the Pantheon? Where must one confront him and how? Evidently, in spite of impressive metaphors, a number of questions remained unanswered. After two years of 'visiting' the Vienna Parliament, Hitler had wrestled himself through to 'this conviction'; this demonstrated a rather 'dwarflike' intelligence. His stature did not suffer because of this, however, since his followers were philistines. The most important ingredient was Hitler's determination to be *Führer;* this attitude was matched by the philistine's determination to let his peer become leader: 1932-3 Hitler was freely elected. He assumed responsibility for all his actions and omissions. He was responsible for the 'fate of the German nation; he was also the highest judicial authority of the German people' (Hitler). Not the 'wealth of theoretical knowledge', but 'the ability and competence of leadership', not the 'gift to shape ideas', but the gift to 'move the masses' carried Hitler to power. Hitler quite correctly estimated the anti-democratic and anti-parliamentarian affectation of most Germans, accumulated over decades, when he predicted: 'A movement that, in a time of majority rule in everything, bases itself on the principle of the leadership concept and the resulting responsibility must, with mathematical certainty, one day overcome the present condition and emerge victoriously.' Adapting Hitler's own 'parable', cited above, it therefore can be said that any incompetent and rascal could come to power if he harnessed the anti-democratic and anti-parliamentarian attitude of the masses, and suggested and propagated his person as the realization of decades of mythical longing for a leader.

Notes

1. See note 2, p.50.
2. *Wandervogel,* popular youth movement founded 1896 in Berlin, dedicated to hiking, folk-dancing and folk-music, dissolved in 1933.
3. Voluntary units of World War I veterans fighting border skirmishes in the immediate post-World War I period with unofficial assistance of the German government.
4. So-called *Ordensburgen,* alluding to the medieval castles of orders of crusading knights.

8 MAN AS PREDATOR

Absolutized irrationalism, not tolerating other views beside itself, least of all reason, had to have a disastrous effect on the political development of Germany. This was so because it did not acknowledge the realization, based on rational thought, of the limitations of its own potential and prepared and respectively countenanced the national *hybris*. Much more dangerous, however, was that the irrational was during the course of the nineteenth century brought down from the summits of metaphysics to the level of the instinctual drives. Darwinism stimulated this. But only selected thoughts of Darwin were used, those that corresponded to or justified the self's urge to primitivity — such as the thesis that 'man hailed from a four-footed hairy animal that, equipped with tail and pointed ears, pursued the life of a tree animal'. Backed by such observations one could comfortably live in the modern jungle!

Darwin fully realized the social and moral aspects of man, even if his reasoning, trying to deduce them too from the biological evolutionary process and interpreting them as end products of the instincts, was very contradictory. For the imitators of Darwin man was a cerebral animal — his animal nature alone was the determining factor; the biological monstrosity, man deprived of his humanity, was posited. But Darwinism alone cannot be made responsible for the 'breakthrough of the instinct'; it was merely apt to be used and abused; the real root of the *furor teutonicus* was very likely socio-pathological in nature. There was the economic and political misery experienced by Germany for centuries, especially during and after the Thirty Years War and during the Napoleonic period. There was the tutelage of the people by a multitude of intellectually and morally inferior princes which prevented personal and communal activeness. These obstacles led to the damming up of impulsive energies which — sublimated — led to the cultural flowering of enlightenment, classicism and romanticism, and — repressed — resulted in the collective neurosis of the *petit bourgeois* nineteenth century. Christian or enlightened humanitarian attitudes alike were handcuffed and tamed by the dual nature (instinct and spirit) of man; Schiller had said: 'only in his physical state does man suffer the oppression of nature; assuming his aesthetic nature he escapes this oppression. His moral nature overcomes it.' Had this maxim, which characterizes Schiller's complete philosophical and literary work, been

136

taken seriously and had it remained the purpose of man's struggle with
himself, it could have prevented the distortion of the German spirit.
Instead, one rebelled against morality, escaped it by slipping under the
false aesthetic front of a cultural façade, and glorified the physical state
of existence, which no longer was to be endured and overcome, but
lived and enjoyed. Once the 'restraining talisman' breaks, said Heine,
'the wildness of the old fighters, the berserker's senseless anger, of
which the old nordic poets speak and sing so much, will come forth
again'. He was thinking of the cross; but more than anything it was to him
the talisman of an enlightened humanism. 'We Germans are of yesterday'
Goethe once said to Eckermann; 'we have been cultivated quite a bit
during the course of a century, but a few more centuries may pass by
before enough intelligence and advanced culture will have spread and
become common amongst our countrymen that we may say of them:
it is long ago that they were barbarians.'

Treitschke observed that Germany retained an ugly sediment of
barbarism. It was uncertain, added Blüher, whether the sacrificial flames
of heathendom really have been extinguished. Foerster noted that
Germany is much closer to the steppes of Asia than the mediterranean —
and its resistance to regression into barbarism — and therefore much
weaker. Such observations, which at times must be regarded as negative
and at others as positive criticism, overlooked the fact that it was not
an outright German archetype which was at the root of the problem
(like the 'Wotanism'[1] dreamed of by Klages), but that the German
inclination to barbarism was caused by historical developments. In
other states the aristocratic or state-church tutelage, which kept the
normal man from culture and spirit and made him into the illiterate
and willing tool, had been broken down in the process of evolution or
revolution. In the Germany of the nineteenth and twentieth centuries
this state of affairs was retained. Intellect was retarded as the instinct
grew rampant. Cultural growth was amiss — it was meant only for the
few.

But there was another reason for the revolt of impulse and instinct
in the nineteenth century. This did not come, however, from an
imposed lack of culture, but rather from an abundance of culture. This
trend aimed at 'a systematic revolt of the impulses in man of the new
age against the former sublimation, against the excessive intellectuality
of our fathers, and their ascetic and sublimating techniques of centuries
which formed man up to now' (Scheler). One felt overly satiated and
cultured. Genuine and genuinely felt culture never can become a
restraint because its nature is to set man free. But when culture

congealed into façade and was passed on as tradition, 'as the people's most sacred possession', difficulties appeared. The poet and philosopher of contemporary life who was interested in the actuality of culture and did not have the ability to transport himself esoterically into the realm of 'eternal values' now showed tendencies 'hostile to culture'. At first, however, he was only hostile to false culture. But eventually his hostility turned into hatred of culture *per se*. The predator then became the symbol of such hatred of culture: the domestic animal, who had been domesticated on the surface only was in the end superior to and more honest than man; in the predator one could 'rediscover his instincts and with that his honesty' (Nietzsche). 'Irrational instincts beckoned beyond the good parlor of the home. . .Instincts range from the heavy urge for a woman to the berserker's behaviour and those wild emotions, the conscious unconscious which was expressed in lyrics by Benn,[2] in philosophy by Klages, and in medicine by C.G. Jung. A heathen spirit emanates from these wishful thoughts, Greek as well as barbarian; however, it was the Greece interpreted by the blond beast, not the Greece of Hölderlin and humanity, nor even the plaster-of-Paris or the grated-window antiquity of the ignorant philistine' (Bloch). Nietzsche's enthusiasm for the 'blond beast', the perfect specimen of vitality, the ignorant and unscrupulous activist and the blind 'will to power' therefore reflected the disappointment of the neurasthenic, the escape from the specifically German 'cultural perversion'. Biographically it was rooted in the petit-bourgeois atmosphere of the German parsonage. The manifestation of the barbaric was explained at this time by Sigmund Freud when he observed that culture basically cannot tame instincts: he considered the 'elemental destructive drive' ineradicable. Freud here was only the representative of the *Zeitgeist,* convinced of the primacy of the instinct. But he was an outsider in so far as he described the sensual world's victory pessimistically. Nietzsche, however, turned from diagnosing and warning to the joyful proclamation of humanity's fall, even though his torn soul was no longer capable of a consistent attitude. This opened the doors for later abuse. The hymns of decline and inhumanity were 'freed' of ambivalence and so could in part be fitted together word by word as the confessions of the cerebral animals. 'Knock down whatever weakens!. . .Who would want to preserve it! Yet I — I want to knock it down again.' 'Only the most noble is thoroughly hard. I place this new law above you: become hard!' 'The weak and deformed shall perish: this is the first command-ment of our love of man. And in that they should be aided 'Restraint has become alien to us.' 'Like the rider on the challenging

charger we let the reins go in face of eternity, we modern men and
semi-barbarians — and we find our greatest happiness only where we
also find the greatest peril.' 'Build your cities near Vesuvius.'

'Who can accomplish anything great if he does not have the energy
and the will to cause great pain? The capacity to suffer is the most
insignificant capacity: here weak women and even slaves can excel.
But not to perish from inner turmoil and anxiety when one inflicts
great suffering and hears the cry of this suffering — that is being great,
that requires greatness.' Man must be able to 'enjoy inflicting pain,
he must be cruel with hand and deed (not only with the eye of the
mind)'. 'The morality of slaves sees the "evil One" as evoking fear;
the master's morality compels the "good one" to evoke fear and to
want to do so. . .Wherever the morality of slaves prevails language
shows the tendency to render the words "stupid" and "good" as similar.'

Nietzsche cannot be exonerated from the guilt of having proclaimed
a philosophy of mercilessness, of titanic life and cruelty; he wanted to
pay homage to 'the roar of life', yet he released repressed instincts; he
wanted to create a new ethics; amorality instead took the place of good
conscience; the 'culture of tomorrow' was his aim, yet the barbarism of
lost generations was initiated. His justification of the strong-willed man
of steel and the 'blond beast' provided philistine wickedness with a
philosophy enabling it to cover the musty world of the instinct with
the mantle of the powerful-demonic. Philosophy now became
Colportage as in Wagner the mythos and in George the beautiful.
Nietzsche did not have to experience the petit-bourgeois Zarathustras,
Hitler, Himmler, Goebbels, Göring, Rosenberg, Heydrich, Ley and
Streicher (vgl. Härtle) as they practised his mercilessness and exercized
the philosophy of being hard in the concentration camps. But he
envisioned the political abuse of his teaching: 'The will to power. A
book for thought, nothing else: it belongs to those who enjoy thinking,
nothing else. . .Today's Germans no longer are thinkers: something else
impresses them and gives them pleasure. The will to power as a guiding
star would of course be comprehensible to them.'

Nietzsche was a 'high-strung professor' who, though he was not cruel
himself, intellectually played with cruelty. He retired into a dream
world of sadism where he, as a deputy also of this generation, openly
indulged in the experience of his twisted urges. This finding of relief on
the 'couch of philosophy' had to be most dangerous when it was no
longer interpreted and declared a neurosis, but a healthy state, no longer
as playful thoughts, but as a political programme.

Oswald Spengler's 'predators' already were suspiciously similar to the ruffians of the SA; though they lacked the element of philosophical 'alienation' they still possessed a veneer of culture. They reflected the view which sees our time in its liberation of instinct and urge as the final stage of cultural-biological evolution. The formative powers of the future for Spengler were 'the will of the stronger, the healthy instincts, the race, and the will to hold property and power'. Thus confronted, 'the dreams that shall always remain dreams, namely justice, happiness and peace', would falter. On the rise would be 'the ancient barbarism', 'realized under the strict forms of an advanced culture which had issued civilization in the beginning. It is that warlike healthy joy in one's own strength which despises the age of rational thinking glutted with literature. It is that unbroken instinct of race that craves for an existence other than oppressed by the mass of consumed books and bookish ideals.' 'Man is a predator. I will say it time and again. All the paragons of virtue and social reformers who refuse to realize this are only predators with defective teeth. They condemn others for the attacks which they prudently evade. . .When I call man a predator, whom have I thus insulted, man or the beast? For the great predators are noble creatures, perfect species without the falsity of human morality born out of weakness.' Biographically Spengler had some 'positive' resemblances to Nietzsche. That is, like generally all the German *Furorists*[3] from Klopstock,[4] Arndt, Nietzsche, Wilhelm II, Blüher, Moeller van den Bruck, to Geobbels, with their cult of the instinct, he has to be granted mitigating circumstances for psycho-analytical reasons. He was an anaemic figure who, compensating for a strong inferiority complex, wielded a very vigorous pen. However, viewed from the text alone, Spengler lacked the discord and perplexity that makes Nietzsche sympathetic. One was a genius ending in insanity, the other a raving pedagogue who indoctrinated his students to despise culture and embrace barbarism. Even though Spengler now and then uses rhapsodic language, the world he proclaims is already the sober world of perfect cruelty: the style of Zarathustra in gothic script.

Hitler's glorification of instincts and urges adopted the image of the hairy four-footed beast from Darwin without paying heed to his biological system. It adopted Nietzsche's cult of cruelty without his internal discord and philosophical many-sidedness; it emanated Spengler's pedantic brutality without taking account of Spengler's nature, which was alien to action; other 'ideas' and especially the style were derived from folkish pamphlets and particularly from Dietrich Eckart.[5] A vicious philistine, acting like an NCO denigrating a recruit, Hitler condemned humanitarianism in *Mein Kampf,* reducing its adherents to a 'miserable heap' cringing at his strapping boots. Humanitarianism, 'as the expression of a mixture of stupidity, cowardice and vaingloriousness, melts away like snow in the sunlight of spring. Mankind has grown in eternal struggles — eternal peace will destroy it.' Pacifism, as a creation of Judaism, was considered by Hitler to keep man from the healthy life of the instincts. The morality of masters is the morality of predators. The first must take what it needs. As the cat has no friendly tendencies towards mice, Hitler observed, so the Aryan does not entertain tender feelings to the subjected peoples or the Jews, who must be subdued and kept down with strong hands. There never has been a culture without Helots. 'First the defeated pulled the plow, and then the horse. Only pacifist fools can consider this a sign of human degradation. They do not realize that this development had to take place. It enabled these apostles today to spout their sanctimonious preachings.' Hitler proclaimed his predator-cult as 'idealism' because it effected a 'genuine elevation of mankind'. The intellectual confusion of the preceding decades thus finds its culmination in Hitler even in this respect: Man evolves 'upward' to the predator, slavery proves to be the basis of culture, mercilessness creates noble humanity! Spengler's 'twilight-mood' of a declining culture had turned into the darkness of night: the 'night of the long knives'.[6]

Notes

1. Wotan, Germanic God of storm and ecstasy, most prominent figure in the Germanic pantheon, also called Odin.
2. Gottfried Benn (1886-1956), German lyricist and essayist of the first order.
3. Relating to the immanent power of the *furor Germanicus* in poetic expression.
4. Friedrich Gottlieb Klopstock (1724-1803), major German epic poet and writer whose emotion-laden work helped pave the way for 'storm and Stress' and German Classicism. A writer of great range, talent and influence, Klopstock had the tendency to overdraw his images; his cult of the Germanic spawned unfortunate epigones.
5. See p.42, n.2.
6. Reference to the mass slaughter of opponents by the Nazi party during the Röhm putsch of 30 June 1934.

9   A GILDED RACE OF GERMANS

A dose of mysticism can gild the life of a nation, Julius Langbehn believed. But this gold of the nineteenth century was really fool's gold. One wanted to return to the 'secret of life' and to seek God. But what was found were artfully stylized deities of heathen origin which, as new idols, took the place of the Christian faith. The disintegration of this faith was substantially aided by the ossification of the churches, which made common cause with the establishment and fled materialism by escaping into the empty rhetoric of edifying sermons. To live in the chill of nihilism was impossible for the petit bourgeois, who was drawn to the idyllic. He did not have the energy to take part in the active life of a materialist world. He did not have the inner vitality and strength to renew Christianity by drawing on his own being. The mythological masquerade therefore was better suited to his mentality, because it retained the fiction of the 'as-if' − that is, as if one had religious values. On the other hand it did not call for too much personal engagement, of which he was not capable anyhow. The Greek Pantheon here was more the concern and (since the time of German classicism) the fashionable genre of the artists who often hid their own creative impotence behind the cheap copies of antique figures. Germanic mythology, though in detail equally alien and 'complicated', could better serve as a popular religion because it came closer to the general national sense of mission and gave it a mystical benediction.

Already the Renaissance-humanists and the men of the Baroque had striven to learn more about Germanic mythology; with the advent of irrationalism, as in Klopstock's cult of the Bard, the attempt was made to infuse the scholarly contents with passionate feelings.

Even though attempts to fuse Germanic and Christian elements in the sense of a national religion were made at that time, they remained without considerable influence on the population at large. This influence came about with the wars of liberation and then especially in the second half of the nineteenth century, when literature, art and music successfully popularized the Germanic. Siegfried as the god of the sun, Wotan as the nordic saviour, the Germans as the actual source of humanity, these were the images which gave wings to the soul of the petit bourgeois, wings which enabled the politically and economically restricted to flutter out into the world of 'Germanic

Ideology'. They freed him from his individual and collective inferiority complexes: he, who had failed to break through to the top, who was threatened with languishing in miserable small-town triviality or irrelevant occupations, was enabled by this Germanic mythology to feel as part of mystic and mysterious greatness. That was the 'gilding' of the nation of which Langbehn had spoken. 'The Germans are the most ancient people. A Nibelung,[1] their king is blood of their kin and at their head has to maintain the domination over the world.' Richard Wagner saw the signs of the day: his *Nibelungenring* 'initiated the most powerful show of the nineteenth German century' (Marcuse). The 'subject',[2] Heinrich Mann said in the novel of the same title, must immediately feel at home in these operas: 'Shields and swords, much rattling tin, loyalty to the Emperor, much shouting and raised banners, and the German oak — one was tempted to play along.' Nietzsche, who in his state of collapse searched his Christian faith for 'new Gods' with great sincerity and at first subscribed to Wagner eventually realized that Wagnerianism, with all its 'to-do and rambling', was no genuine benediction, but a masquerade, the masquerade of Wahnfried. Though he confessed that 'considering everything I could not have endured my youth without Wagner's music', he was made suspicious by Wagner's 'Christian turn-about' in *Parcival.* He realized now that the Germanic gods were used as box office appeal; Wagner's play-acting, complete with 'pompous order' and 'vestments', had to constitute a danger for the German people, especially after the foundation of the Second Empire. German professors, too, contributed to the Germanic dress with which German imperialism now festively garbed itself. They were romantically Germanizing *beaux esprits,* who had the 'confounded mania to idealize and observe historical facts intellectually and to give them a nordic-mythological interpretation' (Schonauer); these people did not later have to jump on the bandwagon, as Thomas Mann wrote to his former friend Ernst Bertram[3] (who himself was a man of naïve characterlessness); they were already on it.

A massive tide of pan-Germanic literature flooded the petit-bourgeois consciousness toward the end of the nineteenth century. The arguments showed little sophistication; using mostly stereotyped phrases, they pounded the reading public with the mythos of being chosen. Incluenced by the racial teaching of the Frenchman Gobineau,[4] Wagner's son-in-law Houston Stewart Chamberlain postulated the 'simple and clear revelation that the whole of modern culture and civilization is the work of one race: the Germanic'. Whatever is not Germanic in this civilization and culture, radiating from Northern Europe and today dominating an important part of the world (though to very different degrees), either is a foreign body imposed on it earlier, not yet expelled, still circulating in the bloodstream like a disease. Or it is alien fare, sailing under the Germanic flag, under Germanic protection and prerogative, impeding our present and future development. . . This accomplishment of the Germanic is without question the greatest heretofore achieved by man. It was not. . .accomplished. . .by the illusion of humanitarianism but by healthy, selfish vitality. No one will have the effrontery to deny that the Germanic peoples have been victorious because of their virtues and not their vices, such as greed, cruelty, treason, and the disregard of all rights but their own. But everyone must admit that especially in those instances where they were most cruel. . .they thereby laid the most secure foundation for the highest and most moral.

The Jews as a particularly inferior race could not have produced Christ; Chamberlain is not yet ready to give up the Christian 'cultural heritage'. So he turns Christ into a blond man with blue eyes, a nordic carrier of light hailing from Aryan Galilee — whereas the German could have mystic experiences, the Jew never could. Although the Aryan, the German has a tendency to be 'merry, mad about life, ambitious, reckless, though he drinks, gambles and smokes', he suddenly

finds himself: the great riddle of existence captures him completely. But it does so not as a purely rational problem, but as an immediate, compelling urge of existence. . .Not to understand, but to be: That is his aim. . .And that he may find this harmony he sings out loud by himself, he tries every scale, practises all melodies; and then he listens in awe. And his call does not remain unanswered: he perceives mysterious voices; all of nature comes alive — all that is human stirring within it. Worshipful he sinks to his knees, not presuming wisdom, not assuming that he has comprehended the source and the final purpose of the world, but somehow feeling that he has a higher destiny. And thus he discovers within himself the seeds of immeasurable tasks, 'the spawn of immortality'.

William Schwaner called his text, which combined similar images with strongly anti-Christian affectations, 'The German Bible'. The All-German League promoted the Germanic cult. In view of the fact that many teachers belonged to this league, the culture was disseminated especially in the schools. ('Our German culture is the ideal core of human thought. Every step gained for Germanness therefore belongs to mankind as such and to the future of our species.') Every positive quality was claimed as an attribute of Germanness — anatomy as well as morality, the form of the skull as well as the beauty of the bosom. If a great populist (like Moeller van den Bruck) committed suicide, even that was 'Germanic' — 'a Germanic death'. Of especial importance for political anthropology were the many petty pamphlets (brochures, tracts) — 'nostalgic literature which found millions of readers. It not only stilled the readers' needs for sugar and sweetness, for torture and cruelty, for sentiment and cheap glitter; it also stilled and again roused urges to hate and to assert power, and it channelled the irrational forces of the dissatisfied and thereby created the riverbeds for later harvests of terror' (Werner). Petty pamphlets appeared in all areas with few regional differences. Often it was the professor of a university, the primary or high school teacher, or a local editor or religious sectarian, having indulged in 'years of private study' and distinguished by a muddled mind, who signed responsibility for them. Of the following two examples the former (little known) came from Franconia, the latter (well-known) from Austria; Franconia was the home of Julius Streicher,[5] Austria was Hitler's home.

Karl Weinländer, a teacher from Franconia, had worked on his racial teachings since 1909. He observed: 'That most able and culturally most valuable race is the Aryan-Germanic'; 'Intuition, vision, perception of nature, the spirit of the discoverer and inventor are almost exclusively formed here. It was and is the only culturally creative race.' The Germanic type, demonstrated by pictures and sculptures of Goethe, the school-superintendent Kerschensteiner *[sic!]*, Queen Louise, Chancellor Bismarck and Hitler, was considered far superior to other racial types demonstrated by photographs of a female Tasmanian, a negroid East-Asian and an Australian aborigine. Tables fixed the results of racial measurements taken in grammar school classes. Size, weight, measurement from nasal bone to occipital cranium, longitudinal axis of the skull, horizontal axis of the skull, proportion and beauty of the body, military fitness, diligence, alertness and political attitude were considered here.

Weinländer asserted that the development of the human brain generally takes two directions: 'One goes upwards and longitudinally to become the idealistic-creative active high-long head. The other is marked by lowness, shortness and compactness and produces the more animalistic and materialistic low-round head.' Behold the racial

superiority also on other parts of the body: he observes that the female
Hottentot has a fat rear, as does the Frenchwoman; the Aryan maid,
contrasted in sculptured form to the photographs of the others does
not, *of course,* have one. But she has 'beautiful, fully developed breasts,
well suited to the nursing of children, a fully formed body and a pelvis
suitable for childbirth'. Her hair is superior to and more durable than
the hair of inferior races: 'Statistical examinations show that the supple
blonde sometimes carries 135 kilometers of hair, while the dark woman
only carries about 70 kilometers.' The Aryan race is 'constructed
according to the law of the golden mean. If the figure of the average
mature Aryan eight or more head tall, is divided according to the rules
of the golden mean, the centre point is at the belt'; Aryan feet are
superior too: 'The Germanic race therefore is better suited for forced
military marches than the lower races.' It was considered characteristic
that Aryans are light-skinned, because 'bright and airy, rosy and blue
are the colours of joy, of the sublime and celestial': 'Blue sky — golden
sun/blue flood and golden field/eyes of blue and golden hair/are the
fairest in the world /Blue and gold the Northland's flag;/ancient law
of Sweden, Schleswig/Hail the Aryans' noble colours/blue and gilded —
true and pure!' Only Aryans can be 'clairvoyant', 'acutely perceptive'
and 'finely tuned': 'It is the divine gift of the most intensely intellectual
vision, it is intuition elevated to actual seeing and hearing.' If such
people at times appear among other races they are of Aryan origin:
'The Chinese philosopher Confucius must, in view of an ancient Chinese
original painting, be considered Aryan; this explains the rapport
between his philosophy and the Germanic. His heir in the 76th
generation still shows some Aryan characteristics.' Weinländer
demanded racial marriages because only they could make possible the
raising of good blood; the Jewish Neanderthals have contaminated
Germany and must be extinguished. 'Thus if Richard Wagner, Bismarck,
Goethe, Thorwaldsen,[6] or Rosegger[7] had chosen partners of equal
qualities, probably dynasties of Wagners, Bismarcks, Goethes,
Thorwaldsens, and Roseggers would have developed.' Gratefully
Weinländer gave credit to his intellectual compatriot, Lanz von
Liebenfels.[8] Pure breeding, Liebenfels wrote, can remove everything
that is unnecessary and harmful from the human body, bringing man
closer to the deity. 'The pure breeding of the Aryan race leads the
path to happy Asgar.'[9] Liebenfels called men of noble race *Asinge,*[10]
Heldlinge[11] or *Arioheroiker.*[12] Those of inferior race he called
Tschandalen,[13] *Warringe,*[14] *Afflinge.*[15] His theo-zoology meant 'racial
struggle including the scalpel of castration'. The heroic man was

recognized amongst other things by the big toe: 'In the heroic man the big toe surpasses all other toes in length and strength.' The heroic wife has the 'most beautiful facial lines, a beautiful, full bosom especially suited to nurse, a full seat and full hips, the characteristics of a pelvis well suited to give birth.' As in all these petty pamphlets, the Jews and the Negroes here, too, are the greatest misfortune for the Aryan race — Liebenfels advertised his journal with the words:

> Are you blond? Are you sick of the mess created by the mob?
> Then read the Ostara-Literature of the blond and the advocates of
> masculine power. . .Are you blond? Then you are a creator and
> preserver of culture. . .'Ostara' is the first and only illustrated
> Aryan-aristocratic collection of writings which proves in words and
> pictures that the blond, heroic man is the moral, noble, idealistic,
> genial and religious man. That he is the creator and preserver of all
> science, art and culture, and the main pillar of the Divine.
> Everything ugly and evil originates in the mixture of races to which,
> for psychological reasons, the woman has more inclination than the
> man. At a time when the feminine and racially inferior is
> meticulously cared for and the blond, heroic kind of man ruthlessly
> extirpated, the 'Ostara' has become the rallying point of all idealists
> who seek beauty, truth, a purpose in life and God [Daim] .

These and similar writings combine lewd wishful dreams with pedantic narrow-mindedness. The sexual aspect will be discussed more extensively later. The fact that the German grammar school was under-developed, its teaching staff insufficiently trained and the required term of schooling too brief now reaped a bitter harvest: the 'philosophical' swindler and the 'political' seducer could be successful in the intellectually poor world of gossip and petty garden environment of the petit bourgeois, especially when he himself exuded the musty odour of repression and deviated instincts.

Some of the National Socialists found it difficult to appear racially 'pure' in the sense of the petty pamphlets. Further pamphlets then served to provide for the 'nordification' of NS leaders. So it was A. Richter who wrote in his 'Our Leaders in the Light of the Racial Question and The Study of Prototypes':

> [Hitler:] Upper skull well rounded, arching harmonically to all sides,
> reflecting good tension; love of all, high religiosity, beauty and
> nobility of being. . .Hitler is blond, has rosy skin and blue eyes,

therefore is of pure (Aryan) Germanic nature and all other rumours concerning his appearance or personality have been sown into the soul of tne people by the black or red press, a fact which I hope to have corrected with these remarks. . .

[Göring:] Upper skull well rounded, broadening to the top and falling off to tne sides with equal tension; high religion, willingness to help, goodness of the heart, strong assertion of faith in the love of the All. . .In tnis respect the marvellously formed right ear of Göring stands out. It speaks of rare harmony and is comparable to the so-called Goethe ear. . .

[Rosenberg:] The explicit long-head tells us that we deal with a pure being of movement and emotion. . .But the complete expression of the eye contains an element of suffering. Also, the left eye is a little larger and more open than the right one. This tells us that our party member takes in everything, but gives it back in form very carefully. . .

[Darré[16] (interpreted on the basis of his ear):] . . .is without question the right man who strives to the end that agriculture will be integrated again with the totality of the people. . .

[Goebbels:] Though the jaw is long, which indicates toughness, it is not sufficiently broad. This helps us to recognize Goebbels as the explicit intellectual. The fine, tender and yet taut neck must be considered as a parallel indication. He must be warned to avoid overwork. . .

[Schemm[17]:] . . .An optimistic, tough, distinctively nordic figure. . . Pedagogues with such attributes win the hearts of children immediately. . .May God give him strength and health so that he may educate Bavarian youth in the national socialist sense, enabling them to meet the great tasks ahead. . .

[Streicher:] . . .Total expression: bold, aggressive purposeful. Woe betide the man who opposes him, he will certainly strike him one. . .

In the race question Hitler's *Mein Kampf* is also only a petty pamphlet amongst others; he was a successor of Chamberlain, an imitator of Lanz von Liebenfels and related political-racial smut literature. Logic, morality and style reflect the generally prevailing abysmal mediocrity.

Hitler proclaimed a truth which, he said, was very obvious: 'The eggs of Columbus are available by the hundreds of thousands – only Columbuses are less frequently found.' Since the titmouse pairs only with the titmouse, the finch with the finch, the stork with the stork, the Aryan shall mate only with the Aryan; if he does not do so, his end as the carrier of culture has come. Hitler lifts one of the 'edges of the enormous, gigantic veil of eternal riddles and mysteries of nature'; this is his revelation: Selection and Extirpation! 'The struggle for the daily bread lets everything succumb that is weakly, sick and lacks decision. The struggle of the males leaves the right or potential to procreate only to the healthy.'

The Aryan stands in the zenith of creation. The 'proof' advanced by Hitler to substantiate this claim is characteristic of the demagogic technique of the *Führer*. 'All we admire on earth today in science and art, technology and invention is the creative product of only a few peoples' – the initial thesis is phrased so that its general formulation does not evoke major objections; '. . .and perhaps originally of one race' – the limitations 'few people' (in the preceding sentence) and 'one race' (in this sentence) are not expressed apodictically, but are turned into vague assumptions by the addition of 'perhaps' and 'originally'; the uncritical reader is thereby made to slip on the treacherous slide of Hitler's logic! After a few passages which amount to diversionary manoeuvring the assertion is interjected: 'What we see before us today of human culture and of the results of art, science and technology is almost exclusively the creative product of the Aryan.' The phrase 'creative product of few peoples' has been replaced with Aryanism; the mental acrobatic is facilitated by the still qualifying addition of the word 'almost'; otherwise the sentence measures up to the assertion at the beginning. 'Just this fact', Hitler continues, 'permits the not unfounded conclusion that he alone was the source of higher human development and therefore represents the archetype of what we understand by the word human.' The involved clausal construction of the sentence is intended to reconcile the reader with the complete absence of proof. A metaphor follows:

He is the Prometheus of mankind whose luminous brow brought forth the divine spark of genius at all times, always anew rekindling the fire that as knowledge lightened the night of silent mysteries and permitted man to climb the path to dominance over all other beings of this earth.

Subsequently Hitler offers additional 'eggs of Columbus', one as bad as the other; there is no section that transcends the usual racism and Germanic mythos! Hitler's upshot then is: the new movement must create the granit foundation on 'which someday the state can rest. A foundation which does not represent a mechanism of economic concerns and interests alien to the people, but an ethnical organism: A Germanic state of a German nation.'

Notes

1. *Nibelugnen,* the holders of a magnificent hoard of treasures of Germanic mythology.
2. Ernst Bertram (1884-1957), writer and professor of the history of literature. As a poet he belonged to the circle around Stefan George.
4. Count Joseph Arthur Gobineau (1816-82), French writer and diplomat. His *Essair sur l'inegalité des races humaines* had a strong impact on racial and anti-Semitic writers of his day and later generations.
5. See p.105, n.6.
6. Bertel Thorwaldsen (1768-1844), Danish sculptor renowned for his figures representing themes of classical antiquity.
7. Peter Rosegger (1843-1918), popular Austrian writer in the mountain genre.
8. Lenz von Liebenfels (b.1874), a confused religious sectarian whose views helped to shape Hitler's mad racial conception. (Comp. W. Daim, *Der Mann der Hitler die Ideen gab,* Munich, 1958).
9. *Asgar (Asgard),* in Nordic mythology the seat of the *Asen,* the Germanic gods.
10. *Asinge:* this and the following terms were part of the terminology of Liebenfels' private religion and ideology.
11. *Heldlinge,* heroes.
12. *Arioheroiken,* Aryan heroes.
13. *Tschandalen* (drawn from the designation of a low caste of Hindus).
14. *Warringe?*
15. *Afflinge,* monkey-like creatures.
16. Richard Walter Darré (1895-1953), Hitler's *Reich* leader of the peasants *(Reichsbauernführer)* and Minister of Agriculture.
17. Schemm, see p.99.

10 OF BLOOD AND RACE

The myth of tne blood is the pendant to the Germanic myth: what distinguished tne German or Aryan above all is the specific nature of his blood. From the beginning of the nineteenth century, a mystique of tne blood was celebrated which partially secularized Christian elements, partially intensified and politically fertilized the folklore superstition of bloodlines which is present in all primitive peoples. The eighteenth-century patriotic cult of blood and wounds had been saccharine, pervaded by sentimental erotic emotions. Klopstock let the blood of youth flow for fatherland and eternal father Wotan; blood 'sparkled and roared deep in the valley'. The bloody binge of words was continued in irrationalism and 'Storm and Stress': 'The youth, aflame to fight, and from his flank he gives/the best blood of his heart to you (the fatherland) with joy' (Herder). The poets of the liberation wars literally sputtered blood; the beautiful blue Rhine was to be dyed by the 'tyrants' chargers' blood, the tyrants' servants' blood, the tyrants' blood, the tyrants' blood, the tyrants' blood!' (L. v. Stolberg).

The struggle in which blood flowed in streams was considered the true test of German character; it was a bath which German man (like Siegfried from the dragon's blood) left newly born.

This blood-ideology also shaped the attitude *(Weltanschauung)* of the fraternities; the duel had to test the 'truth of the blood'. Then

> that sacred, heroic excitement prevails which we admire in the fathers of the past. It is an excitement that everyone must experience who, fulfilling his oath in German loyalty, chivalrously sheds blood for the chosen colours, his blood which after all is a sap of rare quality. Here everything belonging to the nature of our people again comes brilliantly forth from the roots of the personality. Whoever passed the test has become a German man [Bresalski].

Clean, good, Aryan blood, Langbehn said, is aristocratic blood; 'of all human "blood"' he said, it 'is the blood that contains the most moral "gold"'. During the Second Empire, and in the right-wing circles of the Weimar Republic, the 'wellsprings of our blood began to speak louder and louder'. 'The blood in its purity is the true mediator between spirit and deed. It harbours the deepest meaning of our myths, our sagas and fairy-tales. German forests and streams echo in it' (Pechel). The 'great stream of the blood flowed along, a great melody' (F.G. Jünger). Even a man like Walther Rathenau[1] swam in it. Blood for the National Socialists was 'the soul in artful connection with its mode of expression, the body'. Bound by blood and conscious of blood, one was willing to shed it; sacrifices of blood were rewarded by decorations of blood; the blood barrier prevented the contamination of blood; laws protecting the blood extirpated alien blood and inferior blood; emotions of the blood tied together the communion of blood and led to the relation of blood; those who carried the bloodlines appreciated the values of blood and soil; blood poisoning destroyed the once creative races which mixed with racially impure blood (comp. Berning). Blood poisoning was especially practised by the Jews who seduced hundreds of thousands of racially pure German girls (Hitler). But also because they had invented an evil serum, 'a preparation of bloodwater of animals and humans' injected to contaminate the race: 'The Quicksilver serum "Ehrlich 606", invented by the Jewish Doctor Ehrlich, is not only without value. It harms the human organism in the worst way. . . The serum of Dr Koch and Dr Behring, announced with much fanfare, has been proven to be worthless and hazardous' (Weinländer). The prospect of the Third *Reich* began 'to revive the lifeless blood. Under its mystic symbol a new cellular restructuring of the German people's soul is taking place' (Rosenberg). The new faith was faith in the 'myth of the blood, the faith that with the blood the divine nature of man was being defended. This faith incorporated the most distinct awareness that nordic blood represented the mystery which took the place of the old sacraments and overcame them.' The 'new' that had been added was, of course, the blood. 'Here the transformation began. It was the transformation through the blood, namely the German blood. This was equivalent to the realization that all action is without energy if it is not generated by the blood' (Schmolck). The propaganda of the National Socialist was 'blood conscious': new standards were blessed with the 'blood banner' which had been carried during the demonstration of 1923 at the Felderrnhalle[2] and 'dipped' into the blood of the fallen. The dead of the World War and the Movement[3] were 'blood witnesses' who were mystically revered. A religion of the blood was created and practised, including definite rites and symbols; striving for the sublime, the petit-bourgeois consciousness was clouded by a fog of blood.

Notes

1. Walter Rathenau (1867-1922), prominent German business man and politician, Foreign Minister in 1922. He was attacked by nationalistic and anti-Semitic circles for his policy of fulfilment of the Versailles Treaty and assassinated.
2. Site of the abortive Nazi putsch in Munich.
3. The Nazi party and its apparatus was usually referred to as 'the Movement' *(die Bewegung).*

11 BLOOD AND SOIL

Where racial corruption was at an advanced stage, people were to be brought back to nordic standards by the proper crossing with pure blood. This kind of animal culture adopted elements of Darwinism and Social Darwinism: the 'iron laws' of nature were now also to be assisted by the acceleration of the weeding out process or, respectively, the support of the 'superior' in their 'life struggle'. The German race — it was said, was especially suited for this process of blood improvement; even if the bastardization had assumed considerable proportions in the cities, the 'German womb' had remained closed to alien blood, above all in the countryside. Hitler asserted: 'An ethnic state will first of all have to lift the institution of marriage out of the state of permanent racial corruption to give it the sanction of its purpose, that is, to procreate likenesses of the Lord and not the monstrous mixture of man and ape.' These thoughts were reflected in the genetic teachings of Darré, which were later translated into reality with terrible means by Himmler. 'Darré's romanticizing of the peasant and Himmler's romanticizing of authority thrive on the same nordic manure' (Niekisch). Darré wanted to 'gather the best blood'.

> As we have restored our old Hanoverian horse from less pure male and female animals by selective breeding, we will also, in the course of generations, again selectively breed the pure type of the nordic German from the finest German bloodlines. . .We will concentrate on the peasantry, to the extent that it has still retained a remnant of good instinct by confessing to the Movement.

The commitment of the national-socialist certified agriculturist Darré to the peasantry, as that of National Socialists in general, resembles the love of the armchair Tyrolian for the mountains: the native soil to which one 'returned' is perfumed, the blood-and-soil mystique is conceived in the comfort of the bourgeois parlour. The German brawler dreamt of the idyllic pastoral life. 'There was for me only one aim worth working and fighting for', observed the Auschwitz murderer Höss, 'the farm earned through individual effort with a healthy and large family. That was to be the content, the purpose of my life.'

The large new frontier settlements of peasants in the German East,

planned by Himmler, were to reflect the German village idyll: the
Linden trees and German oaks, the German village well and German
Lieder ('At the village well before the gate').[1] The Russian work
animals were allowed to perish by the tens of thousands — only the
German man counted. To twist the necks of geese and Jews from time
to time, to produce healthy blond children with fertile women, to bring
in the year's harvest high on the harvesting cart, to tangle with frisky
maids in the moonlight — that was the wishful dream of the
pan-German sadist. The city with its asphalt jungle was considered
corrupt; it was the home of the Jew and the rationalist, the advocate of
sedition and the superficially civilized. It was 'an inferno of bastardizing
filthy floods of humanity', which deteriorated into the 'seething,
infertile asphalt of a bestial inhumanity' (Rosenberg).

Urbanization, industry and commerce must 'give up their unhealthy
dominant position' wrote Hitler in *Mein Kampf*. He considered a
healthy peasantry the foundation of the nation; it alone could sustain
the nation in times of crisis and war; but German land was too limited
for that: the new *Reich* once more had to begin the march of the
Teutonic Knights of old, 'to conquer with the sword the soil for the
German plow and the bread for the German nation'. Sentimental love
of the soil was thus combined with its practical political appreciation.
The 'return to the father's hearth' was combined with the Eastland
crusade.

The hostility to civilization of Rousseau and of the Anti-rationalists
had fallen on fertile soil, especially in Germany, because it made it
possible to compensate ideologically for the existing backwardness and
provincialism. Other nations, which possessed a more fully developed
rational and democratic attitude, reacted to the shock of
industrialization more casually, and approached the problems with
a greater measure of reason and understanding, planning and realism.
The German soul, handicapped by Restoration and Reaction (of an
absolutism typical for its obstructions in agrarian lands), tended to
react with repression and escapism. As far as the *Junkers* and large
landowners were concerned, they had to react against the increase of
trade and technology — their own economic interests dictated isolation
from the West and active agrarian policies in the East. The intellectual
isolation of the bourgeois was also reflected in their commercial
immaturity, which moreover promoted the perpetuation of a patriarchal
societal order. When the new Germany 'plunged' into the years of its
most intense industrial and commercial expansion during the
Wilhelmian era after the successful war of 1871, the requisite emotional

maturity was lacking. In an age of steam engines and electrical energy, of big cities and world trade, the petit bourgeois retreated into the world of the literary mythos; he relished Siegfried, Brünhild and Kriemhild, and in the shadow of oaks he dreamt of the ancestors' glory. Part of the anti-bourgeois youth, as members of youth movements, indulged in a romantic cult of forest and hiking. The socialists, who above all were familiar with the problems of industrialization, were maligned and deprived of political and social influence. The prevailing 'philosophy of life' adopted elements of Rousseauism and intensified and combined them with ethnic aristocratism. The 'dull and faceless, subhuman urban masses', stultifying in their breeding holes, were considered to be completely removed from the sources of life. As Norne[2] spun the yarn of fate, people like Schuler[3] and Klages spun the yarn of their hostility against intellect, technology and civilization; C.G. Jung made an ideology out of the scientific discovery of the collective subconscious; the motto was: 'Return to the mothers!' – to be an outsider in the technological world really meant, as demonstrated by the case of Ernst Jünger,[4] to be fully within the realm of petit-bourgeois consciousness. This poet, who devoted himself to nature, who, holding an hour-glass, meditated in the forest or at the beach, was an outsider only because of his affected, intellectual-arabesque style, which the petit bourgeois could not understand. The petit bourgeois was more used to the warmth of the heart; he did not want cold portraits of nature, but broadly, colourfully blotched 'warmth'. In the 'process of ruralization' which was desirable (as seen by Langbehn), the Dutch style was considered correct; after all, even Brünhild, the 'warlike maid. . .in the German saga was half Valkyrie, half Dutch'. Warmth was needed – the provincial warmth of the stable:

> The straying soul of the German artist, now roving in all
> directions of the compass, must bind itself again to the native soil;
> the painter from Holstein shall paint in Holstein fashion, the
> Thuringian as a Thuringian and the Bavarian in the Bavarian manner.

The 'ruralized' ethnic literature had nothing to do with the pastoral idylls of the Enlightenment, Storm and Stress, Romanticism, Classicism, Biedermeier and Realism, which were deeply rooted and based on a feeling of insecurity corresponding to Schiller's definition. Nor did it have anything to do with *Heimat* literature, which was rooted in local dedication to nature and portrayed the rural environment with

humour and sharpness. (Ludwig Thoma[5] was a contributor to the
Simplicissimus; when in 1933 the National Socialists did not throw
O.M. Graf's [6] books on the pyre, he challenged them in an open letter:
'Burn me too'.) Gustav Freytag's *Ahnen*[7] marks the beginning of the
fatal development. He himself was still free from the later, offensive
ethnic mannerisms; but his unfortunate cult of the Germanic and his
particular stylistic incompetence made possible a work which, with its
floridity, inspired an army of third- and fourth-rate writers. In the
mirror of the *Ahnen* (his ancestors), the petit bourgeois experienced the
essence of a world in which he was happy or for which he longed: a
chicken in the pot, a shooting-match festivity or the benediction of the
flag, and the romanticism of the family tree which was carefully drawn
on fine paper as he sat at home, sighing that 'he was called to be
something better'.

'The chicken has been cooking long, Godeling', said the little man,
longingly looking at the pot. 'Swing the spoon and put another log
in — this is all we have ample of in this country.'

And a noble at the side of the prince intoned loudly: 'My greatest
treat indeed is such a high festival in the summer, when old
comrades greet each other in the verdant meadow, wearing their
battledress. The grey heads then recall the campaigns of long ago,
the battle-eager youth prove in games that their strength will one
day add to the honours of their elders. The sun is warm and the
hosts's face smilingly beckons the guests. Cattle mill about, the ears
of the grain turn golden in the southern breeze; the man's heart
becomes gay at such times and he thinks of his cares only
reluctantly.'

From century to century the oceans and forests resound the same
mysterious melody, but men came and went, and their thoughts
were changing without end. The chain of ancestors tying each one
to the past, was growing longer. His inheritance, coming from the
ancient days, was becoming ever larger, and stronger lights and
shadows fell from the deeds of the. . .ancestors, into his life. But
under the compulsion of the past his own freedom and creative power
were also marvellously growing.

'My native land' — this was the elemental, longing cry of the pastoral
and homeland literature which resounded over the 'eternal heather' or

through the 'exalted silence of the forest's dome', and 'echoed from the
jagged, glowing Alps to the great, wide sea'. The figures who at the time
of the 'blessed morning prayer' sowed the seeds into the ancestral soil
were proud and defiant men. Rough, pure blood roared in their veins;
the maids' eyes flashed and their figures stiffened with pride —
especially when the sternly beloved returned from the Frenchman's
land of trash to spouse and cottage. Everyone more or less marched
behind the plow, not to forget the long chain of ancestors who were
always along:

> Many are with her, beside her, those who in millenia have trodden
> here behind the plow, serving the sacred soil. They accompany her,
> guide her foot, lead her hand. They pass through her and lift her
> heart close to the sun. It is a festival of the blood, a feast of the most
> intimate communion with the brown soil into which her foot sinks.
> Exertion and joy combine to drive the blood more quickly through
> her young body, flowing through it with unexpected force, growing
> out of the depth of the soil, passing through her so that she must
> stop suddenly, overcome by the exciting sweetness pervading her
> whole body [Tremmel-Eggert] .

The heavenly bodies look down on a land of German grapes, German
grain and German cabbage, miners produce German ore and boatmen
navigate the German Rhine. Peasant mothers place their hands in
blessing on blond children and somewhere in the distance flowers
bloom on a hero's grave. The brow was always turned to the stars:
'Greater Germany you are called, oh native land, shining land! With
green meadows in golden glow, you are the people in the harvest's
wreath' (Schirach). National Socialist art presented the peasant epos
either in its 'eternally valid form, heroic-behind the wooden plow,
fertilizing in every muscle's move, straight forward to the mysterious
end' (Rosenberg), or in its saccharine-lovely form: pastoral bare-
bottoms who, surrounded by field flowers, vegetables or fine knotty-
pine furniture, made an idyllic still-life! 'Good pioneer-novels, creations
dealing with the new German peasantry. . .good artisan-novels, good
regional novels, good novels concerning race and blood' — 'in all these
fields an important and beautiful task was to be fulfilled'
(N.S. Bücherkunde). Orgies of veneration are offered to the 'Blubo'[8]
poets. Succeeding Marlitt[9] and Courths-Mahler,[10] Kuni Tremel-Eggert[11]
and Josefa Berens-Totenohl[12] came to the fore. The latter had, one of
her rhapsodic admirers observed, an especially revealing name:

> You gave your name a harsh suffix — taken from the valley of your birth,
> Totental (death valley) — rather than choosing one that flatters and
> pleases the ear like sweet music. You have let your books appear in severe,
> plain coloured covers. You did not let their principal figures say one
> jestful word. This is how seriously and hard life, art, you, and
> Germany want to be taken [Stöve].

Ethnic home and peasant literature indulged in a special cult of the
maternal, whereby pantheistic (mother nature), Christian (Mother of
God) and psychological elements (The Great Mother) were used and
distorted. While life itself was respected only very conditionally (as far
as it was racial and of pure bloodlines), and war was praised as the great
master and educator of life, the mother and the maternal were
'venerated' in a literally repulsive manner. In reality she was considered
the source of the human material one was ready to sacrifice on the
altars of the fatherland. The style used was half Boelsche, half Goebbels:
on the one hand the vague allusions to the darkness of the soul, the
maternal-Chthonian, to the fertility of sacred birth-giving; on the other
hand the patriotic pathos of hallowed and high words concealing
brutality.

In the story 'Wanderer between Two Worlds' by Walter Flex,[13] the
poet visits the mother of the fallen friend; she asked him 'after a while
of silence: "Did Ernst take part in a charge before his death?" I nodded
"yes, at Warthi!" There she closed her eyes and leaned back in the chair.
"That was his great wish", she said slowly, as if she was glad in her
suffering that something had been fulfilled for which she had long
feared. A mother very likely must know the deepest wish of her child.
And that must be a deep wish for the fulfilment of which she fears even
after his death. Oh, mothers, German mothers!' — In war the mother is
closest:

> How the detonations resound! How the field is torn and quivering
> and full of noise. . .And in all our desperation suddenly a wondrous
> quiet came over us, as if everything, everything now had to become
> good. Someone amongst us it was who spoke the word, silently for
> himself, and we read it from his lips. Like the tone of a bell it
> touched us in all the noise around us: Mother! [Beumelburg].

During the Third *Reich* the life of a German woman finds fulfilment
when she receives the 'Golden Cross of Honour for the German Mother',
when two sons are decorated by the Order of Blood, and she at least can

give one son for the fatherland.

> The sinking sun lit up the golden letters of the headstone: 'They
> died so Germany could live', and Germany lived, stronger, more
> mighty and more glorious than ever, and would live in all eternity.
> Mother Bertha rose and walked home in the light of the evening sun.
> She was full of joy and the happiness of fulfilment [Haas].

When Kuni Tremel-Eggert began work on her novel *Barb, the Story of a
German Woman* during the days of the Weimar Republic, she confided
to her diary: 'I carry the image of a German woman within me. I wish
to give her the name *Barb*. But I do not yet have the energy to shape it.'
But she found the energy, and when she gave birth to her monstrosity –
'the day of Potsdam' had arrived. For four and a half years she worked
on her opus: 'My narrow and silent path went by the side of a great,
sacred and growing faith. Its victory was overwhelmingly beautiful. It
was this faith alone which took my humble gift and carried it amidst
the German people, from where it had come to me. 'The petit
bourgeois – for decades aesthetically miseducated and morally
degenerated – said 'yes' to *Barb* and 'Heil' to Hitler. His spirit was the
spirit of *Blubo* – literature – it was the 'spirit of complete
provincialism' (A. Döblin).

Literary criticism prepared the soil for the likes of Ganghofer,
Kolbenheyer, Grimm, Berens-Totenohl, Blunck and Vesper.[14] Its past
master was Adolf Bartels (1861-1945), who had also distinguished
himself as a writer of peasant life. He received his title of professor from
the hand of the Grand Duke of Saxe-Weimar. With great diligence he
began to distinguish between the work of blood-conscious Germanic
authors and Jewish authors whose blood had been contaminated: 'But
Adolt Bartels is unique in one respect: he was the first to introduce the
segregation of writers according to race and blood into literary criticism,
without ever giving up any factual or critical standards' (Berger). Of
Barlach[15] he said: 'The name sounds too Jewish to me, and the very
success of his plays calls for the mention of his name here; German
dramatists don't succeed here so easily.' In Thomas and Heinrich Mann
he suspected: 'Jewish blood, perhaps via Portugal.' For the care of
culture he founded a Schiller League and a Bartels League; Hitler visited
him in 1925; Chamberlain dedicated his Goethe volume to him with the
words: 'To Professor Bartels with that warm gratitude with which every
Germanic man pays tribute to him.'

Joseph Nadler, another prominent member of the group of ethnic-conscious literary critics, was not as inferior intellectually, but he was equally unprincipled. His *History of German Tribal and Regional Literature,* later called *Literary History of the German People* (1938), again renamed *History of German Literature* (1951), was exceptionally successful. This was in part due to his constant revisions to suit the temper of the times. From the outset he had little regard for Jews. During the Third *Reich* he was free to debase them completely. Now, after 1945, he had to upgrade his estimate again: writers of rural life, whom he always valued, were given uncommonly high rank by him during the Third *Reich* — after 1945 he had to leave out a number of complimentary adjectives and phrases. Nadler's point of view, which attempted to interpret the writer in the light of his regional and tribal association — if used with discretion and without prejudice — would have been useful and fertile as one approach amongst others; but from the beginning his work was based on ideological purpose, which was intensified during the Third *Reich.* His work can therefore rightly be called 'a towering monument to a form of literary criticism which fell prey to chauvinistic and racist delusion' (Muschg).

Notes

1. Franz Schubert's adoption of the popular folk song 'Am Brunnen vor dem Tore' *(Der Linden Baum).*
2. *Nornen* are the three 'sisters of fate' of Germanic mythology.
3. Alfred Schuler (1865-1923), German archeologist and researcher who received prominence because of his intimate knowledge of Roman antiquity overlaid with mystical implications.
4. Ernst Jünger (b.1895), German writer and former front-line officer in the First World War whose war experience occupies a major role in the shaping of his creative work. His views matured from a prolonged nihilistic and defiant phase — attractive to the extremes of left and right — to a philosophical rejection of totalitarianism under the impact of the Second World War.
5. Ludwig Thoma (1867-1921), Bavarian journalist and satirist, biting critic of narrow-minded and phoney philistine morality.
6. Oscar Maria Graf (1894-1967), Bavarian writer associated with the revolution of November 1918 in Munich. He emigrated to the USA in 1933. He said, ironically, 'burn me too'.
7. Gustav Freytag (1816-95), German journalist, university teacher and novelist of national-liberal persuasion. His cycle of novels *Die Ahnen (The Ancestors)* portrayed the history of a German family. Freytag considered the solid middle class as the backbone of the nation. His written work reflected his political convictions.
8. 'Blood and soil poets *(Blut und Boden).*
9. R. Marlitt, pen name of Eugenie John (1825-87), popular novelist of the *Gartenlaube* genre.
10. Hedwig Courths-Mahler (1867-1950), prolific novelist (200 titles) dwelling

on the make-believe world of high society; enormously popular.
11. Kuni Tremel-Eggert (1889-1957), popular novelist.
12. Josefa Berens-Totenohl (b.1891), popular novelist and painter.
13. Walter Flex (1887-1917), poet whose early death in the First World War helped to make his work symbolic in the cause of national regeneration.
14. Will Vesper (1882-1962), editor and writer, partisan to national socialism who dwelt on nationalist and folkish themes.
15. See pp.56-7, n.15.

12 NATIONAL EXALTATION

The Enlightenment was cosmopolitan in spirit. When Moser[1] in 1761 introduced the term *Nationalgeist* (spirit of the nation), he had to borrow from French linguistic concepts. Wieland[2] considered that man a patriot who 'dedicated himself with warm eagerness to the mutual benefit of humanity'. Kant's concept of eternal peace[3] was an appeal to the conscience of the world. To Herder,[4] who perceived the voices of the peoples as a general concert of humanity, nationalism was a negative concept. No people, he said, is God's chosen people; all must seek the truth, all help to till the soil of mutual benefit. 'All peoples shall partake in the weaving of Minerva's[5] great veil, each in its place, without prejudice and free from proud dispute.' Schiller and Goethe considered the nation only an imperfect part of the human cosmos; it was Goethe who coined the term 'world literature'. In pedagogics the principles of education to world citizenship were long at work before they were crowded out by the sense of mission. The universalism of original romanticism did not permit the narrowness and narrow-mindedness of nationalism.

But for Adam Müller[6] eternal peace already appeared as a national misfortune: nothing, he said, was more effective in uniting a people than a genuine war. And Jahn echoed him when he observed that the day that witnessed the establishment of a universal monarchy would be the last day of humanity. Nationalism, 'ignoble and senselessly exaggerated patriotism, which relates to its healthy manifestation as delusion relates to normal conviction' (A. Schweitzer), was the result of Napoleon's conquest of Germany; the people's particular nature, stylized by dreams of the past, was elevated to the stature of the ideal; added to this were hatred of foreigners and irrational fear of the loss of 'purity'. In the final analysis, this nationalism amounted to a lack of normal national feeling: it was compensation for one's own inferiority complex, for the fact that there was no nation and no real state.

However, the roots of German nationalism reach back more deeply; the Napoleonic era and the wars of liberation only freed those forces which had earlier grown in the subconscious. The Enlightenment overcame national *apartheid* in active efforts for the total world and by-passed the stage of national unity for the sake of world-wide unity. The irrationalist meanwhile dreamed of this national unity. But his concept of the nation was here spiritual in nature. Fantasy replaced what reality could not provide. Whereas the nationalist was guided by the idea of progress, the irrationalist was captivated by the eschatology of a kingdom to come. His patriotism was religious or spiritualized. Pietism continued to be influential, as for example in Arndt, who constantly mixed religion and nationalism. 'Fatherland and freedom are an exalted dream, an exultant idea which transcends the earth, a sacred incomprehensible madness which the human heart can never fathom because it is beyond mortal man' (Kaiser). As the 'brethren' had embraced Christ, one now embraced the heroes of the fatherland with 'urgent desire'; out of an air of sacred awe, of suffering and sanguine convulsions the nation unfolded:

> Abounding heart and woe, a sacred air of grace
> a breath of deity! all lives and weaves
> in vernal bloom and force – the glow, the storm
> in every vein, in every arm its pulse!. . .
> Where is more woe, more warmth, more glorious flame
> than in thee, folk of Prussian heroes,
> Thou of one heart, of spirit one
> from throne to hut? – On eagles' wings you fly
> from prey to prey! And clouds of gratitude
> pursue you, raised by the altar of the fatherland
> and every German's sacrificial hearth. . . [Christian von Stolberg] .

Pietism and irrationalism with its great, expansive (superabundant) spiritual energy sought for points of fixation which could aid this spiritual force to form and take shape. The fatherland was praised as one would praise friendship, nature, ice-skating, wine or love; enthusiasm rather aimlessly sought its rhetorical objects. The Napoleonic conquest of Germany and the subsequent 'reveille of the nation' provided this spiritual force with an outlet for hatred and joy, making a tumultous discharge possible. The victory over France gave concrete confirmation to the partially metaphysical, partially folkish-mystical speculations. Thus it came to the extirpation of the German spirit for the sake of the German *Reich* (or the idea thereof), which Nietzsche was to predict for the time after 1871. The word had brought about deeds, the oratorial build-up of the national idea had brought about the building of the nation; but now the deed distorted the word: The national structure held thinker and poet captive; moving in circles they, like their petit-bourgeois sycophants, spent decades within the

cage of nationalistic phraeseology without noticing the intellectual
edifices which were erected next door.

The national feeling of 1813, which was tied to the confession to
and demand for inward freedom, cannot be denied a measure of
greatness. But it was a misfortune that it counted amongst its originators
and proponents men who in their rhetorical aggressiveness no longer
knew sense or reason and who with bombastic nationalist verbiage
extinguished whatever was created by *Klassik* and Romanticism, be it
cosmopolitan morality or, especially, purity of language. The connection
of philosophy and war, lyre and sword, though commensurate to the
intellectual standards of an Arndt or Jahn, was not appropriate to the
intellectual-spiritual breadth of a Friedrich Schlegel[7] or Novalis.[8]
Johann Gottlieb Fichte[9] was a borderline case. His ideas concerning
society, the state and education show enlightened and liberal
characteristics. But with his 'Addresses to the German Nation' he
contributed significantly to the misdirection of German intellectual
development. He wanted to bring 'courage and joy' to the downtrodden,
to 'inject gladness into the depth of mourning'. His was the message of
the 'German Mission'! Jean Paul,[10] virtually presaging a century of
wrongful imperialisms, had prefaced his *Quintus Fixlein* with the
admonition to stay at home ('The most necessary sermon directed to
our century would be to stay at home'). Grillparzer later coined the
no less ominous prediction that the path of German development was
bound to lead from humanity through nationality to bestiality. While
Stifter[11] tried to convince the German people of the fairness of the
golden rule, Fichte believed that he could usher in a century of German
stature: 'For to have character and to be German is without doubt the
same, and there is no special phrase for this in our language because it
is meant to flow immediately from our being without our knowledge or
reflection.' He considered the nation the 'carrier and pledge of terrestial
eternity'. It is possible that Fichte did not aim at an one-sided
chauvinistic nationalism. In his speeches he was often carried away by
the spirit of the moment. Aside from a small group of enthusiastic
followers and exultant youngsters (who, however, had considerable
influence in gymnastic societies, secret patriotic societies and
fraternities), many never comprehended his obscure and suggestive
language. But commentators and successors, who also did much to
popularize him, meant what they attributed to Fichte in the
chauvinistic-nationalistic vein. This became the heritage which led
past the *Gartenlaube,* the pro-Prussians, the conservative historians, the
pan-Germans, the nationalists of 1914, and the folkish of the Weimar

Republic to the National Socialists. Each successive generation, as
Heinrich von Treitschke put it, 'first of all recalled the speaker
who had roused this subjected people with the heroic words: "To have
character and to be German is without doubt the same!"'

Since Prussia after 1813 had been taken in tow by the Restoration,
the reform ideas of the Freiherr vom Stein wasted away. 'Freedom and
unity' was replaced by the motto: 'Through unity to freedom'; the
emaciated bourgeoisie was no longer capable of uniting the two
concepts. The petit bourgeoisie did not desire the realization of
freedom; the petit bourgeois had no conception of personal freedom;
he disliked the initiative of citizenship and political engagement. The
men of St Paul's Cathedral[12] were therefore already outsiders; the
temper of the times had changed from the genuine *Biedermeier*[13] to
bourgeois self-satisfaction. But the aggressive instincts, repressed for
generations, continued to stir within the royal subjects. At the very
least they needed rhetorical satisfaction. If the Rhine could not at the
moment become 'Germany's river', there was always the inspiration of
the melody celebrating it.[14] The *Gartenlaube* called it 'the song which
has given wings. . .to national enthusiasm, the first truly vigorous
folksong in decades, a song suited to keep the sense of fraternal unity
alive in coming generations, and to remind them time and again of the
deeds of the fathers which brought fulfilment to the long-held yearning
of the noblest nation.'

An important mouthpiece of the petit-bourgeois mentality was
Emanuel Geibel.[15] A nineteenth century commentator characterized
him as 'a genuinely Christian man, dedicated to religion, justice and
freedom, who sought the sacred spring of poetry at the rock that carries
the church. . .Unlike the work of the sceptical political-revolutionary
poets, his calm and soulful *Lieder* had a powerful effect' (W. Sommer).
Typical of Geibel's output was his 'German Vocation' (1861):

> Might and Freedom, law and mores
> lucid thought and forceful blow
> will then curb from solid core
> selfish yearning's feverglow,
> mankind once will blessings find
> through the work of German-kind.

The connection of might and 'forceful blow' with freedom, law, mores
and lucid thought was purely rhetorical; these were the values that had
been demeaned for the sake of an uncritical nationalism which placed

might over right, force over freedom, instinct over morality and phraseology over lucid thought. As Ritter remarked, Geibel's 'meagre supply of political ideas did not exceed that of a German high-school teacher during the age of nationalism, of singing, gymnastic, and sharp-shooting festivals. It was especially this mediocrity which made this and similar lyrical poetry so important: not the demonian nature of power but its very mediocrity served as guide and attraction.

Bismarck was the idol of the German petit bourgeoisie because his personality was shaped by a brutal and selfish lust for power, because he disregarded judicial and constitutional principles, because he displayed the superiority of the *Junker* and practised politics not from the ethical but from the tactical point of view. His scornful words deriding parliamentary activity, especially in the West, the opposition parties and the socialists, delighted the subject-mentality, which was equally anti-western, anti-parliamentarian and anti-socialist. Even the formerly democratic forces later on valued success over morality; the victory over Austria, and especially over France, 'cleansed Bismarck's brow' (as Wilhelm Liebknecht phrased it); now 'the halo crowned the laureled head'. Only a few detected the flaws of this development: 'The damage done by the Bismarckian period is much larger than its benefits', wrote Mommsen as an old man, 'because the gains in terms of power were values which will be lost again during the next storm period of world-history; but the enslavement of the German character and intellect was a misfortune which can no longer be undone.' In the words of Nietzsche: 'to gain power is costly, because power stupefies. . . "Germany, Germany above all" — I fear this was the end of German philosophy.' But the official eye saw it as the beginning of world-wide German prestige. The pride and exaltation, the delight and joy 'to be able to call oneself German' was above all to be transmitted to the young: the 'Sedan feeling'[16] (just like the 'Sedanday' as a national holiday) shaped their consciousness. With his 'Catechism for Germans' Kleist[17] had created the model for a nationalistic pedagogy which, with its lack of logic and intellectual clarity, its rhetorical boisterousness and affected naïveté (childish, not childlike), could not be surpassed even in the Wilhelminian period. Kleist established intellectual and emotional processes which captivated national education for generations.

Recite child. . .I am a German! Why do you love the fatherland?. . . Because it is my fatherland. Who can be trusted more, the Kossack emperor or the emperor of Austria?. . .The Austrian, because he is more truthful. For what do the Germans, who are grown-up, now

alone have time?. . .To rebuild the *Reich* that has been destroyed!
What are the highest values of humanity?. . .God, Fatherland,
Emperor, Freedom, Love and Faithfulness, Beauty, Science and Art.

In this sense education fulfilled its 'noble task', to be the 'seedbed of
the love for the fatherland'. After 1813 further adjectives like 'sincerely'
adorned the 'noble task'. After 1870 the school in many ways began to
resemble the barracks where nationalism and chauvinism were exercised.

The nationalism which fused with imperialism during the Second
Reich displayed the same terryfying recklessness as the imperialism of
the other European peoples. But since it was not promoted by the sober
foreign policy of Bismarck, and could not be realized by the
Wilhelminian 'zig-zag policies', and since in addition it was disappointed
by the defeat of the First World War, it intensified itself. What had been
proclaimed and demanded rhetorically for decades now would be finally
transformed into military action by Hitler. The All-German dream[18]
was dreamed and dreamed to the end. It was part of the credo of the
All-Germans that

> In the east and southeast the Germanic race must be assured the
> conditions of life it needs for the complete unfolding of its powers,
> even if inferior nations such as the Czechs, Slovenes and Slovaks
> must thereby lose their existence, which is of no value to
> civilization. Only the great civilized peoples can be granted the right
> to nationality.

Loyally and obediently one was willing to face the enemy's bullets,
but in return one demanded a reward worth the sacrifice: 'but this
reward is to belong to a dominant people which acquires its share of
the world by itself and does not seek to receive it through the mercy
and goodwill of another people. Germany arise!'

In *Mein Kampf* Hitler observed: 'We set to work where others
stopped six centuries ago. We discontinue the eternal Germanic
migration to the South and West of Europe and direct the view to the
land in the East.' He anticipated that the impending conflict would
be carried out with absolute brutality; the master race had to draw its
frontiers 'with the power of the victorious sword'. The NSDAP thrived
in the nationalistic climate of the Weimar Republic, when almost
every one of the many parties solicited the voter's favour with folkish
phrases; it could link itself to the radical nationalists of the Wilhelminian
period who, according to Ernst Tröltsch[19] thought 'in terms of Assyrian

deportations'. Munich's folkish atmosphere of 1918 agreed with the
party. It was a peculiar mixture of bohemianism and chauvinism, idling
artists and upright-reactionary soldiers of the *Reichswehr,* a beer hall
mood and Filser parliamentarianism,[20] petit bourgeoisie, bureaucratic
hierarchies and retired field-marshalls. A large aggregation of
organizations and associations set the stage for Hitler. There were the
Andreas Hofer League,[21] the Conference Group for Truth, Honour
and Justice, the Bavarian Monarchist Party, the Pan-German League,
the Citizens' Bloc, the Citizens' Council, the Bavarian Veterans'
Association, the League for Bavaria and the *Reich,* the German-folkish
Conference Group, the German-folkish Mutual Protection and Interest
League, the Front-fighters' League, the University Circle for German
Kind, the Interest Group of Army and Navy Dependents, the League
for Germanness in Foreign Lands, the Bavarian Homestead and Royal
League, the German-National Storeclerks' Association, the New-German
League, the League of Patriotic Associations of Munich, the Imperial
Banner, the Viking League, the Think Society and the Munich chapters
of the following organizations: the German Officers' League, the
National Union of German Officers, the Union of German Regimental
Associations, the League of National-minded Students, the National
League of War Veterans Studying at Universities, etc. In the midst of
this nationalistic witches' sabbath Hitler mixed his ideological brew.
More successful than the others, he propagated the national myth and
provided his petit-bourgeois electorate with the old faith in the new
Holy German empire. The swastika, already familiar to many folkish
organizations before the war, became the symbol for the reveille,
standing for the 'mission of struggle for the victory of Aryan man and
at the same time for the victory of the idea of creative labour, which
in itself was anti-Semitic and will be anti-Semitic'.

Notes

1. Friedrich Karl Freiherr von Moser (1723-98), political writer and government
   official in Austria and Hesse who opposed despotism and corruption of the
   courts.
2. Christopher Martin Wieland (1733-1813), major productive German poet and
   writer whose work reflects the changes of style taking place during the second
   half of the eighteenth century and was influential in setting the stage for the
   classical period of German literature.
3. Kant's *Zum ewigen Frieden* (1795).
4. Johann Gottfried von Herden (1744-1803), one of the principal figures of
   German literature and philosophy of the classical period whose impact at

home and abroad was epochal.
5. Minerva, Italian-Roman goddess of wisdom and protectress of the crafts.
6. See p.129, n.5.
7. Friedrich Schlegel (1772-1829), major representative of German romanticism, key figure in the development of literary criticism.
8. Novalis, pen name of Friedrich von Hardenberg (1772-1801), one of the major poets of the early romantic period whose work, cut short by his premature death, reflects the finest spirit of the age.
9. See p.15, n.11 and p.59.
10. Jean Paul, pen name of Friedrich Richter (1768-1823), perhaps the most renowned poet of German Romanticism whose often fragmentary work has been of lasting, if less widely felt impact.
11. Stifter, see p.15, n.5.
12. Frankfurt — site of the national assembly of 1848-9.
13. See p.85, n.1.
14. See pp.88-92, 60.
15. See p.60.
16. The Battle of Sedan; decisive German victory during the Franco-German War of 1870-77.
17. Heinrich von Kleist (1777-1811), one of the truly outstanding German poets of the classical-romantic periods whose overall poetic and dramatic work towers over the incidental propaganda pieces referred to here. Nevertheless, Kleist's nationalism in the long run may have had a more lasting and broader impact than his truly remarkable creative writing.
18. See p.56, n.1.
19. Ernst Tröltsch (1865-1923), theologian, philosopher and key figure in the development of religious sociology.
20. Filser parliamentarianism referring to Ludwig Thoma's (1867-1921) *Joseph Filsers Briefwexel* (sic) in which Thoma, a sharp critic of the *Spiesser*, caricatured the narrow-mindedness and 'backwoods' attitude of the conservative Bavarian parliamentarians.
21. Andreas Hoter (1767-1810), native of Tyrol, Austrian-German national hero and martyr in the struggle against Napoleon.

13 THE WORD 'GERMAN'

Nationalism found its highest expression in the word 'German', which as adjective became *the* adjective, and as subject became *the* capital noun *per se*. Whatever was 'German' remained unequalled, whatever was unequalled was called 'German'. Irrationalism,[1] Storm and Stress and Romanticism had discovered the particular importance of the German folk song, the German Gothic, the German forest and the German fairy tale; however, with the exception of some excesses, they had remained conscious of the pluralism and plural voices of peoples. German national literature was considered only as a branch of the 'great tree' of literature.

From 1813 the cosmopolitan-minded German literature was increasingly harnessed, respectively reinterpreted to serve the 'national concerns'. German was Tell[2] (because all Swiss were German), but German also were Joan of Arc, Mary Stuart, German especially were Hermann and Dorothea,[3] German was Faust. Since the 'German was born to live in the realm of the soul' ('There is no civilized people that is more moral than the German' [Harms]), youth had to be guided to the reading of German literature in a German spirit, to realize that its literary heroes were of German spirit. Goethe's *Hermann and Dorothea* became the show piece of folk-conscious German philology; it appealed especially to the petit-bourgeois mentality, because it showed the German small town with its cozy comfort, the patriarchal nature of family life (noble German figures), and the unrest of gallic foreigners. It was a work that 'had to be revered as the noblest garland ever woven by a poet to grace a nation's head' (Düntzer). Goethe's critique of the German idyll within the work remained as much ignored as his fine, somewhat classically alienated humour, which silhoutted the flaws of German man. In addition it had been the intention of the poet to characterize man and humanity; but his work was interpreted as the reflection of Germanness. Heinrich Düntzer,[4] who dedicated his *Commentary to the German Classics* 'to the German people', perceived in *Hermann and Dorothea* 'genuine German competence and inwardness, a plain and straightforward attitude of lawfulness and fair-play, quiet reasonableness, pristine goodfellowship and the comfort of home.' He considered Hermann's parents as representatives of 'genuinely German homeliness, based on competence and inwardness'; as a 'genuine

German' the father's heart was opened by a draught of wine; he has an able and hearty nature. Herman is the product of 'domestic German life'; he is the incarnation of the 'genuinely competent and sincere being'; he insists 'strongly on established values and feels fit to defend them with all his manly strength; as a genuine quiet German he refuses to be enthused by the monstrous movement which has destroyed everything; rather, he is determined to remain firmly on German soil and in German spirit in spite of every enemy'. The minister is the epitome of 'German humanity which, based on pure and noble cultured education, stands above all the limitations of life; unerringly he strives for the good and the true, always searching for the roots of things and not being deluded by superficial appearances'. Dorothea is a German ˙ from the left bank of the Rhine whose 'sense of life reflects a higher, more decisive awareness and open courage'.

This type of interpretation did not change with time. A further illustration from the turn of the century may be cited (Funke):

> To what extent is *Hermann and Dorothea* a genuine German epic poem? Parcival, Oberon and Cid did not become accepted by the people because they lacked the national character. It is different with *Herman and Dorothea*. It is a genuine German epic poem.
> 1. It takes place on German soil, particularly
>   (a) in the vicinity of the genuinely German river Rhine,
>   (b) in a graceful little German town with its white church steeple, its clean street, straight canals, the 'Golden Lion',[5] the 'Angels' Apothecary', etc.
> 2. It takes place within a genuine German family
>   (a) with its morality and strict discipline which shows itself in the distribution of individual tasks (Herman: field and stable; the father: the restaurant; the mother: the household) and in contrast to the gallic neighbour (who lacks morality, discipline and respect for the institution of marriage).
>   (b) in general all main characters are German: the host of the Lions' Inn (who patriarchically cares for the town as much as he cares for his family), the hostess (diligent, tender, devoted), Hermann (attached to the German soil, tender in his relationship with Dorothea), Dorothea (purity in the defence of her maiden friends' innocence; restraint towards Hermann, to whom she reveals her love only under duress).
> 3. Particular small features are also German, especially the drinking episode.

An extensive study of the 'Germanization' of Faust has been presented
by Hans Schwerte. Faust 'from the realm of poetry into that of a
national code'. Aesthetics became ideology (*Weltanschauung*) and
attracted pseudo-religious emotions. The 'Faustian' became a
propaganda phrase, and as 'mythical symbol' of the ideology of
nationalism it became trump in the game with the West. Faust was a
German: he appeared in the mantle of Wotan,[6] in the cloak of Siegfried;
Faust was Aryan, the Bismarck-German; eventually Faust donned the
brownshirt — these were the stages of this derailed development, even
though it did not always follow this direct line. The complexity of
Goethe's work was simplified to fit the national mould; ideological
simplification resulted in a Faust who, unrestrained by petty moral
qualms, resolutely went his way leading to the clearing of the soil and
a kind of Great-German Empire. The doubt, the guilt, the anxiety and
blindness of Dr Faust, his metaphysical salvation, were dismissed as
irrelevant or as Goethe's concessions to the public. Faust was the man
of German action — 'Goethe could not do enough', Alfred Rosenberg
later observed, 'to emphasize the vitalizing nature of action'.

> The greatest hymn to human activity is Faust. Mastering and
> penetrating all of science, life and suffering, Faust is set free through
> the deed. The spirit ever striving for the eternal found in the
> restraining deed, in the damming of the ocean tides in the service of
> humanity, the terminal purpose of life, the last step to the unknown.

The 'Alas, I will' of Faust became 'the confession to a new era which
strives for a new tomorrow, and this will is our destiny'.

Then there was the German Sunday dedicated to the arts ('We are
the most competent people in all fields of knowledge and the fine arts'
[Bley]), which was complemented by the German 'workaday'. The 'old
fighter' Jahn already greeted his compatriots with a 'German handshake'.
The German, German Rhine the French were never to have; it was
shielded by the 'German Guard'. When the 'German month of May'
arrived, the 'German trees' blossomed; the song writers of the liberation
wars already dreamed of 'German oaks'. ('Never shall forsake us/be near
us through all days/the trust of German oak trees/of moon and sunlight
rays [Schenckendorf]'.) 'Which nation can display such mountaintops'
said Wilhelm Raabe[7] in 1860, when he faced the 'German Kyffhäuser'.[8]
The folk poet Ganghofer was enamoured with the brilliance of a
'German pentecost', as were the *Stürmer* and the *Völkische Beobachter*
later on — 'What's firm and noble, true and pure/oh bind it to the

German name;/and crushed shall be the foe's disdain,/forever now so
will it God/at Pentecost, the German feast.' Christmas as the sacred
night was German, the bells rang German; German was the Church
(Luther, the Potsdam Garrison church, the Lenthen chorale), German
was Christ, German was God; 'Let us say it: the deepest religious spirit
of humanity today dwells in us Germans' (E. Bölsche). The new German
man of 1933 was particularly German: 'genuinely, in full measure, and
unconditionally' (Neesse); 'whoever speaks German and wants to master
the German language must think German, and to think German in the
world means to think in terms of German politics.' 'What is the German
fatherland?', Arndt had asked; '. . .the hand's grasp is a sacred vow/
where trust springs brightly from the eye/the heart's love warmly from
the brow/bespeaks what shall be known/that, upright German, call thy
own.' As early as 1858, J. Fröbel[9] warned of mad Germanophilia:

> Which people other than the German constantly uses attributes
> praising its own character? ('German energy', 'German faithfulness',
> 'German love', 'German seriousness', 'German song', 'German
> wine', 'German depth', 'German thoroughness', 'German diligence',
> 'German womanhood', 'German virgins', 'German men' — which
> other people uses such attributes but the German?. . .The German
> specifically demands of himself that he should be German — as if
> he had the liberty to jump out of his skin — just as he asks of his
> men to be 'masculine' and his women to be 'feminine', of his
> children to be 'childlike', and of his maidens to be 'maidenly'.
> The German spirit in a way always reflects itself in a mirror; it has
> seen itself a hundred times and is convinced of its perfections, yet
> a hidden doubt, rooted in the innermost secret of vanity, drives it to
> look again — What else is all this but the masochism of the
> hypochondriac who lacks exercise and can be helped only by
> exercise?

For Nietzsche, part of whose paradox was that his work promoted
what he rejected, to be 'good German' meant to 'degermanize oneself':

> Because if a people progresses and grows it always breaks the bonds
> provided up to then by its national reputation: if it stands still, it
> wastes away, a new bond constrains its soul; the ever hardening crust
> literally builds a prison, its walls rising higher. If a people has much
> firmness this is proof that it wishes to ossify and become completely
> transformed into a monument: From a certain point on this

happened to the Egyptians. Therefore, whoever wishes the Germans well may for his part see to it that he outgrow the German in him. The turn to the non-German is always therefore the mark of the ablest of our people.

But these and other attempts to cure the people of the madness of nationalism were in vain. Moderation, reason and discernment were washed away — 'Germany, Germany above all.' Hoffmann von Fallersleben's[10] 'plain and fervent' song of course sang to the nation and to liberty ('union, law and liberty, these are fortune's sacred band, blossom in this glow of fortune, blossom German fatherland'); linguistically and musically, however, the song invited perversion! The clichés of words and images, the rhetorical banality of sentence structure and rhyme, and the primitivity of the melody corresponded to the 'art-mindedness' of the petit bourgeois. Aside from the fact that most national anthems are lyrical trivia, this national anthem was a particular misfortune for Germany because its liberal and humanitarian content on the one hand and its national content, which could be interpreted chauvinistically, on the other, allowed a state of political ambiguity where clear intellectual commitments would have been appropriate; according to one's intentions the first or third verse could be emphasized or eliminated, or, the nationalism of the first could be assuaged by the humanism of the third. The National Socialists fully recognized the value of this national anthem and utilized it propagandistically even though it was incriminated as the national anthem of the Weimar Republic and in addition had a liberal as its author. Regrettable aesthetic and moral tastelessness was demonstrated when, after 1945, this anthem was again taken up — as if such a weak and common lyrical work-horse could stand another reinterpretation. Here the whole problem of the restored Federal Republic becomes manifest: A song misused and consumed by the Third *Reich* to such an extent should not have been adopted by a democratic state even if heretofore it had been undoubtedly abused. 'Germany, Germany above all' not only contained the national yearnings and ambitions for centuries; the song in itself was the expression of folkish religiosity, which was celebrated under the sign of the word 'German'. The two concluding citations of such 'folkish religiosity' are taken from the work of two relatively unimportant personalities, but they are particularly typical; in the first case for the nationalism of the nineteenth century, in the second case for that of the twentieth century. The second author could only become so well-known and historically influential because so many unknown authors of the past century, including the first one cited here, paved the way for him.

Ours still is the German trust, honesty and energy, our concern is the concern of Germany; and once we have recaptured Germany's inner unity, then blessings will return with the peace, and Germany's banner, adorned with the cross of the saviour, raised proudly and high, will shine forth amidst the peoples to the right and to the left. Amen! [Pütz]

I hold the unshakeable conviction that the hour yet will come when the millions who now curse us will stand behind us and with us greet the jointly created, recaptured, bitterly fought for German Empire of Greatness, and Honour, and Power, and Glory, and Justice, Amen! [Hitler]

Notes

1. Understood as a distinct philosophical theory.
2. See p.75, n.3.
3. *Hermann und Dorothea,* one of Goethe's works (1797).
4. Heinrich Düntzer (1813-1901), philologist and historian of literature, especially the German classical period.
5. *Zum goldenen Löwen,* Standard name of the small town inn.
6. Wotan, see p.141, n.1.
7. Wilhelm Raabe (1831-1910), popular writer of idyllic themes whose work constituted a refutation of the ever more materialistic world.
8. Kyffhauser, Thuringian mountain figuring prominently in German myth and history, including the Saga of Barbarossa.
9. Julius Fröbel (1805-93), professor and politician, one of the leaders of the democratic left in 1848. He lived in the USA from 1849-57.
10. August Heinrich Hoffmann von Faltersleben (1798-1874), poet renowned as author of the *Deutschlandlied,* the German national anthem.

REPRESSION AND COMPLEX

The petit bourgeois is asocial: the fellow human to him is human material, usable subject matter which may be manipulated. The *Spiesser* represses his own humanity; his intimate world reveals a hopeless inner emptiness: his girl as his beloved is sexual animal, as German woman she is a mechanical womb; enthroned as heroic patriarch the man towers over the family. Inferiority complexes are turned into swaggering beer mystique; societal and political responsibility is eased by a collective kind of romanticism. Instincts are not absorbed, nor are they even sublimated; they thrive in the 'forbidden'. Sadism found its first point of fixation in the Orient; it finally liberated itself in anti-Semitism: lascivious cruelty is legitimized as an honourable service to the nation.

The German idyll becomes an abyss: the motive for melancholy disappears; the yearning for security is no longer caused by the experience of inner and external existential perils; cozy cottage comfort becomes an end in itself; cowlike contentedness is the *Spiesser*'s first duty. The homeliness becomes ominous. The petit-bourgeois soul has been swept clean of the primary virtues of humanity. Reduced to the function of a mere 'milieu', the churches are ossified: religiosity becomes part of a 'home and garden culture'.

Political anthropology is in need of social pathology. The German ideological neurosis has not yet been healed.

1 THE GERMAN MAID

The main conceptions of Enlightenment, Storm and Stress, *Klassik,*
Romanticism, of Realism, Naturalism and Expressionism — that is, of
the literary and cultural currents of one and a half centuries —
proclaimed the dignity of man as long as they were not determined and
shaped by official dogma. Man was to be free from prejudices, from
governmental and clerical tutelage; he was to have adequate opportunity
for education and intellectual development. The humanitarian attitude
for which one strove was characterized by a yearning for inner peace
and general happiness. It was marked by the consciousness of personal
individuality as much as by the need of restraint of the individual
through the societal order. In addition, it entailed efforts for social
emancipation and a cosmopolitan spirit. The 'classical' writers, more
than any others, seemed to initiate an epoch of Humanism. There was
Lessing's *Nathan,*[1] Schiller's *Kabale und Liebe, Wilhelm Tell, Marie
Stuart,* his philosophical essays and poetry, and Goethe's *Faust,
Iphigenie, Wilhelm Meister's Lehrjahre* and *Wilhelm Meister's
Wanderjahre.* But the striving for objectivity of judgement, for public
and private rationality, for personal fulfilment and genuine community
spirit, for compassion and empathy, turned into the opposite. The
barbarian did not hear the voice of humanity; 'mutual truthfulness'
did not become the maxim of 'public' thought, speech and action. The
repression of the humane is reflected in the idols which since the
beginning of the nineteenth century have shaped or helped to shape
the petit-bourgeois consciousness. The typical woman, man, and their
relationship to each other reveal the aspects of this repression and the
resulting complexes with their intellectual and emotional perversions.
The process of female emancipation, initiated by Enlightenment, Storm
and Stress, Romanticism and Klassik, was reversed, her degradation and
depersonalization became an element of German ideology. *Mädel*
(maiden) is a key word in this process.

At the time of the Rococo this expression applied mainly to the
'object' of the young men's sexual interest. The bad conscience caused
by this rather matter-of-fact and dehumanized instinct was appeased by
a sweetly sentimental idyll: though the Mädel on the one hand was pert,
forward, rather libertine and therefore easy to 'have', she was on the
other hand touchingly naïve, frightened and troubled. The attraction

of the sexual adventure was thereby increased: the seduction of the
innocent was considered erotic excitation. The socially engaged writers
of the Storm and Stress period — guided by humanitarian interest —
wanted to emancipate the maiden from her intellectually stunted
domestic world and transport her into the realm of culture and
intellectual maturity; many of their dramas are attempts to show the
possibility of such emancipation, respectively the reasons for the
absence of the same. Romanticism and *Klassik* continued this trend and
raised the intellectually sovereign female figure to the ideal. Helena and
Iphigenie are the high points of this development. Yet it was the image
of Gretchen which remained in the German consciousness. Goethe
himself was much attracted to the naïveté of such a being. But for him
the Gretchen figure was at the same time a protest against the
intellectual debasement of the woman who — the captive of ignorance
and 'tidy domesticity' — became the unscrupulous cavalier's facile
object of affection. She became the prototype of the maiden who is
the helpless victim of powerful customs and morality — which are in
reality social taboos.

But this realization is no longer perceptible in the later distorted
image of Gretchen: She has become the 'pure maiden' in the 'neat
parlour' with a snow-white little bed, inspiring Faust's 'sweet yet sacred
shuddering'. 'Gretchen's soul', remarked Heinrich Düntzer, 'reveals
itself to the loved one with all the goodness of her heart, purity and
innocence; her love breathes the air of all her virtues'. She was no longer
the object of pity, which could have made a change in her social status
possible. Rather, she was now the object of 'unadulterated adoration':
a century of 'caring spouses, faithful mothers and pious and chaste
daughters' had begun, reflected in the staple diet of the popular
journals. It was a century of chastity worship which, however, did not
honour purity *per se,* but rather the purity of the maiden coveted by
the male. Marriage, correspondingly, was a patriarchal arrangement:
Gretchen was now safely 'under the bonnet'.[2] Literary works which
included female equality, the idea of partnership, intellectual exchange
or even conflict (of equals) were ignored. *Die Wahlverwandschaften,*
Wilhelm Meister, or *Iphigenie* could never become the standard fare of
the German soul.[3] Wherever the situation was not as clear one eagerly
tried to reinterpret the questionable passages. This misfortune especially
befell Schiller's *Glocke* and Goethe's *Hermann and Dorothea.*

In *Hermann and Dorothea* the strict patriarchal order of the domicile
was revered: the father responsible for the inn, the mother for the home,
Hermann for field and stable, the bride-to-be for the time being hired

as maid. The only difficulty for this kind of interpretation rested in the fact that Dorothea had been engaged once before — so she could no longer be the sweetly naïve girl one desired as the wife of a German Hermann. But her Gretchen-like appearance made up for the damage:

> But let me yet tell you of her appearance so neat:
> for the purple pinafore raises the rounded bosom,
> tightly bound, and the raven black bodice fits her so snugly.
> The ruffled neck of the blouse arranged so neatly
> caresses the features of feminine grace;
> the head's tender roundness rises freely and clear;
> the strong braids entwine the silver ornaments;
> richly pleated and blue the skirt falls from the waist
> embracing her well-formed ankles in graceful stride.

Not to forget that Dorothea also was given the lines so characteristic of the prevailing social structure: 'To serve the wife must learn in time, for that is her calling' (although they included the afterword: 'and only through serving will then she come to rule/to wield the sceptre hers by right at home'). Significant passages in *Hermann and Dorothea* contain thoughts which essentially contradict the prevailing notion of feminine character. But these passages were rarely recognized; rather, one tried to subsume them, to bring them into line with the ideal of submissive chastity, even though the work clearly spoke of mutual respect, of man's and woman's dignity. When, walking home in the moonlight, 'not familiar with the path and its rougher edges', Dorothea almost fell, the 'thoughtful youth' extended the arm and

> supported the loved one; and softly she leaned on his shoulder,
> their faces were touching in tender embrace. He stood
> a statue of marble, tamed by his earnest will,
> his grasp was light, he stemmed the heavy longing.
> And he so felt the lovely burden, the pulsing warmth
> the soothing balm her breath gave to his lips,
> and man thus bore the weight of Venus' glory.

But future generations of maidens in similar circumstances were always to fall into the sinewy, vigorous arms of their lovers, pressed firmly to the broad and bulging chest of mighty man without restraint. The graceful creatures, however, whose charms were viewed with glowing eyes, the maiden with velvety cheeks and swanlike hands, with lilywhite

bosom and curly tresses graced by pretty bows, the joyous soul that
held the God of dreams, she bowed to HIM in still delight; and he
enjoyed it. The maiden and woman image of the *Biedermeier* already
stood at the borderline between idyllic genuineness and cheap sweetness
and affectation. 'There is no beauty like the beauty of love, and every
day our hearts and souls grow closer', confided Klara Schumann[4] to
her diary. 'Noble, German, pious features, deep-blue eyes with brows
of indescribable charm, but especially the forehead so childlike, pure
and good, and yet so full of thought' — this is how Lenau[5] described
his idol. Heine characterized the typical woman of the *Biedermeier*
period with the words: 'You are the heart of flowers,/so sweet and pure
and fine.' Courtship found the maiden bashful and ashamed. As
Kalkschmidt observed,

> Kleist's 'Käthchen von Heilbronh'[6] has been called the prototype of
> this maidenly existence. But a number of other poets also espoused
> the type. It was above all Chamisso[7] who (around 1830) in his cycle
> on woman's love and life sang out: 'Behold him, the most glorious
> of all, so mild and so good!' Robert Schumann's music then made
> this precious song fully popular.

Schleiermacher's fiancée'[8] implored her lover: 'I have a deep longing
time and again to hear from you that you love me — love me in the
fullest meaning of the word — for I still can hardly grasp it, you so
magnificent and I so miserable.' And Sally von Klügelgen[9] confessed
to her diary:

> My heart is full, it wants to burst. The time I usually spend on these
> my recollections I'd rather sit with folded hands and thank the
> Lord who made me, and made me so happy. Since Wednesday I am
> a bride. All I think of now is HE. It is four o'clock in the morning.
> Sleeplessly I have turned and found no rest for happiness. It promises
> to be a beautiful day — the sun already rises glowingly over the trees
> and frosty dew rests on the young and fragrant greens. For an hour
> already a little finch jubilates in the tree before my window, and a
> hundredfold echo answers him out of the forest.

Blossoming roses, nightingales' singing, 'echoing to and fro' when love
captures the maiden's heart: 'Of wild blood in impatient days,/she now
strides deep in thought/and from her hand her bonnet sways/she suffers
still the sun's hot rays/her wondering is for naught' [Th. Storm] . At the

wedding the girlfriends wove the 'virgin's wreath'; a part of life came to an end, a new one, the most important, had its beginning. All of this did not lack poetic feeling. Often it reflected genuine romantic idealization; marriages were happy or unhappy depending on the fact of the emotional professions expressing genuine feelings or mere metaphors of the correspondent; moreover, it mattered whether they were observed after the wedding. Reality, to which Schiller addressed himself so purposefully in the *Glocke,* was excluded from this conceptual world. When the reality then showed its face, these celestial natures demonstrated a good degree of courage.

Political repercussions began when the unreal idealization of the woman was retained as façade and became part of the nationalist catalogue of phrases, eventually to assist in the concealment of political brutality. It is true that since time immemorial problems of insurmounted puberty had driven poets and troubadors to recite aesthetically unbearable love songs; this manifestation of bad taste became politically dangerous when it attempted to shape the picture of the German woman in its own image. Goethe's literary sins of youth with their whisper of maidens were different from Theodor Körner's[10] songs; when the latter poetically adored his 'sweet bride' this was — at least in the judgement of his later commentators — the ode of a patriotic hero and divine youth to his German maid. When Adalbert von Chamisso revealed his poetic love life, this still was an affair of private aesthetics. ('I will serve him, live for him/always be his own/ will give myself and find/myself transformed by his reknown;/A golden pledge of love,/has graced my finger fine/and piously I touch the lips/ hold close you to this heart of mine'.) But when these verses became public possession of German feeling via the *Gartenlaube,* they quickened the heartbeat of the German man. 'The heart and mind of German maiden, of German womanhood' — this is what his majesty's subject the *Spiesser* saw in it, and it was this unconditional submission he demanded from his betrothed.

The *Gartenlaube* by and large contributed substantially to the degrading and stupefying of the German woman. As a family journal for the German home and the German family, seemingly unpolitical, using the backdoor of emotion, it unloaded step by step social and aesthetical misconceptions into the German consciousness. Its star author, Eugenia Marlitt,[11] a liberal *Fräulein,* bravely championed the cause of maidenly virtue against mean and mostly aristocratic seducers and playboys. The fact that she compensated for her rheumatic sufferings by writing novels should not be of concern to political anthropology.

But the solutions she offered were, from the liberal point of view, dubious compromises: the poor good girl found the wealthy good aristocrat, or the evil rich aristocrat at the last moment was purified by pristine maidenly love; the deserted palace once more had a mistress; the servants and peasants breathed with relief. There was much joy in the final pages of these novels, but also considerable suffering.

The reporter of the *Gartenlaube* who one day visited the author[ess] and shook her hand, pressed the creative gifted hand which had painted, sculptured and evoked the most delightful figures of literature. It was the hand of a writer who, in her work, 'had taken up a fearless struggle with colourful, glittering hypocrisy, with a miserably heartless religiosity which bloats itself in outward formalities and boring self-adulation'. It was a struggle against 'the long rotten, the long condemned claims of a class which was in futile opposition to the liberal demands of the modern day'. But to experience this kind of 'attitude' the German could also have read Büchner,[12] Keller,[13] Gotthelf,[14] Stifter,[15] Fontane,[16] Hauptmann,[17] Marx, or Lassalle;[18] but Miss Marlitt pleased the petit-bourgeois consciousness because she presented the liberal content of her novels in just this style of colourful hypocrisy, linguistic misery, outward formalities and boring soul-adulation — i.e., rotten bombast; this helped the reader to forget the content with dispatch and ease.

The aesthetic varnish glazing maiden and wife, noticeable already at the beginning of the nineteenth century, was growing heavier with every year in the *Gartenlaube* and other popular journals. Glowing sweet joy pulsed in the tender hearts as one kissed and carressed, as the hands of the lover (always strictly innocent) groped along the contours of the back, 'the wonderful line from the armpits over the softly rounded hips'; these German maidens and youths strode hand in hand through the parks, sat in arbours or wandered across the hills. 'From rugged rock there beckoned/the Alpine rose so small/I took it from the moss/ and graced with it/the finest rose of all.' The pristine maiden, only recently a child, now became the budding flower of which the poets sing. At eighteen she stands in the maidenly bloom of May:

The world is in full flower, the heavens are adorned by garlands of roses and everything, everything is in festive garb — eighteen years of age! The curious look seems to ask pensively, what will the new year bring? Oh, certainly only lots of beautiful things! How could it be different? A young girl's heart, if it is right, is after all like a chamber of heaven where the angels give a concert with flutes and shawms, making for pure joy and merriment. A gay little imp blinks from the eye, and the dimples in the full red cheeks serve as the hiding places for another frisky one who is at play with his comrade upstairs.

And — lo and behold, who comes up the stairs into the virgins' chamber, to play along in impish fashion? It is none other than the dashing junior clerk of the court, with duel-scarred face, the trim lieutenant of the reserves, his eminence the doctor of officialdom — the German marriage vow will soon be sealed.

Such and similar prose was complemented by the lyrical poetry of the maiden's world. Still shy, when she hears of love she is mortally terrified — 'wild you are still,/and still so shy,/tamed only by the mother'. But once touched by love, 'amongst the noisy crowd,/ within a golden cloud,/the Lord's arm guides her'. When they toast each other this is 'oh so difficult': 'For both were trembling oh so much,/one hand can't find the other,/and purple wine wells to the ground.' Dreaming of the loved one, she slumbers in the heavy air, 'lightly covered, smiling at rest, she breathes warm and softly,/yet her thoughts are travelling far'. The bride with 'white shoes, white bows, the virginal myrtle wreath adorning her soft tresses'; she stands 'confronting all dangers that come our way'. There is the lover, 'his hands/prayerfully placed on the fine head' of the loved one (compare Gregori). Countless maidens' prayers and rhapsodies of love's delights like this were spread abroad; a national fountainhead of such trivial lyrics was found in the book of German fraternity drinking songs. 'Maiden and *Schätzel*[19] now were objects of poetic commonplace ready for general consumption, and the "old-German beer hall" around 1900 may perhaps be seen as the temple of this muse' (Sternberger).

To return once more to the *Gartenlaube*, this representative journal, indeed at times attempted to curtail the stultification of the German woman, which, later on, under the label 'idealistic dedication to sacrifice', was so shamelessly exploited, especially by National Socialism. Along these lines an especially popular regular feature was entitled 'Medical hints for girls and young women concerning feminine beauty and its care'. Here 'thinking, correct (logical) thinking, that is reason', which 'most women unfortunately (because of their misguided education), lacked, was recommended for the beautification of ugly faces in particular: '. . .it could make women into angels, because then they would be able to understand and judge properly those things that occur around them, and would not ruin their own and others' lives with their twisted beliefs, assumptions and feelings.' The eyes, usually

shyly lowered or languishing, should be open, expressive and thoughtful;
the turned-up nose was not to be recommended: 'The nose, in a way
the extension of the brain, is the feature which characterizes the human
face most decisively.' In his letters to his bride, Bismarck warned of the
'nebulous phrases' which frequently caused harm because they were
used as criteria for reality by women and girls who saw life only
through the eyes of the poets. This was implied criticism of the
education girls received; this education was in a particularly bad state
because of the patriarchal German societal structure. Girls had to be
provided with an education building 'emotional' qualities: embroidering,
knitting, cooking, the recital of poetry and some moral theology. The
'solid foundation' of the woman was the family: At the hearth and in
the quiet of the home, the German housewife and mother went her way.
The man's wishes were the unwritten law. 'A girl already puts herself in
the wrong when she does not avoid the suspicion of doing wrong. All of
nature does not have as delicate a plant as virginity. The dust on the
wings of a butterfly is less perishable than the reputation of a maiden.'
The ossified churches of the nineteenth century with their 'preaching
of purity' had the power to tie the frightened souls to themselves and
thereby prevent the intellectual emancipation of families: 'Mind and
disposition of the growing girl are directed to those factors, questions
and duties which partially have practical importance and partially serve
as adornment of the individual's life.' The curriculum of a girl's finishing
school was described by the *Fliegende Blätter,* which was otherwise a
stupidly philistine and entirely uncritical and unironical magazine, as an
instrument teaching the composition of love letters and 'marital aids' in
proper German;

> Geography:. . .the knowledge of the finest routes for wedding
> trips. . .Europe's most famous spas. . .Kitchen geography: Munich:
> Beer; Pommerania: Goosebreasts; Strassburg: Goose-liver; Frankfurt
> and Ratisbon: Sausages. . .Physics: Lightening conductor for
> domestic thunderstorms; the right tone to communicate with young
> men. . .Zoology: Marten, sable and other animals with valuable
> furs. . .Fine Arts: To stand as a model. Kitchen-dough and Liver
> dumplings. (Haute cuisine and delicacies).

The future bride should be a connoisseur of music — demanded the
marital advertisements; she should long for Goethe, Schiller and
Rückert, venerate Bismarck, come from an acceptable family and
possess the requisite 'earthly belongings'; light blonds were preferred

as long as they were perfect in cooking, interested in the family's bliss, responsive to legitimatized lust and of German mind. The literature of the turn of the century and the following decades has unmasked the phoniness and artificiality of that velvety world; Sigmund Freud's works show this society's anatomy with its twisted instincts and perverted cravings; the crust of civilization could hardly withstand the pressure of these repressed and unsublimated urges. But wherever the crust broke, it immediately concealed the breach. The Romanticism of the 'gentle maiden' was in a way too narrow to capture the 'great intoxication of existence', the 'great yearning'; the sensuous passion of the velvet era found outlets in aestheticism, exotic airs and the cult of the superman − Parnassus[20] becomes Montmartre, the philistine flirts with the demi-monde and fashionable world, pleasure in the red-light district; but then he is drawn back into the 'inner sanctum', the conjugal bedchamber, the bliss of wedded life.

Copies of the Venus de Milo were popular and representative pieces of bourgeois interior decoration. In influential sociological literature and in the world of 'official' fine arts, this 'classicism in the tender abode' was expressed in a peculiarly odd style: it was a mixture of petit-bourgeois fustiness and aesthetic Renaissance intoxication − Gretchen[21] and Lucretia Borgia, Scheffel[22] and Boccaccio were interlaced. 'Woman', Richard Wagner philosophized, 'realized her full individuality only in the moment of surrender; it is the nymph which soulless roams through the waves of its domicile until it receives its soul through the love of a man.' Raw sexuality hid behind Tristan's suffering, as in Wagner's personal life the harmony of souls became the cover-up for adultery. Wagner's myth of Germanic deities became for Bölsche[23] the mystique of the cell. As the one celebrated the ecstatic mating of celestial and heroic figures, the other rhapsodized the loveplay of the Ichthyosauri, the lovelife of the mammoths, the primeaval history of the worm, the amorous philosophy of the tapeworm and the Tristan-raving of the insects.

A moment of bliss and spring is gone. Now it flutters down like a withered leaf. The female casts the fructified eggs into the stream and dies, a victim, as if the poor, soft, sylphidine body was mortally struck by too much bliss, the joys of love and motherhood in the span of one brief moment. Driven far away by the first breath of the thundercloud, the male, too, pushes on, struck by the lightning of love which drove his senses to their peak and then took them away for ever with this storm that broke the fragile life in the instant

when it reverberated with the most powerful melody of an
unprecedented harmony.

The bubbling, grinding and orgasmic activity is such that one does not
know whether the 'sacrificial death of a mother' is that of a folkish
heroine or a protozoan, whether the 'new melody' accompanies the
mating of racially akin humans or the lovetale of the bee (but not the
tapeworm, because this creature 'cannot experience the majesty of
love, the tête-à-tête').

The pseudo-scientific trash productions of a Bölsche were matched
by the cheap love rhymes of the earlier and later blood-and-soil poets:

> The proud lips smile and then one hand grasps the other as never
> another hand has grasped hers. Never! And she too has only the
> one desire to be kissed by these lips, to be caressed by these hands.
> So that is love! This heavy sweetness of the blood, this intoxication
> over another being. Yes — that is love! Barb Vonberg! The 'I love
> you!' 'I love you'. . .I think of you only day and night! Of you! I
> see you, your dear eyes, your sweet, sweet lips. Never will I tire of
> kissing them. I love everything, everything about you, Barb, you
> sweet, dark, pure, German maid. . .Barb! My sweet, austere, tall,
> beautiful Barb. . .And so you are my Barb, my Barb, my slender,
> tall, beautiful, brown, good, prudent, tender, passionate, dear,
> beloved Barb [Tremel-Eggert] .

The National Socialists retained these 'portraits of women' and
perverted the motifs further. The personal biographies of the NS
leaders are often revealing. Hitler comes from the rude, excessive,
unsublimated petit-bourgeois sexual environment; his 'adolescent
existence' was erotically frustrated; the normal crisis of puberty
remained unresolved. In *Mein Kampf* he glorified the brutality of
marital union for the sake of breeding; in reality he yearned for
heroines; wealthy women of upper society like Winifred Wagner,
Magda Quandt, Elsa Bruckmann, Helena Beckstein paved his way.
As a 'heroic nature' he himself was anti-feminine, lonely, without a
familiar nest; this he secretly built for himself in the mountain world
of Berchtesgaden; the loved one is a genuine German maiden, without
intellectual *niveau*, a treasure for the bed, sweet to look at in her
Dirndl-dress — but with provocative underwear. The physical
shortcomings of Goebbels, his small size, the deformity of his foot,
intensified his sexual excessiveness, which sometimes made him long

for 'magnificent wenches' and 'passionate dames', at other times for 'sweet maidens'. 'Every woman arouses me to the core of my blood. Like a hungry wolf I roam around. And yet I am bashful like a child. Sometimes I hardly understand myself.' 'Goebbels did not only take what he found along the way, he also unscrupulously used his power position. He did not conceal his way of life, openly drove up to his mistress's residence and even practised adultery with his wife under the same roof' (Heiber).

Göring's first wife was a *'Biedermeier* figure' — at least that's how she was portrayed by NS propaganda: 'Carin lived her life as if she were in two worlds. Looked at with mundane eyes, she struck the beholder because of her majestic and yet maidenly lithesome appearance. . . she was familiar with the heavenly world from earliest childhood. She had the gift of introspection.' In her maiden-chamber she dreamed of her great union: 'There I have a little corner with my organ, a few pictures, a few little things that remind me of creation and the heavens, for which I always long, a little oval table always with a flower from Hermann and a few souvenirs in the drawers' (Wilamowitz-Moellendorff). After her early death, Göring built her an 'eternal monument': 'From Berlin to the north the broad expanses of the *Schorfheide* extends itself. In this truly majestic forest on the shores of its fairylike beautiful dreamy lakes, Hermann Göring built his dead wife a memorial site of rare impressiveness: Carinhall.' The thoughts of the sweet maiden, however, did not only fail to curb Göring's inhumanity; they intensified it: 'In his outstretched mailed fist he carries her colours. . .' A 'pure, German youth was the commander of Auschwitz, Rudolf Höss. Already a soldier, he had his first love experience during the First World War': 'Up to this point love to a woman, to the other sex, still had been unknown to me.' Then he found himself in the 'magic circle of love'. 'This affection became for me a marvellous, undreamed of experience on all levels including sexual union, which it brought for me. I myself would not have brought up the courage for it. This first love experience in all its tenderness and sweetness became the guiding principle for my entire later life.' The murderer of Jews never could 'speak about these things trivially; sexual intercourse without deepest affection became unthinkable for me'. When he married his girl later on, he built himself a bourgeois idyll complete with *villa,* flowers and a wading pool for the little ones; the smokestacks of Auschwitz's crematoria fumed in the background. 'My family was my second sanctuary. I am firmly anchored to it. I was always anxious to provide for its future. Later on a farm was to be the homestead. In our children my wife as well as I saw the

purpose of our life.' Of course, Rudolf Höss' thoughts did not only
revolve around his duty and his family; he also had a distinctly
pathological interest in sexual perversions.

Had the efforts of the Enlightenment to 'improve the civic status
of womanhood' only been somehow continued, had one endeavoured
to cultivate and educate the girl and accepted women as socially and
intellectually equal, had she not been allowed to be stultified as an
object of erotic desires, a sweet maiden, the progenitress and
housemother, the 'maidenworld' of National Socialism probably would
not have come to pass. The 'National Socialist Maid' displayed empty
idealism with the pathos of folkish arrogance, which was reflected
especially in trashy sentimental songs; athletic and fertile, her being was
shaped by the strong joys of comradeship and hysterical devotion to
the leader, the 'longing for beauty', the willingness to serve and the
readiness to do battle. This 'sense of purpose' was in reality intellectual
and spiritual emptiness stuffed with the straw of ideology. The youth
movement leader was either a super-Gretchen with the allures of an
Amazon, or an Amazon with Gretel-braids. 'Faith and Beauty' was the
password; in the many illustrated volumes, newspapers, journals and
other publications propagating racial purity this motto was often
depicted: well-built girls danced and jumped barefoot over sandy dunes
and the meadow's green toward the sun; blond and blue-eyed, girls
in native costumes sat pensively on rocks awaiting the SS man;
female comrades dispatched to aid in the harvest, the swastika-pin
attached to their bosom, they raised their pitchforks with bundles
of grain; on joyful hikes these female mountaineers stopped to
reflect at the sites of Alpine crosses; but there were also aristocratic
maidens galloping on their black steeds across the heather (in the
background, thunderclouds): or there was the blond mother with
the blond child at the piano complete with candle-holder and nordic
pomp.

Girl and woman were viewed with the eye of the breeder of races:
'To breed means to create, by means of deliberation and planned
utilization of all aids, a generation which at least is not below the value
of the progenitor, and, if possible, will improve the stock from
generation to generation.' Woman, Darré[24] stated, is the carrier of the
blood; that is 'the sexual animal'. 'The sexual glands with their impact
on desire and will, will take care that in a marriage where man is man
and woman is woman and both are of the same race each will get its
due.' Should the woman show the desire to go further than this, indeed
should she show the desire to be emancipated, this would be an offence

to 'her essential feminine nature'. 'Should obvious un-Germanic blood
not be the cause of this attitude, one could say. . .that there is some
form of glandular malfunction in this woman.' Going by the method of
the cattle breeder, Darré divided girls into four classes: those well-suited
for procreation, those less well-suited, those hardly suited, and those
unfit.

> Where exactly legitimate daughters and illegitimate daughters of
> known parents would fit into these four classes does not have to be
> decided here. It is not at all contrary to human dignity if in this
> respect animal breeding and human breeding also are compared. In
> the breeding of animals too, the proper classification of the
> offspring's breeding value is one of the most difficult tasks. But
> difficulties exist in order to be overcome; also, the writer sees no
> other way than this classification to help the best of our new
> generation of girls to enter matrimony. . .

Amongst the elite of maidens were the select ones who received an
hereditary estate to found a racial dynasty; valuable genetic treasure
thus would be preserved: 'Her noblest way to be is to be mother.'
　　Hitler's point of view in *Mein Kampf* is that of the arrogant anti-
feminist, the petit-bourgeois patriarch who looks down on 'womenfolk',
though he has need of them for pleasure and procreation; racially pure
they were allowed to share his bed. Marriage served 'the multiplication
and preservation of race and kind'. 'Only that is its meaning and
purpose.' Because of his procreative faculties man should marry early;
'woman after all is here only passive partner'. 'A folkish state. . .first
of all will have to raise married life from the level of permanent racial
desecration, to give it the sanction of that institution which is called to
create men in the image of the Lord and not miscegenations of men and
apes.' It was considered reprehensible to deprive the nation of healthy
children; fertility of the healthy woman had to be promoted;

> folkish ideology within a folkish state finally had to succeed in
> bringing about the establishment of that more noble age when man's
> concern no longer focused on the selective breeding of dogs, horses
> and cats, but the genetic improvement of man himself, an age in
> which the one silently knowing stands back while the other gladly
> gives and sacrifices.

As a soulless and anti-intellectual movement, National Socialism could conceive of love only in terms of lust and procreative mechanics. So it was only consistent that for the time after the war, since 'so much genetic mass had been lost', a veritable national bordell of fertility was planned.

The higher the birthrate of a people, the more secure is its life and future. . .After all, women who after this enormous war are not or will not be married to a man cannot conceive their children from the Holy Spirit. . .We must wish that those women who after this war have no husband or will not have one will enter a preferably monogamous relationship which will produce the largest possible number of children. To safeguard the future of our people we must practise a veritable cult of motherhood. . .Pursuant to special application, men shall be permitted to enter permanent marriage bonds not only with one woman, but with one additional woman, in which the woman without question receives the name of the man and the children the name of the father [Bormann].

Notes

1. Gotthold Ephaim Lessing (1729-1781), principal figure of the German *Aufklarung* (Enlightenment), dramatist and scholar whose works on literary criticism had universal impact and significance. His play *Nathan der Weise* was an early and eloquent plea for toleration.
2. *Unter der Haube,* the marital bonnet – a popular German phrase.
3. Three of Goethe's works.
4. Klara Schumann (1819-96), wife of the composer Robert Schumann and a virtuoso pianist in her own right.
5. Nikolaus Lenau (1802-50), Hungarian -German poet, the 'German Byron'.
6. Käthchen von Heilbronn, principal figure and title of one of Kleist's dramas, completed 1807/9.
7. Adalbert von Chamisso (1781-1838), German romantic poet.
8. Friedrich Schleiermacher (1768-1834), prominent and influential Protestant theologian and philosopher, he was personally close to, and his work was part of, the early German Romantic movement.
9. Sally von Klügelgen, an obscure minister's wife whose diary was published in 1936.
10. Theodor Körner (1791-1813), popular romantic poet whose patriotic verse was widely hailed. His death as a volunteer soldier in the Wars of Liberation gave his work a prominence exceeding its artistic merits.
11. See pp.159, 161, n.9.
12. See p.15, n.2.
13. See p.81, n.3.
14. See p.81, n.4.
15. See p.15, n.4.
16. See p.15, n.6.

17. See p.15, n.4.
18. Ferdinand Lassalle (1825-64), gifted political writer and early German labour leader and rival of Marx.
19. Sweetheart, 'little treasure'.
20. The seat of Apollo and the muses.
21. Faust's tragic love.
22. Josef Victor Scheffel (1826-86), painter and poet of jovial and happy themes of nature and life.
23. Wilhelm Bölsche (1861-1939), influential popularizer of scientific problems, writer and philosopher of nature. Using poetic language he transmitted revelations of biology in the context of the teaching of 'development', however emphatically rejecting materialism. His view of the world was idealistic-panosychistic.
24. See p.150, n.16.

2 THE MAID'S HERO

'The maiden' — Hitler said in *Mein Kampf* — 'shall meet her knight';
she always prefers the soldier to the non-soldier. The idol of the maiden
was the hero. 'I am a frail maiden and you a vigorous man. . .with her
left she embraced me and with her right she pressed the iron cross to
her lips, like a worshipper her medallion in the moment of danger'
(Clauren). Youth was raised in heroic illusions. For decades patriotic
educators, poets and philosophers hammered their staccato of
fatherland, nation, sacred war and heroic death into the consciousness
of the young man. In Klopstock's[1] rhetoric the fatherland was 'more
than mother and wife and bride'; Goethe as a twenty-year-old already
ridiculed the 'heroic youth' which was close to Klopstock: 'The glowing
courage flashing from the eye, the golden hoof sprayed with blood,
the plumed helmet, the spear, and a few dozen terrible hyperboles —
taken together that is unbearable.' The patriotic youth either longingly
seeks death on the sacred battlefield, or he returns victoriously to
the enthusiastically waiting bride: 'Hermann! Hermann! Thusnelda/
never loved you so' (Klopstock). The youth of the Wars of Liberation,
comforted at the soothing spring of war, man by man desired 'to stain
the iron purple,/with hangman's blood, the blood of France — /oh day
of vengeance sweet!/a fine refrain it is for Germans;/it is the greatest
deed' (Arndt). 'Through Youth we are rejuvenated, because it teaches
us to love and to hate', proclaimed *Turnvater* Jahn;[2] 'Our highest
earthly good is people and fatherland, everything that is exalted and
sacred appears in these words.' The youth of 1813 did not 'joke and
fool around'; at least in the eyes of later interpreters it consisted of
Spartan youths, 'striding with defiant gait, with hardened bodies,
dressed in old-German garb, reciting words of angry moral pathos and
patriotic enthusiasm' (Treitschke). Gymnastic societies, fraternities
and militant student organizations, especially after 1848, helped heroic
nationalism to assert itself; more will have to be said about that. The
foundation of the Second Empire in 1871 steeled the 'new generation'
in the consciousness that 'the sword must hold what the sword has won,
and to the end of all days the manly word must stand:. . .force is
conquered by force'. War, Treitschke said, 'makes men'; and even if
the youths fell on the field of battle, 'fathers and brothers would say:
much mourning means much honour'. 'A house thus bereaved then

owned a leaf in the swelling wreath of German glory.' Christendom
and the warrior's world could now no longer be separated from German
kind, proclaimed Julius Langbehn;[3] he was convinced that documents,
written in blood, would keep for centuries. At times with pathos
('blood and iron'), at times in a folksy manner ('pep and ooomph'),
the image of the youthfully trim officer was propagated. His stature
was considered immeasurably superior to the weak demeanour of the
civilian. He was the incarnation of forceful manner, moral purity, iron
nerves and brilliant beauty. Surrounded by girls, 'the lightly wounded
arm in a sling, firmly in the saddle, he is a leader, a victor in front.' For
the pan-Germans, war was the finest educational experience of youth,
an experience of 'careful renewal and preservation, the great doctor
and gardener accompanying mankind on its road to perfection. . .Woe
betide the people which for a longer period is deprived of its healing
and caring hand.' Ever since its foundation, through the crowning
experience of the First World War and the disappointment of the
Weimar Republic to the days of National Socialism, the pan-Germans
unerringly intoned the bardic song of an equestrian aurora to the
edification of defiant youth, spread abroad in many brochures and
pamphlets. Youth had to find its way back to the sources of enthusiasm,
that is to war-loving patriotism. Woman (whose political emancipation
could be considered neither justified nor useful) had as mother to raise
her children to be future heroes:

> Woman's strength is in her instinct — the German woman, as long as
> she is conscious of her nationality and proud of its history, greatness
> and deeds, by her instinct for mood and feeling, will take care that
> her fatherland means so much to her that, once intellectually
> awakened, she cannot help but love it.

When the First World War began, the hearts of poets and youths, as in
1813, were immediately aflame. Now they vied with each other to sing
in praise of war, jubilating with deeply welling cries (Thomas Mann).
The flower of German youth 'showed itself masterful in charge and
death. . .Rosy dawn, rosy dawn. . .No finer death is in this world, than
by the hand of foes. . .' (Beumelburg). The hero's prayer called for
daylight's aim: 'Oh hold the swords' cold length/and pray — to maim!/
Lord give us force and strength:/and daylight's aim' (Flex). Klopstock's
romantic youths, their cheeks reddened by the joy of battle, blessed by
the prayers of battle virgins, had in the trench warfare of the First
World War become 'natures of steel':

sharp-eyed and weather-beaten, mercenaries of love too. . .men as
the world had never seen them before. . .it was a whole new race,
energy incarnate and charged with most potent power. Lithe, lean,
sinewy bodies, striking features and eyes under the helmet numbed
by a thousand shocks. They were conquerors, natures of steel,
conditioned to warfare in its most horrible form [E. Jünger].

A man's courage was, as ever, the most sublime: 'Like divine sparks
the blood pulsed through the veins when, conscious of one's own
audacity, one crossed the fields in clattering arms. The cadence of the
storm blew away the values of the world like autumnal leaves. What
could be more sacred than the fighting man?' For Jünger[4] the fire of
the massive battles of attrition had opened the soil and fertilized it
with torrents of blood; a new relationship to the elementary had
thereby been created.

'As Siegfried fell under the treacherous spear of the grim Hagen,[5]
so fell the exhausted front.' With this lie Hindenburg managed to plant
renewed hopes for a martial future into the hearts of German youth
after 1918: one day the treachery (and the desecrating peace of
Versailles) should be washed away with blood. 'In this sense I
confidently put away my pen and firmly trust in you, German youth.'
That was not building on sand! The anti-democratic thought of the
Weimar Republic further nourished the consciousness of the 'beauty
and moral force of the death for the fatherland. . .the more passionate
the battle, the closer one came to God; and as one came closer to God,
death became more beautiful' (Eckert). Under the three-fold ringing
of Battle, God and Death, the youth should grow 'as his father had'.
With the Third *Reich* heroism, 'full of passion as the coming creator
and leader of political destinies' (Hitler), triumphed over dissipated,
decadent democracy. The National Socialist Heroes' Memorial Day
combined the 'heroic' elements of the nineteenth century in itself:
Fichte's idealism was celebrated at Treitschke's altar of the fatherland
by notorious petit-bourgeois sadists who posed as Rembrandt Germans[6]
in the style of a Ganghofer.[7] The education of the German youth to
the heroic took place under the sign of certain *Leitmotifs* from History
and Literature. One was called to be a Spartan, and to die 'as ordered
by the law'; or, like the ancient Roman, return from battle carrying or
being carried on the shield. Favourite subject matter for Latin lessons,
and also for lessons in history and Germanistic, which were dominated
by classical philology, was found in the glorification of patriotic
peasantry: 'The daughter of the peasant adorning the altar.' Also

celebrated was the chauvinistic deed: 'It is sweet and honourable to die for the fatherland'; or reverential patriarchy: 'As the ancient approacheth, oh youth, arise.' Representations of the Greek Olympus, in painting already expanded to gigantic panoramas of trash during the early nineteenth century, were the beginning of later battle portrayals which then outlived German heroism as 'living pictures' and journalistic reflections of history in marvellous colours. Beginning with pedagogic visual aids like wall posters and textbook illustrations, such pictures deeply impressed themselves into the consciousness of young people. Sedan-art[8] eventually found its highest fulfilment in the 'blood-and-soil' paintings of the National Socialists.

> When we demand today that the standard of German idealism again be raised in Germany's provinces, we do not preach the submission to feelings, the idle dream or intellectual pleasure — our greatest men were idealists, but also men of thought, of passionate hearts and action! Armin,[9] the Great Charles, Martin Luther, the Old Fritz,[10] Friedrich Schiller, all the heroes of Prussia's rebirth, and Otto von Bismarck — all of them, you men without drive and love, all of them were idealists [Frymann].

Three examples from the German gallery of idealists and heroes shall demonstrate some aspects of such national pedagogics.

The 'Knight of Bamberg'[11] was considered as the biological incarnation of the nordic-masculine-heroic and genuinely German being. His devotion could be transformed to the secular world, relating to the sword more than to God; he was all man, but it could be expected that a chaste gentlewoman awaited him in the ladies' bower. Siegfried was reborn in him; the crown became him 'as the steel-helmet suits the German soldier' (Schultze-Naumburg). The German maid, always having her 'proud and beautiful soldier' before her eyes, was right to ask: 'Doesn't he look like the Knight of Bamberg Cathedral?' (Tremel-Eggert). The Knight of Bamberg as motif of 'racial selection for everyman. . . incorporating the ideal of the nordic hero in a purity never to be equalled', at the same time foreshadowed Hitler:

> You monument, elevated by National Socialist doctrine to a granite testament of the Germanic race, you eternal German who, shaped by artist's hand, manifests the immutable law of the fatherland, which can only be national-socialist, you have found a master. Though he does not have your features, he even more than you

represents the inner voice of the fatherland, as it was he who
fulfilled that for which you, sitting for centuries on your steed,
have waited [Anacker].

Martin Luther, too, was an arch-German — a Christian warrior (more
warrior than Christ), always obedient to his authorities. He was no
decadent thinker and philosopher, no pacifist and humanist, but one
who packed a strong and forceful wallop (as in the case of the
'republicanizing' peasants). In his warrior-like nature, 'quite different
from Lessing,[12] for example', the whole man was shown: 'The strong
hatred which Luther at the time held for Erasmus was not at all
accidental or personal; it was the hatred of the man of honour against
dubious character, of the loyal and plain man of the people against the
deceptively polished intellect; genuine and false greatness never agree'
(Langbehn). Luther knew that 'dear Christ had no more bitter,
poisonous and severe enemy' than 'a Jew who seriously wanted to be
a Jew. There may be those amongst them who have the faith of the
cow or the goose; but all of them are marked by blood and
circumcision'; in this fashion some Luther citations and writings were
incorporated into the German Catechism of anti-semitism (Fritsch).
The 'Germanic Luther', had he lived in the Third *Reich,* would have
'pointed to the brilliantly luminous nordic saviour-figure and disallowed
German loans in matters of faith from the East. And he would point to
the rune designating the god-man and say: This is our, the kindred
German nordic God' (Bergmann). A 'gigantic Luther' (Beumelburg) led
the way to the Third *Reich;* Hitler completed Luther's work — they
were 'partners in the service of the German people's welfare'. There was
no tastelessness of which the 'German Christians' were not capable.

The forger of the 'German Empire's Unity' was Bismarck the defiant,
a product of old Germanic peasant stock. Even if the 'ancient Gods are
gone', for Bismarck Wotan's oaks still echoed the storm; the brilliance
of his heroism 'once more sanctified the ancient shrine' *(Die
Gartenlaube).* The 'gushing fullness of his energies knew no higher aim
on earth than to become the Eckart[13] of his people. He had filled the
world with his name that even in centuries hence the heroic saga would
resound, a German song of joy and jubilation' (Herzog). 'Gloriously
fulfilled' he stood before his national worshippers:

Bismarck! Your sacred name, never before this day appeared it so
large before your people, under the thunder of adversity the seed
grew to iron, the seed you planted intuitively into our hearts.

Unbreakable is our energy and courage, unbreakable our will to victory; unbreakable is our faith in the immortal deed — Behold it, oh radiant one, from your sublime silence and bless the harvest of time as you have blessed the seed [D. Eckart].

It was due to Bismarck's work, Hitler wrote in *Mein Kampf,* that after a series of victories without precedent an empire arose for future generations, 'a prize of immortal heroism'. 'Not in the chatter of a parliamentary debate, but in the thunder and noise of Paris under siege, the solemn act, the profession of the will took place.' Hitler wanted to preserve Bismarck's heritage: 'What the fathers gained with their heroic blood in the battles from Weissenburg to Sedan and Paris, young Germany now once more had to earn.' Young men were obliged to strive after such and similar examples, which mostly were formidable re- and misinterpretations; then it became clear to him that 'Luther and Bismarck, Frederick the Great and Moltke,[14] Goethe and Richard Wagner, Bach and Beethoven could only be Germans' (Houston Stewart Chamberlain). To be a hero was to be German, to be German to be a hero. Like the Knight in Dürer's etching 'Knight, Death and Devil' (compare Schwerte), German youth should bravely go its way, its God a national bastion.

In the person of Hitler the hero of all heroes arose. *Mein Kampf* became the National Socialist 'Emile' — a German youth portrays his life. As a child he one day found a popular text of the Franco-German war of 1870-71: 'It consisted of two volumes of an illustrated journal of the day and now became my favourite reading matter. It did not take long before the great heroic struggle became my greatest inner experience. From now on I ever more adored everything connected with war and military life.' Like the Hitler Youth who later emulated him — 'tough as leather, hard as Krupp-steel, and quick as whippets' — Hitler in his youth was a 'little instigator — anything but a stay-at-home'. The 'young madcap' had only one great concern: to be born at a time when the temples of glory were empty because of mercantile peace. But, thanks be to God, a war broke out and the youth was given a chance to prove himself.

Each hour now was for me like a salvation from the unpleasant impressions of the youthful days. I am also not ashamed to admit today that, overcome by stormy enthusiasm, I then went to my knees and thanked the heavens from an overflowing heart that I was granted the happiness to be alive in these days.

When his petition to be allowed to serve in a Bavarian regiment was approved his 'joy and gratitude knew no bounds'. His heart swelled in the proud happiness to share the moment when the 'merciless hand of the goddess of fate would begin to weigh the nations and people as to the truthfulness and timbre of their spirit. 'So often I had sung "Germany, Germany above all" and shouted *Heil* out of the fullness of my throat that it almost appeared to me as an additional grace to be allowed as a witness in the divine tribunal of the eternal judge, to proclaim the truthfulness of this conviction.' For young Hitler there began 'as perhaps for every German, the greatest and most unforgettable time of his earthly life'. So it was that Hitler, who always had felt within himself the urge to fight, became the incarnation of decades of heroic education and later became the idol of a generation of youth which was systematically alienated from humanitarianism, peaceful work and competition, whose senseless and blind readiness for battle was exploited, in the end to be sacrificed to the national idol. Before the war magnificent graveyards of heroes were already planned by the National Socialists for all European lands. German youth was meant to take the 'grand stairway to the Pantheon'; instead it landed in the national morgue, the cursed boneyard of a blinded nation.

Notes

1. See p.141, n.4.
2. See pp.15-16, n.13.
3. See p.40, n.4.
4. See p.161, n.4.
5. In the Nibelungen Saga.
6. See Langbehn, p.40, n.4.
7. See p.60, n.15.
8. Again referring to the 1870 battle.
9. Arminius (18[16] BC – 19[21] AD), the tribal leader of the Germanic Cheruscans, victor over Augustus' legions in 9AD in the Teutoburger forest, ever since celebrated as the man who kept Germany from becoming a province of ancient Rome.
10. Frederich the Great.
11. Statue in Bamberg Cathedral.
12. See p.191, n.1.
13. Referring to Ekkehard, a medieaval German figure symbolic of heroism.
14. Helmuth von Moltke (1800-91), chief of the Prussian and later German General Staff 1864-88.

3 BEER-MUG MYSTIQUE

An academician aspiring to heroic-national humanity had to join a
student corporation – or so it was said. Towards the end of the
eighteenth century the corporations included especially members of
the aristocracy and those students who emulated the exclusive feudal
way of life. In contrast to this concept, Friederich Ludwig Jahn
conceived the plan for a 'German *Burschenschaft*', which during the
Wars of Liberation soon assumed firm outlines as the Freecorps of
Lützow. *Burschenschaft* members returning from the war were in a
national and democratic mood; at the Wartburg festival of 18 October
1817, they burned a Prussian drillmaster's whip, a whig and the uniform
of a cavalry officer. The feudal corporations were now partially
absorbed by the democratic *Burschenschaften.* A progressive student
movement demanded the dissolution of the corporations and the
creation of general student associations. The student assembly at
Eisenach in 1848 was the high point of this progressive development.
The principle of a united democratic Germany was proclaimed; a
reform of university life was to serve the general democratization which
was hoped for. But this endeavour collapsed with the revolution of
1848.

The democratic element in the upheaval of 1813 was omitted in
later interpretations. Ferdinand Hodler's[1] paintings, for example,
reflect this distortion:

There is the painting in Jena of students marching out into the
war of liberation, and there is the painting at Hanover portraying
the pledge to the new teaching. To my knowledge there are no
other paintings which are related to our rebirth, renewal and
purification through the revolution of 1933 in so uncannily
revealing a manner as these. The artistic accomplishment corresponds
to the marvellousness of the German event. In the Hanover painting
one sees a leader inspiring a number of compatriots, by the utmost
exertion of intellect and body, to make a sacred pledge: all hands
are extended, all muscles taut. Everyone seems to feel that he is
pledging himself to something new, everyone unconditionally
participates with his whole being [Burte].

However, this nationalistic and elitist interpretation was in many ways
caused by the inherent spirit of the *Burschenschaften* —even in its very
beginning. If the conception of the National monument to the battle of
the Nations at Leipzig as a Gothic cathedral was anachronistic,
dedicated to the great dead of the fatherland, the entrance hall decorated with motifs drawn from German myths and history — so were
the conceptions of democracy: they were idealistic-utopian notions
of folk community and folkish unity. The absence of any experience in
self-government in Germany further promoted these exaggerated
conceptions; a rational conception of society, including a pluralism
doing justice to humanity in giving and taking, was considered as alien.
'Suddenly my eyes were opened, my soul was strong again, beckoned
by a divine symbol. As the sun breaks through dark clouds after a heavy
storm. . .and appears in eternally youthful clarity. . .our people too
shall pass through the portal of peace in renewed youthfulness'
(Kohlrauch). This kind of romanticism could not serve to found a
democratic state, a state which most of all would have required calm
deliberation, the exclusion of emotion, cool logic and pragmatic
sobriety. In addition, the white heat of national passion scorched some
of the democratic shoots — even though democratic reforms were part
of the *Burschenschaften* programme at least until 1848. The language
used was more revealing than anything else:

> Dear friends, do not let this sacred hour with its moving and
> beautiful mood pass and die away in futility [such Wartburg
> festival speeches were remembered for decades with pride and
> emotion] a German fraternity you shall become and be. And do
> not deceive yourself to think that you are the soil, the root, the
> trunk of German unity's oak; this you are not, you are only the
> green shoots of its hope. Not on you alone does Germany's
> existence, permanence and honour rest. . .Always strive for the
> whole, and if you yourself cannot become a whole, become a serving
> member of a whole [Bechstein].

It was in October of 1820 that the national fraternity member Karl
Hase, commemorating the battle of Leipzig, addressed the following
words to his audience:

> And all of Germany pulsed like one heart, full of love, hope and
> confidence in the promised greatness, freedom and unity, in the
> fulfilment of the words: 'Lost independence shall have to be

regained, the German *Reich* will have to be reborn in venerable form, and, rejuvenated, revitalized and unified, the German Nation again shall stride before Europe's peoples.' These words from the prince's lips tore the husband from his spouse, the youth from his bride into the thunder of battles and joyful death. And as everything beautiful blossoms most beautifully in youth, this century too has seen no more beautiful festival than the one celebrated by our brothers five years ago at Luther's castle, at the Wartburg. Today is the day of the third year, tonight the night when flames and songs and hearts glowed warm. Bleak and dark it is around the turrets and mountain tops of the Wartburg now, bleak and dark the graveyard where we stand, and bleak and dark are Germany's hills, and all that once was Germany's *Reich,* and sin it is today to think of Germany's past and to celebrate her liberation. And we, my friends, alone we stand at the site of the nations' battle, no flame joyfully guides our way to tell the people that there still are youths, German youths. Biting the wind cuts through our hair, lonely we stand around the battle's mound like spirits of another day.

Although the symbols of reaction and absolutist patriarchalism had been burned and revolutionary demands were being made, one still spoke in the style of oblivious aloofness, in the manner of falsely youthful paternalism; the dialectically clear and honest language of enlightenment and *Klassik* had remained without influence. The clouded language of Fichte, but especially that of his successors, proved to be fateful. Heine called the Wartburg festival a demonstration of narrow-minded, nationalistic, religious and racial hatred, in short an 'obscene tirade of the ravens'. The mania of racial hatred and racial pride began to spread; anti-Semitism showed its face. The *Burschenschaft* member Wolfgang Menzel[2] has with justification been described as anticipating National Socialism (see Schuppe): nationalism, chauvinism, hatred of France, anti-intellectualism, Germanism and anti-Semitism were here united in a 'complete' German ideology. The Germans were considered 'still [the] most powerful race on our entire planet'; France brought 'immorality and irreligion'; the lower race must become the slave of the higher 'if mankind is to prevail'. 'God grant us intense and tough warfare, which we. . .sorely need if our soaring spirits shall not turn sour and consequently make us succumb. Then one shall see what deeds our German nation still is capable of doing.' After 1848 the mood of restoration prevailed all along the line in the fraternities. The once dislodged 'corps' formed an umbrella organization to oppose

attempts at reform, which after 1855 was called *Hoher Kösener
Senioren Convents-Verband*. The formerly democratic *Burschenschaften*
split into various sections. Some became conservative groups which
could hardly be distinguished from the 'corps'. Others turned into
radical-democratic organizations which soon completely disappeared.
Yet others again joined the liberal parliamentary opposition with a
national-liberal programme and later submitted with it to the power
politics of the new German empire. The duel and the preparation for
it became the actual focal point of a perverted sense of honour, aiming
to make the instinct for red-necked brawling academically respectable.
The rise of the Second Empire brought the climax of neo-feudalism, of
a 'tradition of trash, the cheapness and inner falsity of which only
reflect the period which produced it'.

What are the elements of this 'tradition'? More than anything it was
ideological gymnastics: Byzantine harangues, the suppression of
humane conscience and civic reason as moral cowardice, a feudal
cult of honour and an elitist ritual of form. All in all, it is
compensation for the political importance of the subject and a kind
of 'sacral' preparation for the master's manner of existence. The
'bouquet' of attitudes and prejudices which went into the make-up
of a mature *(ausgefuchst* = no longer *Fuchs,* i.e. fox) member of the
student corporations consisted of: class and cultural superiority,
faith in authority, hatred of mere civilization (contrasted to
wholesome *Kultur),* anti-humanism, nationalism, militarism
(including the ideal of the Prussian lieutenant of the guard),
imperialism, German-folkish pride, combined with contempt for the
masses, rejection of female emancipation as well as modern art ànd
literature, denunciation and ideological terrorizing of all minorities,
and a double standard of morality which could manifest itself in
prudishness as well as in utter profanity. In sum total it amounts to
contempt and rejection of all rational, democratic and humanistic
endeavours. From a force and power of enlightenment, German
students in their incorporated majority had turned into the darkest
element of obscurantism. The dot of the i was provided by the
anti-Semitic 'Leagues of German Students' which had been inspired
during the 1870s by the Berlin court preacher Adolf Stoecker[3]
and which constituted themselves as the *Kyffhäuser* union[4] in 1881.
As precursors of the National Socialists, these leagues propagated
the 'Aryan racial principle'. With this they found fertile soil amongst
the students of the corporations. By the turn of the century all

leagues were 'clean of Jews'. This racial mania fanaticized especially the organizations composed of middle class elements such as *Burschenschaften, Landsmannschaften,* etc. [Finke].

The attacks of the *Simplicissimus*[5] on this world of falsehoods was as tireless as it was fruitless, which is usually the fate of satire and caricature: 'And when we receive the call to arms, we are there man by man. This we pledge to our beloved fatherland with our sudsy word of honour!'. . .' "How was the trip to Rügen?"[6] "I tell you, did we drink and fool around with the old gentlemen from Berlin – it was plainly ideal."'. . .' "Who are your officers in charge now?" – "The first in command is Count Schönhoff, the second Baron Pahlen, the third is called Meyer – but he has three horses."'. . .'The duel is a grand institution! – Otherwise anyone would come around to call me a dumb bub!'

   The unpolitical character of the student corporations before the First World War, that is, their undifferentiated national, folkish and imperial attitude, changed after 1918 into a political activity which was directed against the 'undignified' democratic state, against the 'rule by the inferior'. Folk-mystique and élitist biological thinking paved the way for National Socialism. Style and content of many utterances with their relishing of kinship and their jargon of consanguinity, correspond to Rosenberg's[7] 'Mythos'-thought. Anti-Semitism further strengthened itself; evidence for this is of especial importance.
The students of the corporations wanted the Third *Reich:* 'We want the Third *Reich,* we want it with all Germans and for all Germans!' *(Akademische Blätter).* Baldur von Schirach,[8] in his capacity as the leader of the National Socialist German Students' Union, pointed out as early as 1929 that:

> It is no accident that the National Socialist German Students' League and the dueling corporations *(schlagende Verbindungen)* unite in their ranks a certain elite of human material drawn from contemporary students: The will to act and the will to fight here brought together the only valid activist elements. And why do activists unite in leagues which in the final analysis are dedicated to battle? Because genuine youth wants to do battle.

The year 1933 then became the realization of what *Burschenschaften* and *Korporationen* 'had longed and struggled for since 1817'. Fully garbed in their ceremonial dress, the *Korporationen* also participated in the book burnings; for them this was indeed a very meaningful activity, because it involved the destruction and proscription of the writings which were based on humanism, enlightenment, rationalism and the principles of democratic freedom and human dignity. These were 'things' from which the *Korporationen* had been estranged for decades, which ran counter to their 'essence'. As he officially transferred the remnants of the *Burschenschaften* into the National Socialist Students' League during a ceremony on 18 October 1935 at the Wartburg, their leader Glanning commented:

> The objective of the German *Burschen*, the unity and power of the German people, has been brought about by the *Führer* and the NSDAP in a manner which the men of the Wartburg festival of 1817 in their fondest dreams could not have conceived more beautifully. Their German *Burschenschaft* no longer has to fight for this objective. To retain what has been established is not its task, but the task of the NSDAP.

He was correct in the sense that the spirit of the Wartburg festival already contained the beginnings of the faulty development; he was wrong in the sense that the spirit of 1817 (until 1848) also would have permitted democratic-liberal development. However, since the spirit of 1870 overcame that of 1848, 1933 triumphed in the end — the hero overcame the thinker. Tucholsky[9] once said: 'Brain and brawn are unevenly distributed amongst us: the one has the brain and the other the red neck. There hardly is intelligent energy. They do not only have the louder mouth, the thicker stomach lining, better muscles, a lower forehead and more nerve: they have more vitality.' The maiden deserved her knight in armour: for the girl of better family it was the fit academician. Of immaculate manners and rigid behaviour, he took her to the reunion where ladies' grace enhanced the festivities for the colourfully capped *(buntbemützten*[10]*)* celebrants. Flowery toasts to the ladies' grace on the one hand, and contempt for women's intellect on the other, are part of elitist fraternity philosophy; a division of language took place. The 'higher form of expression' at festive occasions addressed itself to ideals above the belt with noble pathos (personality, bravery, style, demeanour, honour, freedom). The more 'vulgar jargon' dealt with matters below the belt in the drunken comfort of student gatherings in old-German style. In duelling the inner coward was suppressed, anti-Semitism and chauvinism then set him loose again. Authority is based on brutal force. Reason is considered as the dialectical undermining of ethical principles through alien intellectual influences. One of the most popular expressions characterizing this process was the word *Vermassung* (proletarization, plebeianization). There is so much 'courage' that one doesn't dare to utter a word advocating the reform of the incorporated fraternities; however, if someone yet dares to do so, he offends the collective sense of 'honour'. Any examination of one's own or the whole people's nationalistic or national-socialist mistakes is avoided. So one posits the honouring of the war dead but rejects the honouring of the victims of fascism. It is all right to celebrate the anniversary of unification, but not to commemorate the victims of Belsen or Auschwitz. Even convinced Catholics take part in duels — often with a bad conscience — yet nevertheless, 'one goes along'. If a senior member recites a dirty joke, no freshman dares to complain; ordered by the foremost senior to drink, all empty their *Stein.* Since 1848 all opportunities to demonstrate civil courage and earn honour were rejected as a matter of principle: as minorities were discriminated against, no one objected. As German culture, spirit and politics was destroyed, no one resisted. As the *Führer* commanded, one followed. Jews were hunted and gassed, and yet even now silence is usually the response. Heroes are honourable men, but their honour is the philistine's honour. At the merry round with foaming brew, accompanied by the beer-organ[11] — *ad exercitium salamandris* — the joyful song of heroes rises: 'Where courage, strength still glow in German souls/the gleaming sword is near the merry round'. . .'For fatherland and honour we raise our arms/for Hermann's trust and good/we shed the blood'. . .'German maiden, German frau, finest jewel of German meadow.' The *Weltanschauung* of the incorporated fraternities as much as that of the National Socialists flourished in the beer-mug mystique of barrel house and barrel song, of duel scars and political brawls; both ideologies were expressions of the petit-bourgeois character's eternal longing for submission and partnership in dominion (Adorno). They were symbols of inferiority complexes rising from individual and collective repression, finding outlets in nationalistic, folkish and anti-Semitic actions. Glorification of the heroic was compensation for the complexes of 'cowardice' and 'servility', under which one suffered more than enough, especially in the upper strata of society.

Notes

1. Ferdinand Hodler (1853-1918), Swiss painter of monumental art.
2. See p.15, n.12.
3. See p.125, n.4.
4. Named after the Thuringian mountain near the Barbarossa cave.
5. Influential Munich satirical journal, published there 1896-1944 and again from 1954.
6. Island in the Baltic Sea.
7. See p.39.
8. See p.56, n.10.
9. Kurt Tucholsky (1890-1935), journalist and poet, articulate and effective critic of society, co-editor of the *Weltbühne*.
10. The caps traditionally worn by university students.
11. Beer organ, the piano.

4 MOB ROMANTICISM

The youth movement was originally a reaction to the authoritarian thoughts and actions of the Wilhelminian era: youth wanted to escape the world of school and the adults, wanted to be free from the tyranny and dependence on pedagogues and fathers. It was a 'young-bourgeois' revolt, an uprising of a minority of *Gymnasium*[1] pupils who thought of themselves as the élite. German education had failed to solve the problem of freedom and authority in the sense of a rational interplay; rather, it had hidden behind institutional authority, which either turns youthful individuality into servility or drives it to a revolutionary explosion.

Literati, vitalists, apostles of culture and other preachers of reform soon approached the youth movement and took it under the wings of their confused ideologies. It was especially under the influence of Hans Blüher,[2] whose repressed sexual complexes sought an outlet, that a youth movement ideology with strong homosexual leanings developed. This ideology was moreover characterized by a narcissistic longing for an 'adolescent culture', wherein one attempted to raise the pubescent 'mood of a new beginning' to the norm of existence *per se.*

Adolescent culture owed its radiant force 'to the combination of three elements: first of all, to the innate social structure of the horde; secondly, to nomadic existence; thirdly, to the cult of fire which was initiated by the wandering horde' (Pross). The fraternal way of life was anti-democratic; for the 'community bound by a sacred pledge', the declaration of faith in the *Führer* grew out of 'the erotic experience of a passionate enthusiasm'; 'dedication to the leader, readiness to sacrifice' was the motto. Nietzsche, Lagarde and George were heroes of the youth movement; their works were read, cited and duplicated. The paradigm was the medieval knight, the soldier, the lansquenet, the peasant settler, the brethren of the sword or the wandering scholar. With anachronistic naïveté, one tried to emulate them by letting one's hair grow long, wearing Germanic garb, health sandals and carrying knapsack, dagger, tent, standards and mandolin.

> The game of war! We do not scuffle with each other, tearing each other's garb. Game of war! We fight only with the enemy. The first glimpse of the enemy brings the blood to my head, and howlingly I jump into the fray, the chaos still before my eyes, and ignorant of

the enemy's strength. And now the youngsters break through the underbrush, scuffling and grinding my teeth I lash into the first one, to break the tension and clear the view. . .With the back of my hand I brush my hair: Blood! My blood! An insane anger rises in me because I realize: We are wearing the blue coats – that's why they attack me, us, so. And I storm forward, threshing with the club around me, and a wave of joy is within me as I draw the first blood from the enemy. Streaming blood; because we wear the blue coats. Victory! There is a rising tide within me when I feel the cadence of the youthful team, when I know that with me there are hundreds, thousands of soldiers with the same aim: a team of German youth. It is marvellous to be part and parcel of a power. But still more marvellous it is to be the leader even of a minute part of power [Hebs].

Hiking – 'to be blended into nature' – meant for the horde life outside of society, away from the avenues of civilization. Eichendorff's[3] poetry of moonlight and romantic forest solitude, which in the original romantic setting must be seen in contrast to the realization of the demonic nature of the world and the nihilistic endangering of humanity, now became part of the ideology: hiking manifested opposition to the older generation, the city, technology; the view from the mountain top became a panorama of the nation: it was not the beauty of nature at one's feet, but the beauty of *German* nature.

The horde rested at the campfire: 'As the song echoes in the evening sky of the solstice festival – behold as pairs we pledge/at flaming altar's edge/to be German – the movingly devoted love for the homeland and the strongly felt moral obligation to the people then give these words a deep and genuine sanctification' (Stählin). At campfire discussions, one thought about the meaning of the word – however, these were discussions which overstressed the discutants' capacity; schooling of rational intellect and conceptual clarity were lacking. Sitting in the darkness of the night under the glistening stars at the crackling fire, one was inebriated from speculative dreams – well-meant webs of verbiage which fell apart in the face of reality. The intellectual incest of the leagues promoted such development; the grown-ups whom one trusted or to whom one confessed were themselves arrested juveniles, incapable in their own immaturity to guide others to reason.

The 'community bound by a sacred pledge' was ready for action. 'To be ready for action' was a popular catch-word; but one was not sure for what one was to be ready. There was no awareness of the pressing political and social problems; a generation was caught in a romanticism which found its climax at the *Hohe Meissner*[4] in 1913. Here 2,000 members of the youth movement met to celebrate the first Free German Youth Festival and to proclaim guide-lines for a life 'based on self-determination, individual responsibility and inward honesty'. The proclamations of those days are read today only with dismay: they were framed in the very language of the petit-bourgeois reactionary world against which one claimed to be fighting. The youth movement had attempted to break free from the *Stammtisch*,[5] veteran's organization and singing society; but the campfire, scuffling in the woods and mandolin songs were expressions of the same mentality — only clothed in different garb. Urbanity, an unideological openness, the endeavour to make political judgements, the interest in the societal and social problems of the state — that is to say, civic manners and mores — were equally alien to the 'old' and 'young' of the Wilhelminian era.

Many important men later 'gilded' their juvenile years in retrospective sentimentality — as a grown-up looks back with a certain fond nostalgia to the favourite literature of his youth. This does not change the fact that the spirit of the youth movement was essentially anti-humanitarian; it helped to undermine the Weimar Republic; in 1932 there was only a small group which stood by it. In the same vein, many members of the youth movement made themselves available to the National Socialists, especially as leaders in National Socialist youth organizations. Here, however, they were soon replaced by more brutal types. The National Socialists were propagandistically clever in adopting the cheapened romanticism of the youth movement. The existence of the vagabond — and outsider — was, however, too individualistic, too fragmentary for them; they therefore pulled the pubescent irrationalisms together by means of military regimentation, and in the Hitler Youth and the League of German Maiden created the perfect totalitarian youth organization. The youth movement was now itself 'moved' — manipulated in whatever manner the *Führer* commanded.

Notes

1. The German High School, at the time stressing humanistic subjects.
2. See p.50, n.2.
3. See p.80, n.2.
4. Hoher Meissner, Hessian mountain.
5. The Spiesser's fixed weekly round-table at the corner tavern.

THE ENIGMA OF THE ORIENT

'Repressive tendencies' and 'incapacity to sublimate' were the prevailing characteristics of the German's relationship to the dynamics of his instincts. These must be understood not only in terms of the psychoanalytical make-up of the individual, but more so in the sense of social pathology and social psychology. The patriarchalism of medieval societal structure, which was effectively unchanged in Germany almost up to the present day, was especially unyielding. The concept of absolute rule as the guiding star was imposed on society until it freely identified with it. Thus institutionalized, the father image strengthened the paternalistic spiritual make-up, which in this fashion became the dominant element. The egocentrism of the German man, which reached new heights during the wars of liberation, brought about a bipolar ideal of equality. The other pole was the projection of the already elevated male ego in the woman as the super-ego: the virgin who encompassed all values within herself. It was an image which was supported and apparently objectified by a form of medievally stylized historiography *(edle Minne, edle frouwe*[1]*)*. All this was connected with a sort of Oedipus complex: the man considered the woman's purity as destroyed, violated by a man (the father), his equal; however, since the male was above any doubts of his morality because of his narcissism, the woman, in spite of her angelic nature, had to be responsible for the destruction of her own purity ('purity', which was a central conception of Germanic ideology). The woman was now as much denigrated as she had been earlier idealized. But the awareness of the 'evil woman' (as a sociological type) ran counter to the norms of society and therefore had to be repressed. Outlets had to be found wherever the denigration of the woman was not *taboo*. The 'dishonoured' woman's uninhibited sexuality at the same time especially attracted the male; the result was the attraction to the whore, the witch, the female demon and heroine, an attraction which was, however, concealed as revulsion. Although these types were only rarely existentially realized, they reflected the general conscious attitude of the male as psychological points of fixation, and he used them to confront the woman as collective being.

The Baroque age, creating a metaphysical baldachin, had still managed to balance the tensions generated by the contempt for instinctual drives on the one hand and their glorification on the other. It was able to bear, to endure the tensions because the baser drives were considered concessions to the all-too-human in man, their conquest an important step on the path to God; equilibrium was reached *sub specie aeternitatis,* even though in its manifestation in man it was accompanied by passionate spiritual struggles. The emancipation of the human urges during the Rococco was an uncommon solution. Unhinging the spiritual pendulum and finding 'peace' in unchecked pleasure, this solution was possible only for those who functioned in terms of an unscrupulous feudal rationale. The general conscience remained intact, but in the face of a demoralizing aristocracy and beginning religious decay it could no longer play a regenerating role. The morality of the Enlightenment was the antithesis *per se;* it offered new principles of a moral order: it replaced Christian commandments, which had usually been accepted without reflection on the basis of fear of punishment (not only metaphysical, but — because of the close alliance of throne and altar — physical punishment), with the morality of the autonomous rational man. The norms of the Enlightenment were rigorous. To act against the 'urge' was for Kant the very test of moral action. However, since metaphysical and physical fears were stronger obstacles to man's eudaemonic[2] striving than the appeal to reason and the proclamation of humane and moral maxims — especially since the Eng!ightenment was soon repressed by the ruling forces — the attempt at moral renewal was without much effect. The association of morality with the feeling of happiness, of ethical conduct with sensuousness, was attempted during the German *Klassik;* but Schiller's philosophy and Goethe's existence were too much for the moral standards of society; Goethe and Schiller fit into the framework of the later petit-bourgeois understanding of art and philosophy in a distorted form. Morality and the feeling of happiness, ethical conduct and sensuousness, therefore, were considered irreconcillable; medieval, baroque and Enlightenment factors hereby received a common point of reference. The metaphysical explanations of this dualism were now only conditionally accepted. The rigorously rational explanation of the dualism by the Enlightenment, based as it was on the awareness of the forcefulness of human instincts, which had to be overcome rationally, was not realizable without a pronounced rational disposition. Elimination of the dualism by means of classical *Kalokagathie*[3] would have required the acceptance of sensuality and at the same time a considerable capacity to sublimate. The progress of technology and industrialization with the accompanying easing of workloads, led in

those classes most favoured by this development to a surplus of vital
energy which press:d for relief. Tne urges thus reinforced were
considered as animalistic. The lack of real education, and the repression
of the autonomous rational man for the sake of the subaltern subject's
loyalty made tneir sublimation impossible. Since religious prohibitions
(even tnough wavering) and societal taboo (even though only as
façades), were still in effect, repression continued.

These complex processes brought about social-pathological neuroses
and led to confusion. When the animalistic nature of man was finally
legitimized (as for example in Social Darwinism and National Socialism),
and played out against 'decadent' culture, the hour of 'liberation' for
the petit-bourgeois mentality had arrived: the predator had broken the
remaining bars of its cage. The interim between repression, respectively
elimination of instinctual urges and 'liberation' from them, witnessed
revealingly modified manifestations of the same; spiritual imbalance
here and there permits a glance into the subterranean development and
growth of bestiality. The 'enigma of the Orient' is here especially
revealing. The longing for the Orient during the nineteenth century
seems at first to have been a rather harmless, fashionable fad.
Preponderently during the sixties and seventies, Cairo, Egypt, Nubia
and Asia Minor were visited by travelling German painters; one indulged
in the intoxicating experience of Oriental splendour, exotic
picturesqueness, and more than anything the secret of tne harem,
Egyptian slave-girls, Turkish singers and dancers, and 'legitimate'
nudity: for in the Orient certain sexual liberties, at which one's own
culture looked askance, seemed to be natural and part of the way of
life; whoever enjoyed it thereby did not leave his own culture but
rather had to adapt to another one. The exotic Orient entailed sadism:
whatever was romantic was brutalized, whereas the cynical elements
were romanticized:

> Reflecting local colour, how many of the portrayed, described or
> plainly imagined slave markets of Cairo and other places evoked the
> viewers' lustful pity with the frightened yet passionate eyes of their
> olive-skinned slave girls and his impulsive revulsion from the brutal
> and cynical demeanour of their sellers and buyers. For here sweet
> suffering and cold cruelty, sensuous compassion and humane outrage
> are inseparable. . .The beholder feels a hidden pleasure in the whip
> and tne cold eyes of the slave dealer. . .He needs his own cruelty to
> feel pity. . .Virtue and sin are inseparably bound together in the
> milieu [Sternberg] .

Inseparably? Virtue ever more moved into the background, it became a pretense only, making the enjoyment of sin possible.

As early as the 1820s this one-sidedness was visible in Philhellenism; though in miniscule fashion it corresponded to the nationalism of 1813, because in both cases the 'good cause' made the release of overflowing aggressive energies possible. The liberal Philhellenist often took to the revolting nature of Greco-oriental warfare rather casually; the Greeks, who chopped off the Turks' heads and sent them to their commanders in return for loaves of bread in the same baskets, were representatives of another culture, which apparently could be fully reconciled with the educational ideal of the humanist. The fact that the Turks held slaves and slave-girls, Christians and Greeks, was considered terrible; when the Greeks did the same, however (Moslem slaves in their case), this was considered less disgraceful. Shameful or not, it was 'fascinating' anyhow; slave-girls somehow captured the imagination of the *Spiesser.*

Journals, books and paintings offered the genre representations already mentioned: pictures of everyday life; it was this aspect which made them so attractive to the petit bourgeois; what was here presented as usual and normal his bad conscience had suggested as uncommon, not normal and abnormal. Torn between the taboo on the one hand and the emancipation of the flesh on the other, he looked at them with craving and yet askance. Their dress was such that they 'could hardly cover their nakedness', a fact which became part of the stereotyped vocabulary. They had to suffer all sorts of maltreatment, which was shared with lascivious pleasure. 'It is a shame of the nineteenth century', read a headline of the *Gartenlaube,* commenting on events in the Dutch colony of Surinam in South America. Needless to say, the typical phenomena of the oriental enigma manifested themselves in any other locality. A prison routinely accepting slaves and slave-girls from their owner for chastisement was the subject of the article.

> The slave or slave-girl is immediately forced to take off his or her clothes and retains only a cloth to cover his loins. . .Lydia is disrobed; though she tries to cover the mounting breasts with her hands, these are torn away by brutal guards and firmly bound together. Then she is pulled up at the stake by her hands. Her cheeks are flooded by tears. . .Yes, one wouldn't believe it, there are ladies in Surinam who do not stop at examining the torn thighs of their slave-girls to see if the wounds measure up to the price, ladies who rub spanish pepper into the wounds.

Cruelty and sensuality, brute force and lust, practised with the 'abandon of the desert', linked with the idyll and homely comfort of the *Gartenlaube,* were the characteristic features of the bourgeois German sadism of the nineteenth century; the slave as girl and the girl as slave: the idols of passionate sensuality converged.

But the Orient also entered the German comfort of the home in other ways: Oriental carpets, Oriental fabrics and Oriental decorations graced the bourgeois habitat — 'here we find the home of opulence and every dream' (Sternberg); the 'solid' bourgeois world is interwoven with wild phantasmagoria. Writing his last will in 1840, Schinkel[4] observed:

> In future the conception of barbarism will assume an entirely different character. It is no longer complete crudity and lack of mores; rather, an extremely thin, external culture which has no firm basis. Taste will be governed by the conventions of the day without a trace of genius. All naïve and original attitudes will be eliminated and the laws of society will be cleverly evaded for egotistical purposes.

As Schinkel died, Makart[5] was born; his red velvet became the standard for interior decoration, his paintings epitomized the petit-bourgeois sexuality of this epoch. He transferred the French exoticism, sensualism and sadism of a Delacroix into the German 'Oriental' — sensuality. 'The death of Sardanapal'[6] by Delacroix was of especial influence.

The representation of the pleasure felt by the Asiatic-Assyrian King at the slaughter of his favourite horses and women, the anatomical accuracy demonstrated in the carving of breasts and bodies by eager servants was an aesthetically sublimated concentration camp painting. Makart softened such motifs and thereby so much more won the heart (i.e. the thus quieted conscience) of the *Spiesser.* Reviewing Makart's 'Moderne Amoretten'[7] (which were friezes for his own atelier), the art historian Pecht commented in 1888:

> The combination of semi-nude and fashionably dressed figures against a gilded background interwoven with trees and bushes is in its mad mixture of delightful beauty so intoxicating that the exhibition created an uproar even in an otherwise so phlegmatic Munich. Only Delacroix' showing of Dante and Vergil at the Paris Salon can have matched it.

Makart's 'Florence Plague' showed the 'blossoming of feminine beauty';

the mixture of death and sex — the original title of the painting had been the 'Seven Mortal Sins' — corresponded to the *Spiesser's* longing for the bordello and harem. Ordinarily his sexual urge could assert itself only in hiding: here, however, prostitution as lewdness and nakedness were 'in order'. 'Charles V's entrance into Antwerp was also crowded with alabaster females who shamelessly enjoyed their nakedness and thereby delighted all viewers.' In Makart's and his cohorts' work, women were usually found in the process of more or less advanced disrobing: it was the striptease for the bourgeoisie of the nineteenth century. It was fully in character, therefore, that during the Third *Reich* Makart, as antecedent to the National Socialist blood-and-soil nudist cult in painting, 'was given an eternal place of honour in German art' (Göring at the 100th anniversary of the painter's birth). He was assigned a niche in the national pantheon of culture, which in reality was an overly decorated panopticum of cheap sexuality. The Makart style in literature shows similar features — not the usual pornography or Rococco-cynicism, but an orgasmic style which, with its combination of myth, the cozy warmth of the nest and small-town sentimentality, gave even to sadism a Germanic pathos or idyllic veneer. An always slipping dress of rugged linen covered the sweet figure, the figure celebrated in song. Yet, when approaching the woman, one should not forget the whip (as both will enjoy it). The woman was conceived of as a sort of nymph. 'A mermaid thou art to me' says 'HE' in Hans Heinz Ewers' *Alraune*,[8] after he kissed the rosy lining of her thighs; and these mermaids, as sweet and delicate and slender as they were, always remained soulless. One took a sharp knife and began to slice — 'right into the fishtail. It hurts, it hurts a lot, but the mermaid hides the pain for the sake of her deep love.' Human she would like to become but mermaid she will remain; the operation is in vain. And the German man really doesn't mind: had she possessed a soul she really couldn't have been a slave girl of the passions:

> Oh, yes and as she put her arm around me and kissed me with her lips and breasts, what came of it? The slave-girl embraced me and dragged me into an empty affair. And in my despair I did not defend myself. And so it came that we carried on as never in our lives before. Some call it marriage. She threw her legs around me and panted between kisses that she wanted a child, now. . .now [Hausmann].

The blond German male, who after all wanted to be Siegfried and

Troubador, who 'performed heroic deeds for his loved one and killed dragons' (Lanz von Liebenfels), was quite rude, at least toward women of dark complexion who were 'destined to be prostitutes anyhow'. But the racial pamphlets of the nineteenth and twentieth centuries now reflected a fully orientalized sadistic sexuality in other respects: that is to say, in the process of 'nordification' the enigma of the Orient has disappeared, it has lost its neurotic character. It now was not only allright but actually necessary for the man to have intercourse with many women. However, the same was not true of the woman, who is stained by the male sperm. 'From this it follows that virginity does not only have sentimental value; it has most important bearing on racial substance. For only a virgin of monandrous genes could serve as wife and mother of racially pure children. Experienced in racial breeding, our ancestors therefore considered virginity of the bride an essential precondition' (Liebenfels). For Hitler, too, the woman was only a bundle of instincts whose blood could be whipped to passion, and the 'whipping' here could be taken quite literally at times. Racist lunacy and the dominance of the National Socialist superman made it possible to consider the sadism of the concentration camps as an honourable service to the nation: the maltreatment, torture and murdering, especially of women, was almost always connected with lascivious lust. 'I clearly remember the first flogging I witnessed. . .as the screaming began, chills ran down my spine. . .The first execution at the beginning of the war did not excite me as much as this corporal punishment' (Höss). E.G. Reichmann was justified when she remarked that the relationship between National Socialism and crime was not accidental but rather necessary, in so far as crime is no more than the consequential satisfaction of urges by the asocial. The asocial, however, must not be understood as the characterization of a sociological class; rather, it must be seen as the feature of a certain type of human behaviour: so it was the petit-bourgeois who was asocial more than any other because he saw in his fellow citizen not the human being, but − as shown in his relationship to the woman − an exploitable, usable object that could be manipulated. Torture and even fatal rape now somehow became institutionalized as part of an official ideology; the *Spiesser*'s dreams had been realized in a way which, however, repulsed all those who now considered the transition from the fictional to the real Orient as too drastic.

Anti-Semitism must be mentioned in this connection because it gave 'inhibited' spirits an even more legitimate opportunity to release aggressive and sadistic urges: that is, it made it possible to project one's own sadism onto a symbol of the other; then one could attack in the symbol of the other all those things one secretly cherished. Streicher's *Stürmer* (the only paper Hitler read in its entirety, as he remarked to Rauschning), was a striking example of this kind of pornography, which had been especially widespread since the end of the nineteenth century, and which was finally officially sanctioned by National Socialism. By thundering against the 'Jewish pigs' who dragged one Aryan girl after the other into the dirt, one really emulated the act in wishful thinking. The reader was regularly presented with scandalous tales of racial shame, which served to please his fantasy and bedroom pleasure as much as it documented his folkish outrage.

> He thought he could entrust his daughter to him. He did not know that he had given her into the claws of a pig. . .Today he knows. Today she is back home with him. But she no longer is the child looking into the world with clear, pure and innocent eyes. The Jew Dr Schoeps has violated her body and murdered her soul.

According to Hitler, the black-haired Jewish youth waits for hours, satanic joy marking his face until, stealing her thus from her people, he can violate the innocent, blond German girl with his blood. 'Systematically these black parasites of peoples violate our inexperienced German girls and thereby destroy something which in this world can never be replaced.'

German 'purity' had been fought for since the days of *Turnvater* Jahn; obscenity, that is 'un-German' sexuality and sensuality, had been rejected with anger. The complexes and perverse outlets which grew out of such repression and tabooing of urges could have been successfully mastered only by an 'enlightenment' of the self and the social environment. When Freud made the diagnosis of his time, it was probably too late for collective therapy. Love 'no longer was blessed by roses'; weeds had to do.

Notes

1. Medieval: courtly love, noble lady.
2. Eudaemonic, producing happiness.
3. The fusion of physical and intellectual perfection as conceived by the Greeks, the term was adopted by German classicism.
4. Karl Friedrich Schinkel (1781-1831), prominent painter and architect.
5. Hans Makart (1840-84), prominent Austrian painter whose ornamental style influenced the taste of the age.

6. Sardanapal, Assyrian king.
7. Amoretten, winged children's figures modelled after Eros of antiquity.
8. Alraune, German for the Mandragora root used in witchcraft; the name of the title figure of Ewers' (1871-1943) eccentric-erotic horror story of 1913.

6 ANTI-SEMITISM

As the scapegoat, the Jew enjoyed a peculiar form of 'sympathy': the Jewish minority in Germany was large enough to serve as the general garbage dump of resentments and as an outlet for uncompensated feelings of inferiority. On the other hand, it was so small and encapsulated that discrimination would not bring about any particular damage to the socio-economic fabric of the people. Centuries of ghetto life had set the Jews so far apart from the general tenor of society that the ignorance of Judaism could be exploited; that is, that the vacuum of unacquaintance could be filled with cruel stories and horror tales. The attempt of the Jews to gain on the upper classes in the process of the emancipation initiated by the Enlightenment promoted a parvenu mentality. This was not so because the Jew was racially a parvenu; rather, it was so because the upstart is more common in classes on the rise. The anti-Semite, however, had found renewed 'sources' for his hatred.

The term 'anti-Semitism' had been coined only in 1879 by Wilhelm Marr[1] who provided labels to lump together all anti-Semitic motives and arguments of the preceding decades and also to conceal prejudice by a veil of science: 'Thereby he only gave to an era which wore an aura of enlightenment and science a correspondingly superficial rationalization of the ideologically, emotionally and in the final analysis somehow religiously rooted, and as such often manipulated rejection of the Jews' (Goldschmidt).

Anti-Semitism as rumour about Jewry (Adorno) gave the underprivileged and frustrated petit-bourgeois a chance not only to release his sexual-sadism, but also to give vent to his overall anti-humanitarian tendencies; the Jew was the subject of rhetorical and actual assault. The foundations of a bestial anti-Semitism were laid in the shadow of confused myths and a racially inspired demi-monde romanticism on which National Socialism could then base its firmest ideological pillar.

All the baseness of which humans are capable was condensed in the flock of Jews (H.S. Chamberlain); a visage of vice and venality, each Jew shamelessly stared into the German's face. The 'relatively low situated upper lid' was already said to reveal the 'sensuously brooding or stalking' nature of the Jewish soul, especially of the Jewish doctors

220

(Fritsch). Jews were not considered to be capable of being real soldiers because they lacked the 'heroic body-frame'; in addition they had flat feet and chicken hearts; they were not capable of feeling and a warm heart; rather, they were cynical agents of decay and degenerate intellectuals. In his *Handbook of the Jewish Question,* Th. Fritsch denied the existence of Jewish children as such: 'There are no Jewish children; each Jew is born an old man.' At their feasts the Jews slaughtered children; in their miserable department stores they only offered inferior merchandise.

Since the Jew was not Germanic, was neither blond nor blue-eyed, and 'lacked the elongated skull', he was characterized as immoral. 'Our German concepts of loyalty, humanity, dedication, and sacrifice for a cause are incomprehensible to the Jew and evoke his scorn. The only virtue to him is that which brings personal advantage or pleasure.' Fritsch proclaimed ten commandments of self-help — for the German should know that, with all his fellow Germans, 'regardless of creed or political opinion he had one common irreconcilable enemy: his name is Jew!'

Very early in the nineteenth century 'Love plus Humanitarianism' was considered as 'a way of thought which decomposes all living forms and laws of a people and state' (Hitler). Nature revolts against it: the 'nature' of the *Spiesser* was revolted by it. He enviously attacked all those who were intellectually or materially superior to him (except for those connected with governmental authority) with venomous hatred, and indulged himself at the expense of those below him; the Jews often served as the two-fold object of hate: they were economically and intellectually 'superior'; socially, however, they were inferior. Humanitarian, liberal, democratic or socialist arguments against discrimination of the Jewish minority were doubly distorted: on the one hand they were considered as unnatural, as contrary to the essence of man as cerebral animal (a thesis which was 'scientifically' supported by Social Darwinism); on the other hand they were considered as 'outcroppings' of Jewish 'humanitarian propaganda' designed to protect them from their impending elimination. The Jews were thus supposed to have invented the 'myth of conscience'. . . . 'Conscience, this Jewish invention', Hitler said to Rauschning.

'To strive for human tolerance and brotherhood,' for the aims of humanity, is to kill off any racial, kindred and familial feelings in the people and to transform them into a helpless stew of humanity which will willingly bow to the Jewish people, a people governed

by anything but brotherhood and humanity. . .It is somehow like
this with the concept of 'pacifism': it leads via the genocide of
peoples, to the disarmament of peoples under the supervision of
an executive authority which is governed by Juda. . .'Liberty' is the
licentious, uninhibited, unscrupulous tyranny of the Levite, the
privilege to do anything conducive to the Jewish lust for power. . .
Equality is the undifferentiated, coerced, equal enslavement of all
Gentiles by the Jews [Ludendorff].

Such claims were typical examples for the focus of attack that anti-
humanitarianism found in humanitarian Judaism; had it been any other
delusion than the hatred of Jews, had it not been initiated by the upper
classes of society, had the educational level of the population been
more advanced, anti-Semitism would have been subject to general
ridicule and would have disintegrated in the fresh air of natural reactions
and understanding. But the stupor of the people was institutionalized;
the ruling classes did not adhere to the ideal of the gentleman (as in
England) or the citizen (as in France); with their condescending joviality
or abrupt 'monocled' forwardness, their affected fancy of straw-hat
fineries and club comfort, their velvet decor and mentality, they were
not a moral élite but rather anti-humanitarian fanatics and 'cultured'
anti-Semites.

Be it in the Court of Law, the professor's lecture hall, the teacher's
classroom, the officer's mess or the pastor's synod, here as anywhere
the humane was declared weak and defamed as un-German. The
designation 'people of poets and thinkers' served, as much as an
affected, rarely really lived, Christianity to calm the conscience.
One basked in the sun of a great past of which the individual was
part only in so far as he was forced to memorize biblical verses and
German classical poetry at school. How could Jews be acknowledged
in such an intellectual and human atmosphere? [Ehrlich].

The myth of the Jewish Satan, partly Germanic ideology and partly
German *Ersatz*-religion, was systematically created by the 'intellectual
élite'; it was no 'wild fruit', not the product of the gutter even though
it dwelled on the level of the gutter. It had sprung from the calculated
thought of ideological sadists. By raising their individual venality to a
general norm, they freed themselves from their own amoral alienation.
The anti-Semitism of those jumping on the bandwagon was in effect
often more brutal; in conception, however, it was more naïve than the

racism of the 'signal callers'. The fashionable anti-Semites and
intellectual instigators wanted later on to dissociate themselves from
the gutter-level anti-Semitism of the National Socialists, which was too
bloody for their aesthetic sensitivity; but it was just this group which
had committed 'treason to Germanness', as the Hölderlin scholar
Wilhelm Michel called it. Theirs was treason because they would have
been well capable of recognizing the criminality of their actions. Instead
they handed the 'raised cudgel to the raving', the 'slashing blade to the
mass-murderers'; they demanded and promoted the 'abandonment of
due process, readiness for any kind of cannibalism, the intoxicating
warmth of a shouting mob and, deep inside, the comfortable and
cowardly awareness of a facile escape into the irresponsible masses'.
German anti-Semitism was thus an essential part of the German 'official
way of life'; here one could be for Goethe and against his humanity at
the same time.

Since there is no such thing as partial humanitarianism, since it either
envelops the whole man or not at all (unless he only pretends to possess
it), the moral accusation must fall on the 'moderate' anti-Semite as
much as on the radical; that is to say, the man of 1813 is as guilty as
the man of 1933 or 1939. A few examples shall illustrate the German
cultural schizophrenia of 'love of intellect' and hatred of Jews.

Fichte was an idealistic professor who, with the treasure of his ideas,
knew how to set the students sitting at his feet ablaze in the service of
the true and good; but he did not want to grant civil rights to the Jews:
'To that end I see no other means but to cut off all their heads in one
night and replace them with others containing not one Jewish idea. To
protect ourselves from them I again see no other way but to conquer
their promised land for them and to send them all there.' The genial
good-natured Jahn (whom Heine, however, with more justification,
called an 'idealistic rowdy'), feared that the Jewish monsters would
erode the forest of German folklore. Though animals and trees could be
cultivated and bred to higher stages of perfection, the Jew could not be
ennobled; here nature (that is, German nature) refused to co-operate.
'Poles, Frenchmen, priests, Junkers and Jews are Germany's misfortune.'

After 1810, Christian Friedrich Rühs was professor of history at the
newly founded Berlin University, and later on he became the official
historian of the Prussian state; so that the hebraic enemy could be
recognized, he suggested they wear a yellow patch on their clothing.

The *Burschenschaften* fought against suppression and for freedom.
So it came about that some of them also defended the freedom of the
Jew, as for example in 1819 at Heidelberg, where they fought a popular

mob with drawn side-arms; but the germanophile *Burschenschaften* with their racial hatred prevailed in the long run. They organized Vehmic[2] leagues and called for 'crusades against Judaism', led by Wolfgang Menzel.[3] The battle-cry of such 'brethren in Christ' was: 'Up to revenge now! Our battle-cry be Hep, Hep, Hep! All Jews death and perish, you must succumb or vanish.' The 'warmth of the heart' was the *Gartenlaube*'s concern; but when it came to Jews it was as if this tenderness had been blown away. 'All of world history knows no other example of a homeless people, a physically and psychically decidedly degenerate race, who, merely by cunning and craft, usury and huckstering, dominate the globe.' Wilhelm Busch was a bright and witty poet and cartoonist who knew the weaknesses of the philistine, a pessimist and humanist; the love for man left him when it came to Jews: 'And the Jew with crooked heel,/crooked nose and baggy slacks/ to the bourse on high he will/rotten deep a soul he lacks.'

The *Fliegende Blätter*[4] never offended anyone; its plain and honest humour remained aloof from all contemporary problems. But it became more pointed or cutting when it was time to sock it to the Jews. Jews were dirty, yellow, vain, sordid, unsportsmanlike, not as dashing as the proverbial lieutenant, but also of course not as stupid, which made them even less liked.

Richard Wagner wanted to penetrate the cosmic secret, create sacred stage events and open an added dimension of depth to German music and culture in general; but in the evaluation of Jews he did not shy away from the most banal superficiality and intellectual slander: he considered Jewish musicians as characterized by fundamental incompetence; always dwelling in the trivial, the Jew was indifferent to art; a Jewish artist could not address himself to the heart and the soul. Wagner considered the Jewish race the 'born enemy of pure humanity and everything that is noble in it'; 'that we Germans especially will perish because of them is certain, and perhaps I will be the last German who managed — to remain upright. . .in face of an all powerful Judaism.'

Wagner's son-in-law, the 'very learned' Houston Stewart Chamberlain, despised the Jews especially because they were a mixed race, a race with impure blood:'. . .A mongrel dog not uncommonly is very smart, but never reliable; morally it is always a tramp.' Heinrich von Treischke was a serious historian proud of his nation, with profound knowledge and striking insights. This man, of whom the Jewish philosopher Hermann Cohen[5] said 'that we younger ones all owe him much in terms of understanding and impulses', found it necessary to raise the racial issue against the Jews. 'To satisfy and protect Germanic instincts in days of uproar and incited popular passions, he exposed his Israelite fellow citizens to real insults and conspiratorial suspicion.' Treitschke's *A Word About Our Jews*[6] was not as clumsy as the anti-Semitic pamphlets of the day; after all, Treitschke was an educated historian who 'did not tolerate the filth and crudeness of the anti-Semitic movement at all'; his smut was fine-grained: 'Even in the circles of most refined culture, amongst men who would reject any thought of religious intolerance or national pride with revulsion, the refrain today comes as if from one voice: the Jews are our misfortune'. Theodore Mommsen described anti-Semitism as 'the very core of the madness which has now taken hold of the masses, and which has found its right prophet in Herr von Treitschke'. To Mommsen, Treitschke was the 'epitome of the moral brutalization which is endangering our civilization, as he has become its most powerful exponent in the field of literature'. He called him

> 'The father of modern anti-Semitism.' His programme, the pamphlet *A Word About Our Jews,* which had created a public stir, he characterized as contradictory as well as damaging, and he did not hesitate to come forward with. . .an answer. 'The times change and nothing is eternal but stupidity and meanness.' In fighting anti-Semitism he fought the 'abortion of national feeling', the baseness and brutalization of human nature [Wucher].

The later president of the Pan-German League, Heinrich Class,[7] on the other hand considered it an 'inestimable good fortune' to have been exposed to the passionate Treitschke as a student. Expressions like 'perfidious Albion'[8] or 'the Jews are our misfortune' remained for the rest of his life a kind of Evangelism for him. 'For me Treitschke was the master who governed my life.' Class and the Pan-German League wanted to enhance Germany's rating in the world: this could very well be combined with an anti-Semitic campaign which in its demands anticipated National Socialist anti-Semitic legislation in almost every detail.

Paul Bötticher, who went under the name Paul de Lagarde, was known as a diligent professor (of Oriental Studies) and a Christian proponent of a national Evangelical Church. In his *Deutsche Schriften* he let go of his atavistic hatred in the form of an especially venomous anti-Semitism: 'As Jews the Jews are aliens in every European state, and as aliens they are nothing but carriers of decomposition.'

He thought many Germans were too cowardly to stamp out the Jewish vermin. 'One does not negotiate with trichinae and bacilli, nor does one "educate" them; they are being rendered harmless as quickly and as completely as possible.'

Karl Eugen Dühring[9] was a political economist and above all a philosopher; his love of wisdom did not stand in the way of his vile anti-Semitism; under the influence of Count Arthur Gobineau[10] he represented a racial-biological point of view. One of his writings was entitled: *The Substitution of Something More Perfect for Religion and the Expulsion of all Judaism by the Modern Spirit of Peoples.* Against the Jews there is only one kind of politics: that of restriction, confinement and segregation.

Teachers concerned with the welfare of youth, plain and honest German representatives of culture turned out to be uninhibited violators of the people's soul. They included Nietzsche's brother-in-law Bernard Förster,[11] who organized an anti-Semitic petition handed to Bismarck in 1881 with 267,000 signatures (of which 4,000 were by students), Ahlwardt,[12] Dinter,[13] Krieck[14] and the many local Nazi leaders[15] who during the Third *Reich* planted the spirit of anti-humanism and racial hatred into the hearts of children.

German-national pastors[16] and religiously oriented national and nationalistic publicists and politicians 'were revolted by the new Judaized Germanness' (Frantz). The conservative theologian Adolf Stöcker founded the petit-bourgeois Christian-Social Party in Berlin which sought to attract the Christian educated masses with anti-Semitic watch-words. The 'blood-poisoning' of the German people's body by the Jews was to be cured. The discomfort of that era's capitalist situation he attributed to the Jews. 'Much is not right with our modern economy, politics and morality; it was necessary to find the guilty one, to remove the onus from the king and his servants, from the productive capitalist and attach it to the Jew at the bourse, the huckster's shop and the newspaper's editorial office' (G. Mann). The German Reform Party demanded the 'Christian and national education of youth' — the carriers 'of decomposition were the essentially alien Jewish people'.

In Austria it was Georg Ritter von Schönerer[17] who from 1890 spouted forth 'unadulterated German words' in the journal of the same name against the Jews — he was a German national and Christian fighter 'of genuine calibre'. 'What the Jew believes is neither here nor there — it is in his race, the pig is everywhere.' In 1897 Karl Lueger[18] became Burgomaster of Vienna; at the same time he was chairman of the Christian-Social Party of Austria which in 1907 became the strongest party in the Austrian Chamber of Deputies. Lueger operated on a higher level than Schönerer — thus he became even more influential and dangerous; many Austrian Catholics and clergymen remained faithful to his anti-Semitic principles up to the days of the *Anschluss:*

> Only Christian anti-Semitism is national and effective; it measures up to every standard of culture and humanity and proceeds naturally from the 1800 years of Christian life and teachings. . .Christian anti-Semitism judges by the standards of positive intellectual attitude, not by genealogical tables or the quality of blood.

German conservatives, who were concerned with 'lasting values' and wanted to preserve what was 'inalienable' (and whatever else their slogans were), entered an alliance with the anti—Semitic hate-mongers to make their politics more popular; needless to say, racial hatred also reflected their attitude. The affinity of conservatism and anti-Semitism has been pointed out by (among others) Th. Adorno.[19] Moreover, the Jews, concerned with emancipation, usually belonged to the political left. But this was not so because of any racial aptitude for leftist liberalism, as was immediately implied by the right. Rather, they belonged because the left with its demands for democratization and constitutionalism wanted to put a stop to the discrimination of minorities. 'Ten *Ahlwardts*[20] rather than one progressive' was the motto of the conservatives; if it meant opposition to liberalism, one was willing to tolerate political immorality.

All the examples cited here, which could be extended *ad infinitum,* manifested themselves on the lowest or gutter level; but they nevertheless represented the thinking processes of the cultured German bourgeoisie. The war against the Jews was organized by forces which belonged to the German intellectual 'élite'; they functioned as the whips of the hate programme which appealed to the masses of the semi-educated. What Alexander Rüstow[21] once said of conservatism also goes for anti-Semitism, as both after all were in close mutual contact:

> We are dealing. . .with a quasi religious manifestation which shares with confessional religiosity the characteristic that its teachings and views are transmitted at a completely uncritical, blindly faithful stage of childhood, devoid of logic, which later on is protected and isolated from criticism by taboos of loyalty.

Anti-Semitism was the ideological and therefore rationally unassailable foundation of a *Weltanschauung* which reflected the brutality and narrow-mindedness of the *Spiesser,* regardless whether he was a member of the Imperial or Royal family, the aristocracy, the clergy, the bureaucracy, the academic world, a clerk, an artisan or a merchant. The workers, themselves constantly discriminated and defamed, were almost completely immune to anti-Semitic hate-mongering.

Chancellor Count von Caprivi had urgently warned of the dangers of anti-Semitism in a *Reichstag* speech in 1893:

> The movement, initiated in Germany and flowing from various motives, in my opinion already goes in many ways beyond the limits reconcilable with the welfare of the state. One doesn't know whether the spirits which are being awakened can be curbed. What guarantee have the men who evoke these spirits that the current which drives them on will not one day unite with other currents directed against property and public order. . .It seems to me that history gives many examples of movements which initially doubtlessly wanted the best, then went beyond their intentions and eventually could no longer be stopped.

The justification of these discerning words was to be fully borne out during the following decades. At the same time, however, in a certain sense they reflected the very spirit they set out to combat: not even in the beginning had the anti-Semitic movement aspired for 'the best'. It could not because it was anti-humanitarian to the core. Its especial dangerousness was not rooted in the fact that one day it could turn against property and public order, but in the fact that it always and at every time turned against the human order and the dignity of man. But such insights no longer could be expected of the official cultured bourgeoisie, to which Caprivi belonged too.

When the Third *Reich* erupted, the legion of anti-Semitic German thinkers fell into step with the National Socialists in the march into a better future (free of Jews). 'The promiscuity of the thinkers and murderers saddens us', Wulf said; however, we must face it because it reveals the most shattering problem of German political anthropology of the nineteenth and twentieth centuries.

The anti-Semitic principles of many centuries were commensurate to the petit-bourgeois mental capacity of Hitler: 'The Jews are responsible for it all!' 'The Jews are our misfortune!' 'The Jews are evil incarnate'; the simplifications rendered complex thought processes and the need

for reflection unnecessary — intellect was a Jewish invention anyhow!
For Hitler, the epigone of the earlier anti-Semites, the Jews had only a
very primitive herd instinct. And this was a commonplace argument.
The Jew chokes in filth and garbage; his culture is a false culture; there
is no Jewish art — 'especially the two queens of art, architecture and
music, owe nothing original to Judaism'. 'Great' Jewish actors also do
not exist; they are only 'imposters and imitators'. 'No, the Jew does
not possess any culturally creative energy because he lacks idealism,
without which there is no higher development of man.' Hitler of course
also cited the forged 'Protocols of the Elders of Zion'. He does not
present any justification for his anti-Semitism in *Mein Kampf;* he does
not even try; he knows that the person enraptured by fanaticism rejects
even the attempt at proof, because after all he does not have to be
converted like an infidel, but rather wants to be led, faithful and
narrow-minded.

After 1935 the anti-Semitic aims could be realized; during the war
the 'hour of the final reckoning with Juda' had come. Paraphrasing
Goethe, the *Stürmer* recited in 1943:

Quiet is in the bourses' halls
from the children of Israel falls
hardly a sigh.
Over there still a few cryers
soon you too, Abraham Meyers
will quietly lie.

A commentary was added: 'This wish and this prophecy is being
fulfilled in our days.'

Notes

1. Wilhelm Marr in *Der Sieg des Judentums über das Germanentum,* Bern, 1879.
2. See p.76, n.17.
3. See p.15, n.12.
4. *Fliegende Blätter,* humorous weekly published from 1844-1928 merged with
   the *Meggendorfer Blätter.*
5. Hermann Cohen (1842-1918), neo-Kantian professor of philosophy at
   Marburg University.
6. Published in 1880.
7. See p.51, n.1.
8. Albion, ancient term for England.
9. Karl Eugen Dühring (1833-1921), positivist philosopher and economist who
   opposed the religious beliefs of his day as well as a socialist system.

10. See p.150, n.4.
11. See E. Salin, *Vom deutschen Verthängnis. Gespräch an der Zeitenwende: Burckhardt-Nietzsche,* Hamburg: 1959, p.171.
12. Hermann Ahlwardt (1846-1914), elementary school principal, pseudo-scientific author of anti-Semitic tracts who became a member of the Reichstag and was engaged in the most venemous sorts of anti-Semitic polemics.
13. 1876-1948, author of *Sünde wider das Blut* (1918) (*Sin Against Blood*).
14. Ernst Krieck (1882-1947), professor of pedagogy at Frankfurt and Dortmund who attempted to establish a philosophical foundation for National Socialism.
15. Glaser refers here to the *Ortsgruppenleiter,* the links in the party structure between the street level organisation (*Blockleiter*) and the district leadership.
16. Of a new, National Socialist oriented Christianity.
17. See p.125, n.6.
18. See p.125, n.7.
19. Theodor W. Adorno (1903-70), Frankfurt professor of philosophy and sociology; prominent social critic proceeding from Hegel and Marx. He spent the Hitler years in exile.
20. See n.12.
21. Alexander Rüstow (born 1885), liberal economist, historian and sociologist from 1933-50, Professor in Istanbul, from then on in Heidelberg.

7 THE GHASTLY IDYLL

The spirit of the French Revolution did not take hold in Germany; the citizen remained dependent on absolutism. The proclamation of liberty and human dignity, of civil rights, of the revolt against feudal forms in state and society, and of the emancipation of discriminated classes was left to literature — these were declamatory pronouncements without practical effect. Territorial particularism moreover prevented economic expansion: 'In a land where the majority of the factories have notoriously either succumbed or infirmly linger on, where fairs and markets are filled with the goods of other nations, where the majority of merchants is almost inactive, is there any need to bring further proof that the evil has reached the highest degree?' (List).[1]

The citizen therefore was left only the 'free' realm of the intellect. As early as 1796, Jean Paul[2] had given the 'programme' for future generations in the preface to his *Leben des Quintus Fixlein,* wherein he described the romantic as well as *Biedermeier* solution to the general misery. Man, he said, cannot be fully happy, but he can be 'more happy':

I never could detect more than three ways to become more happy (but not fully happy). The first, striving upward, is: to transcend the clouds of life so far that the whole external world with its pitfalls, charnel-houses and lightning conductors, lies at one's feet like a little *Kindergarten.* The second is: to fall right down into that little *Garten* and there to nest so comfortably in a furrow that, looking out of one's warm lark's nest, there are no pitfalls, charnel-houses and antennae to see but only the fruits of grain, each one of them being a tree or an umbrella against sun or rain for the nesting bird. The third one at last, which I consider the most difficult and wisest, is as follows: to alternate between the two. . .It is my intention to show the whole world that small joys of the senses should be regarded more highly than great ones, that the nightrobe rates more than the formal coat. . .As one can see, I urge that man become a settled tailor, not dwelling among the storm-whipped branches of the roaring, bending, immeasurable tree of life, but rather stitching a nest on one of its leaves and there dwelling in cozy warmth — the most necessary homily for our century is the admonition to stay at home.

For the man of the nineteenth century, the 'idyll' was the refuge from the imposing powers of interior as well as external, religious as well as political threats. To be satisfied with one's lot and ask no more, to turn inwardly and perfect the self, to free oneself from the external forces of fate and to remain an inwardly free and joyful man in spite of heavy pressures – this 'introversion' was the motif of a world view and philosophy of life which can be met time and again from the Enlightenment until the late nineteenth century. The idyll meant gaiety on the basis of melancholy, gaiety which came from resignation tempered by melancholy: 'Lord, send what you will,/of sorrow or of love;/it comes from you above/by your hands I am still/would'st not with joy/and not with pain/you fill my lot these days/for in the golden mean/the blessing rests always' (Mörike). The idyll meant to wrestle for one's 'quiet existence', the endeavour to escape the gravity of being, without in the end being able to evade it anyhow. It was often a desperate attempt to gain control over oneself, to curb and sublimate the urges, to submit them to a 'milder law'. In Grillparzer's 'dramatic fairytale' *Life, a Dream,* Rustan, an ambitious youth, stimulated to active life by the Negro slave, is cured from the urge to live this life, to long for power, glory and prestige, by a dream which anticipates these things. 'The evening before his planned exit, shortly before his dream and awakening, he jubilantly' saw the wide expanses of the plains before himself. 'Every fibre of his body reacted', his fists were clenched, 'and from the lowered brow shot the lightning of wild-fire'. Next morning, however, he only wants to stay at the side of the loved one in the peaceful hut to find his happiness. 'Oh spread it forth with yonder rays,/instil it deep in every heart:/of all the earthly happy ways/ there is but one, its inner peace/and an unburdened heart!' All action is in vain: greatness 'is dangerous', glory is 'an empty game'; the deed casts 'lowly shadows'. Exile was the only alternative for revolutionary fervour in Germany. Goethe commented in *Wilhelm Meisler's Wanderjahre* with the words of Leonardo that 'the highest and most ample values of life are rooted in change and in those things gained through the active life'. Thereby he wanted to speak for the 'general migration' into the distance, to the land beyond the great ocean. Concerning the 'longing for America', which had spread more and more since the beginning of the nineteenth century, Hegel remarked in the *Lectures on the Philosophy of World History:* 'America is the land of the future where in coming epochs the essence of universal history shall reveal itself; it is the land those long for who are bored by the historical armory of ancient Europe.' Whoever did not want to

be 'bored' in the German narrowness, the nooks and crannies of the
mountains, who wanted to remain man in the all-encompassing sense
of that word, had to isolate himself from his trist environment and
erupt internally, had to free himself for the 'ascent to the spheres', the
'life of the furrow': real existence was nothing but desolate flat
desert. Schiller has characterized this mode of thought in his essay
concerning naïve and sentimental poetry. He considered it the attempt
of the sentimental spirit, that is, not the naïve but the calculating spirit,
to reconcile himself with all evils 'he must endure in a world of culture'.

> The culturally committed man is therefore immeasurably concerned
> to find a material confirmation of the feasibility of this concept (of
> an innocent and happy humanity) in the world of the senses, of a
> possible reality of this state of being. However, since practical
> experience, far from nourishing this faith, rather constantly
> contradicts it, poetic license here as in many other cases comes to
> the aid of reason to conceptualize this idea and to bring it to
> realization in one single instance.

The *Biedermeier* era was a period not only of melancholy dreams, but
also of hopes for an innocent and happy humanity, even if narrowly
confined. A sort of purring comfortableness was part of it, 'secularizing'
the idyll and metaphysically cheapening it. Life in the village is quiet.
The summer evening finds one sitting on the garden bench, one child
on the lap, the others jumping about; the pipe in his mouth, grandfather
holds the beermug in his hand. In the cold of winter, looking through
the frosted windows, one views the 'virgin snow', goes sleigh-riding and
prepares for the Christmas season. In the evening the family gathers at
the round table in cozy harmony as the water for the inexpensive
peppermint tea is simmering in readiness. At midnight the watchman
calls out the hour, but everyone is already fast asleep; only a tomcat
wanders along the old wall in the moonlight. Remembering the 'blissful
days of childhood', Storm[3] later spoke of the 'midday solitude' of rural
existence. 'Now it is silent in yard and barn,/no longer grinds the mill;/
the pear tree with its lustrous leaves/ in the sunlight stands so still.' The
little town lies off the beaten path in silently sleepy bliss. 'We look
down the lanes, into the cozy corners, at the steeply slanting roofs
around the ancient churches, at the market-place with its fountain
before the town-hall opposite the restaurants "The Elephant" and the
"Golden Lion"' (Kalkschmidt). Spitzweg[4] has portrayed the 'small
town', and many poets have praised it in their songs. The *Bürger*

inhabiting the small town is diligent, frugal and concerned with order and cleanliness. 'Does not the stranger praise our reconstructed gates/ and whitewashed tower and renovated church?/Does not the pavement praise each one and the canals well planned and covered, rich in water, serving safety's sake,/so that the Roman candle be snuffed out on first appeal?' So did the host of *Hermann und Dorothea*'s Lion's Inn, 'who himself served six times in the council', take note with satisfaction.

Inward attitudes correspond to the external picture. If everything is to come out for the best, one must display a 'pure and always evenly quiet attitude and common sense'. 'Virtuousness' alone counted. Beginning the 'diary of their marriage', Robert and Klara Schumann made this first entry: '. . .All happiness of life rests on these three words. Let's voice them as a talisman: "Diligence, frugality and loyalty".' But in 1857, in his first work the *Chronik der Sperlingsgasse,* Raabe[5] already 'mourned for a Germany which could then be found any longer only in sidestreets and attics, a soulful Germany of faith, goodness, humility and patience' (Burger). In his search for bygone days, Raabe time and again placed the plot of his short stories and novels into old and weather beaten cities, into villages and quiet and comfortable regions. Raabe paints the 'old nests' and their inhabitants with affection and vividness; his sympathy is with those poor in body and intellect, the melancholy loners, the eccentrics and the old-fashioned, alienated odd fellows. Raabe fully realized that the 'German Idyll' often left man stunted in philistine narrowness. He did not overcome this narrowness by romanticizing it, by attributing an elevated meaning to the common, by giving it a mysterious appearance, by giving the dignity of the unknown to the commonplace, or by making the finite look infinite, which could be done in the confinement of the furrow as well as in the vastness of the celestial spheres. The charnel houses and pit-falls disappeared from sight, melancholy waned and one came to be at home and comfortable in the world of generalities (later the world of the profane), the common and well-known and finite. The transition from the true to the false idyll was often very smooth; what appeared as such a superficial feeling of happiness in reality often was obtained by the individual only after perilous effort. However, in the second half of the nineteenth century, a 'harmless' emptiness prevailed, the cultural contentedness of the cow, which politically was most dangerous. Epigones of Romanticism and *Biedermeier* usurped journals, popular fiction, calendars and primers, in short, the public media with their influence on the masses. The silently quiet turned into cobweb-mustiness, the world of the village and small town into idealized stupour, and the proverbial night-watchman into a costumed reactionary. The *Leitmotiv* was the image of the philistine who never left his four walls and 'maintained his composure', come what may. 'The sustaining hand, cultivating and caring for the little garden. . . already is the hand which refuses asylum to the fugitive' (Adorno). Keller[6] (with his novels about the people of Seldwyla), Wilhelm Busch and especially Heinrich Heine have exposed the superficial nature and narrow, often already malignant *Biedermann*-morality of the bourgeois idyll. Provincial, small-town Göttingen was characterized by Heine in his *Reisebilder*[7] as 'famous for its sausages and University. She is beautiful and pleases the beholder most when he turns his back to her.'

> She must be very old because I remember when I matriculated there five years ago and shortly thereafter was expelled; she already then looked grey and precocious and was fully stocked with freaks and poodles, dissertations, *the-dansants,* washwomen, compendia, roasted doves, Guelph-lodges, fancy carriages, pipes, court-counsellors, judges, disciplinary deans and other fools.

'The German', Heine mocked in the *English Fragments,* 'builds his house behind his stove and comfortably dwells within it reading the news.' The Philistine, 'the white nightcap on his head, the white clay-pipe in the mouth sits at his doorstep in the mellowness of the summer evening and thinks right comfortably: wouldn't it be nice if he could keep on sitting there and vegetate into blessed eternity without losing the spark of pipe or life?' This image would transport the sensitive Heine into angry anxiety; the thought of a Germany like this could cause sleepless nights: the sensitive had turned into the sentimental idyll, the struggle for security had turned into escapist bliss; the time had come for the homely Germans to turn into unholy Germans. The general intellectual depravity was virtually transported into the world of the arbour. To be unpolitical, which once was a bitter sacrifice, had now become the most exalted aim, because it was in this manner that one could become most pleasing to the powers that be; one was concerned with security and career. 'The political tune is an ugly tune'. Political satirists of the day commented: 'The ostrich and the German man/are veritable twins/the bird reflects the camel's head,/and he the philistine's. . ./the one conceals his head in sand/his rear the wind's oasis,/the other digs with learned zeal/in literature and phrases' (Dingelstedt). Yet this unpolitical withdrawal from public affairs was complemented by a no less unpolitical veneration of power.

The Germans, Schopenhauer observed, are followers like sheep, and they follow the asses. Laziness and cowardice, Kant once said, are the reasons why a large part of humanity long freed by nature from alien guidance prefer to remain in lifelong nonage.

The Germanic Philistine, Raabe observed about a hundred years later, is comfortable in his 'state and municipal tax paying, church-pew assured, police guarded, total and glorious security supervised by all the princely authorities'. Journals of bourgeois humour reflected this apolitical dullness in text and illustration, quite contrary to the anti-bourgeois journals like the *Kladderadatsch* or later the *Simplicissimus.* A few examples should illustrate the kind of humour contained in the *Fliegende Blätter,* a humour which was always without point and at times utterly without taste.

A contemporary ad: the unknown lady to whom I became engaged at the dance last night is requested to reveal her whereabouts. When in India a worker loses or forgets his workstrap this doesn't matter much; he quickly catches a snake which must perform the services of the workstrap.
'Just think, Miss, today I have seen many snowgeese.' 'Tell me, lieutenant, are snowgeese edible?' 'Oh yes, when they are young!' 'But aren't they terribly cold?'
A father's suffering: 'Too bad that my little Pepi passed away! Today he would've been just four years old — by now he could have nicely gone to get my beer!'

The apolitical subject of the Second Empire and the unpolitical 'citizen' of the Weimar Republic represented stages in the development of the apolitical *Volksgenosse*[8] of the Third *Reich.* The political animal had drifted into the apolitical idyll, but this 'false idyll' could not absorb the impulses, no less sublimate them; they dwelled in a void and sought new connections. National Socialism served the purpose because its collectivist view of life released the individual from responsibility and thereby seemed to safeguard bourgeois quiet and self-satisfaction. Incapable of genuine mutual existence, one fell for a movement which condemned the ideal of a society of justice and human dignity.

The unfulfilled existence of the housewife for whom Hitler became the idol; the old German National anti-Semite, for whom the whole movement served as compensation for his unbalanced drives; the teacher who elevates his self-imposed loneliness 'as the archetype of

a universal existence' and, conscious of the final solution, posits
and helps to bring about 'a fundamental new order'; the 'enthralled'
lady with the fad for handwoven materials; the frustrated advocate
of German colonies whose once firmly directed impulsive private
imperialism now seeks room to live in the party cells of the NSDAP —
all of them are the expressions of internal instability, unrealistic
expectations of life, spineless speculations, emotional sloth and
misery: these are the subterranean foundations of the ideological
shambles [Kurzrock].

Through the surrender of his individual autonomy, the petit-bourgeois,
delivering himself to authority, gained four 'advantages': by rendering
himself as morally not of age he eliminated most of the potential for
conflict; he took part in the narcissistic omnipotence of the external
authority under which he had placed himself; he gained its protection
and without feelings of guilt could relieve himself of his aggressive
instincts as long as he abreacted them on official enemies; the pursuit
or killing of the enemies of *Führer* and party became a sanctioned
witch hunt: by hexing the others one's own devilishness could be
neutralized (compare H.E. Richter).

    The National Socialist mass murderer too was first of all the
apolitical subject, filled with a sense of duty, 'solid' in the execution of
the crimes, showing devotion to those above him, always concerned
with his career, a worshipper of power who turned loose the beast in
him wherever it was opportune and entailed no risk. Rudolf Höss, the
commander of Auschwitz, was the prototype of this attitude. His
autobiography reveals the eagerly diligent conscientiousness of a man

who is forever serving some authority, who always does his duty,
be it as executioner or as confessing culprit, a man who always lives
a second-hand existence, who always sacrifices his own self and
therefore willingly surrenders his innermost self, a terrifyingly empty
self, in the form of an autobiography to the Court to serve 'the
cause' [Broszat].

Since childhood days Höss was raised to a 'firm sense of duty'.

In my parents' home, strict emphasis was placed on the exact and
conscientious fulfilment of all orders. Everyone always had a certain
number of duties. My father took special care that I followed all his
orders and wishes meticulously.

'Raised to unconditional obedience, a most meticulous sense of order and cleanliness', Höss later on 'devoted himself fully' to his given task, the mass extermination of the Jews, with 'unselfish dedication'. Although the order to make Auschwitz 'into the largest plant for the destruction of humanity ever' was to him somewhat unusual, unnatural, 'the order had to be executed correctly'. 'At the time I did not contemplate — I had received an order — and I had to execute it. Whether this massive extermination of the Jews was necessary or not, I could not venture to judge, I could not see that far.'

Like his superiors, 'fellow fighters' and subordinates, Höss had 'to obey the laws of war and the flag.' The trials of the post-war period have time and again confirmed the image of the bourgeois murderer in terrifying manner. 'For me an order by the *Führer* was just that: an order by the *Führer*. I was a National Socialist and did not think about orders. These shootings of Jews I considered necessary for the welfare of the fatherland.'

The National Socialist executioners privately lived a humbly respectable existence. They were home in time for dinner and the women often had no notion of their husbands' activity. After 'business' was done, one submerged oneself in the solid well-being of a neo-bourgeois existence — as if nothing had happened, as if the slaughter of men, women and children in a way belonged to the daily duties of a conscientious public official. The many small occasional offenders, such as respectable merchants, bureaucrats, teachers, clerks, workers, faithful heads of families, showed the same character. Enjoying a happy family life in their homes for years or even decades on the occasion of pogroms or other organized inhuman activity they would exchange their bourgeois garb for the brown shirt and wreck the homes and stores of Jews, manhandling the owners. Then they returned to the loving wife and the children's happiness, cleaned their brown shirts of Jewish blood and continued to face life — correct, conscientious and reliable — German men without flaw or blemish. The model of them all, Heinrich Himmler, was the son of a well established, strictly Catholic bourgeois family. In high school he was an exemplary pupil, highly esteemed by the teachers as an ambitious student. 'His entire being breathed loyalty, even if in a somewhat exaggerated manner' (Hallgarten). His father, a servile high-school teacher who was sycophantical especially when faced by aristocratic pupils, had raised his son to a 'sincere sense of duty'. Only in gymnastics was Himmler a failure; in spite of the utmost exertion, he never mastered the knee-circle on the horizontal bar. He relieved himself of the resulting inferiority complex by retiring as a youth into a pubescent dream-world of ancestors and élites. Corresponding to his petit-bourgeois mentality and background, he oriented himself here in line with the dominating feudal class; except for the colour, the later uniforms of the SS bore almost complete resemblance to the uniforms of the 'pages', that is, the sons of the Bavarian aristocracy who attended the Wilhelm High-School with Himmler. As potentate of the National Socialist Party and the SS, Himmler later built himself a little gymnasium in the vicinity of his office in the Gestapo Building. Here he exercized eagerly and he finally managed to fulfill the requirements for the sports-medal of the SS. Unknown to hi, the sports instructors of the SS had altered the measurements to enable him to obtain the desired trophy.

> Finally, finally he has mastered the feared knee-circle and thrones on the horizontal bar, looking down at the class with nearsighted eyes. But the one who sits up there is not the sweaty half-dead creature shamed by the vulgar roaring of the Wilhelm High School's class A. It is the other way around. The man up there, a cheated cheat — looks about gaily and beneath him more than his former class cringes in the dust: there are whole schools, and cities and continents. Before him, flat on its belly, there lies the Third *Reich* [Hallgarten].

It is part of the absurdity of German history that the failed knee-circle of a man's youth could become a pregnant factor in history, and that the road to Auschwitz began in Köpenick.[9]

However, the bourgeois murderers were not only correct, but also sentimental, full of feeling and even good-natured; adjacent to the crematoria of the concentration and extermination camps, flowerbeds were located. Visiting the commander of Auschwitz, after having satisfied himself as to the functioning of the plant destroying human beings, Himmler in the evening spoke 'with a happy voice about the education of children, new dwellings, paintings, books, visits to the front with the *Führer*. . .Everyone was absorbed by his refreshing tales and his carefree mood. I had never seen him like this!' (Höss).

During the executions, when mothers tried to save their children, Höss would have liked 'to disappear from the earth for sheer pity', 'but he could not afford to show even the slightest emotion'. 'Those in the chamber already became restless — I had to act. Everyone looked at me — I motioned to the non-commissioned officer in charge and he took

the wildly struggling children in his arms and brought them, with the
mothers who sobbed heartbreakingly, into the chamber.' Höss showed
especial affection 'to his gypsies'. 'They were optimists, I never
encountered dark, hate-filled looks by gypsies. Once one entered the
camp, they immediately left their barracks, played their instruments,
let their children dance and performed their usual tricks.' But, they too
had to be gassed. Höss was a great lover of animals. In his youth he was
drawn to horses: 'I could not do enough petting them, talking to them
and offering them fancy treats.' After he had moved and it had become
more difficult for him to be near horses, Höss was 'sick for weeks,
longing for his animals and the mountain forests'. At Auschwitz Höss
often 'found relief walking through the stables at night' after the
exciting work of a day. His children too always had all manner of
animals which they raised and cared for. Hitler was an opponent of the
hunt, an animal lover *par excellence.* So he reports in *Mein Kampf* that
during his Munich years he became used to the game

> of throwing the little mice entertaining themselves in the little
> chamber a few pieces of hard left-over bread or rinds and watching
> how the cute little animals chased each other around the few
> delicacies. During my life I had suffered enough want so that I
> could fancy their hunger and therefore also their joy only too well.

Such animal love was sweet and nice, it showed heart as it touched the
hearts. Pictures of Hitler with the shepherd dog were present in
millions of homes and minds – just as earlier the chicken coop of
Emperor Wilhelm I had been advertised by the *Gartenlaube:*

> Whoever enters the vestibule of Schloss Babelsberg early in the
> morning becomes witness to a scene which shows the eminent master
> of the castle, whom the world knows as one of the potentates of
> Europe, from the purely human side and as a simple and plain private
> citizen. Emperor William in his chicken coop. Could he, who after
> all is known to have a warm regard also for the world of small things,
> when building his country home, could he have forgotten a chicken
> coop, the symbol of German well-being? And the emperor is a loyal
> caretaker, a friendly provider of his feathered wards – each morning
> after taking his coffee he takes some of the remnants of the bread
> served to him and steps out into the vaulted hallway which leads
> directly from his room into the garden. From here he has a
> magnificent unobstructed view of the park, Glienick bridge, all of

the Heiliger See up to its distant wooded shores. There is already much excitement; the cackling inhabitants have already noticed their lord and benefactor, and come quickly running from all ends and corners of the yard to receive the eagerly expected morning snack from his hand. We see that in the person of the Emperor the dignity of sovereignty and the plain life of the citizen can also come together.

Wilhelm I was not of course a sadist or a hater of men. But the citation refers to the 'genealogy' of official German animal love as a symbol of German sensitivity and style of life; the conviction took hold that 'we Germans alone in the world have a decent attitude toward the animal', as Himmler later put it; the inhuman attitude toward man could thereby be compensated.

The apolitical citizen was the citizen of the *Stammtisch*.[10] 'At the *Stammtisch* he passes the evenings with rumours and small-talk; he learns only from those like him and he does not bother to think' (Bloch). More than anything the *Stammtisch* is the sociological and anthropological *locus* where the energy of repressed urges can be released, where one can rage and rant, call God and the world to order and wildly overwhelm all lands and parts of the world with warfare. Hitler thus was an explicit barrel-house type who was most comportable at the *Stammtisch* among old comrades; here his language was most 'uninhibited'. Hitler's speech of 8 November 1942 in the Munich Löwenbräu Hall *in memoriam* of the beer-hall putsch of 1923 may serve as an example.

Even if Mr Stalin expects that we attack in the centre, I did not want to attack in the centre. Not only because Mr Stalin perhaps expected it, but because I saw no reason for it, because I wanted to reach the Volga at a certain location, at the site of a certain city. By chance it bears Stalin's name. But don't think for a minute that this is the reason why I marched here [Laughter].

It could have any other name. Only because there is an especially strategic point. . .I wanted to take it, and you know, we are humble, we have it already. There are only a few small remnants left. Now the others say, why don't you fight there; because I don't want to create a second Verdun, because I would rather take care of that with very small units. Time does not matter. No ship any longer goes up the Volga. That is what counts [Applause].

Hitler sometimes rehearsed his speaker's poses for the *Stammtisch* before the mirror; they were of great influence because they reflected exactly the beer-happy passion characterizing the talk and cursing of the philistine: the pointed finger, the cynical smile of superiority, clenched fists, appalled shock, hate-filled pounding of the table, gesticulating protest — and the waving of the beer seidel and its imaginary use as a club.

Stammtisch — mentality, conceived of as a general political anthropological classification characterizes anaemic types, unstable, spirits, political cowards who inebriate themselves rhetorically and then find relief in wild ejaculations of verbiage. One should only remember the 'noble youths' of the Hain League,[11] who on the one hand dissolved in mildness and sentimentality, on the other worshipped a noisy *Furor teutonicus.* Here their venerated mentor Klopstock led the chorus: 'To go and take the lands only half possessed completely, to spare false culture nowhere, to run the plow over all mere flower gardens, to wreck all structures built on sand, and should whole cities stand on such foundations, to set them aflame from all sides, and not to leave until smoke rises everywhere.' Heinrich von Kleist, one of our most subtle poets, a man of self-destructive hyper-sensitivity, at the same time behaved himself as the 'stalwart' bard. 'Every vale and every site/you dye with their bones so white;/bones despised by fox and raven/shall become the fishes prey;/let the Rhine become their haven/ heaped their bones divert its way,/that around the Palatine,/a new border be the Rhine.' Verses like this were the fruits of his hatred of Napoleon. Of a visit with the composer of the *Wacht am Rhein* the *Gartenlaube* reported with caution. The fact that he appeared to be without much spirit or vitality, that he frequently broke into tears and thus hardly demonstrated any soldierly virtues, was only hinted at, that is, it was concealed with nationalistic pathos. Nietzsche's call for the 'blond beast', for the 'dangerous life', for 'dwellings at Vesuvius' grew out of an internal instability which heightened itself to madness. The *Stammtisch* speeches of Wilhelm II must be seen in connection with his physical handicap,[12] which he psychologically never overcame. Thomas Mann, delivering himself of his anti-western sentiments in the *Betrachtungen eines Unpolitischen,* did not hesitate to call this a wartime service — 'I made myself suffer, I fought and sacrificed'; but very likely he, too, favoured the pen in the hand to the bullet in the belly. Moeller van den Bruck,[13] the prophet of an anti-democratic, anti-liberal Third *Reich,* a man fascinated by the mythos of the heroic, was called to the colours as a militia man during the First World War.

But he 'proved not to be up to the demands of barracks life and after a
prolonged recuperative leave in Berlin, he was transferred, thanks to the
efforts of his old friend Franz Evers, to the foreign department of the
Army High Command created by Ludendorff.' As an occasional war
correspondent, Ludwig Ganghofer[14] glorified war as the German soul's
fountain of regeneration. His heart beat with the genuine spirit of the
Bavarian brawler, as when they broke the skulls of Frenchmen with
the butts of their carbines: 'Take the butt and crash it down/that was a
little bit too light!/And as I brought it down again/the butt-end broke
from all my might/the devil, said I, let's not stop/spit in the hands and
grab the barrel/four Frenchmen stretched out on the top/a man must
help himself in quarrel.' Protected by such masculine virtue, the
complacent Ganghofer in back of the lines could well sing of 'The
Fatherland that rests reassured'.

Hans Blüher[15] 'experienced both wars in a fully militant mood,
which only because of my physical weakness could not find military
expression'. 'Anyway: nothing is further from my mind than a pacifist
attitude'; he emphasized that his work *Die Rolle der Erotik* was written
during the First World War — apparently he considered this a sort of
war service; the *Achse der Natur* was created during the Second World
War — 'and time and again it happened that I half finished a sentence
of the manuscript when the sirens began to howl. This meant for me to
get the steel-helmet and the gas-mask, and out I went into the terrain.
For I had charge over seven houses in my neighbourhood. Once the
situation calmed down again, I returned to my desk and finished the
sentence.' Incidentally, this passage may also be shaped in the image
of Hegel, who completed his *Phänomenologie des Geistes* during the
days of the battle of Jena, for Blüher loved to sidle up to the example
of great ancestors. Blüher and the other anaemic but vocal individuals,
however, were no more than symptomatic samples from the catalogue
of the German *Stammtisch* — and barrel house spirit.

Even where brutality was not the compensation for physical
weakness or repressed inferiority complexes, where the individual
himself had experienced the worst during the war, he returned
unchanged to the *Stammtisch*. The wine 'delighted the tongue and
the great deeds of the war were remembered with sincerity,
loquaciousness and naïvité', Friedrich Nietzsche already observed in
the *Unzeitgemässe Betrachtungen;* 'much then comes to the light of the
day which otherwise remains anxiously hidden'. Fürst Hohenlohe[16]
noted in his *Denkwürdigkeiten:* 'All these philistines shouting "hurray"
under the flag while indulging in beer and roast veal were repulsive to

me, and the sound of the song *Die Wacht am Rhein* was for me joined by the voice of the wounded Frenchman, whom I found lying in the garden of the hospital in the grass, crying *mon dieu, mon dieu.*' But both after 1870 and 1918 the *Stammtisch* rhetoric proved to be stronger than the terrible experiences of the war. Not the trenches' stench of decay remained in the consciousness, but the domesticated rabbits one cared for while out there; one did not see the mountains of cadavres before the barbed wire, but the well-being of romantic comradeship in the bunker; not the mutual slaughter was remembered, but the 'calm glow' of the battle.

> Without rest or breather the Siberians storm at us and do not cease even as the bodies of their dead tower before us like a wall. Our boots burrow in empty shells and clips. We fire and fire. As the right arm swells from the backfire we rip the uniform open and insert a folded sand-sack under the suspenders. And then we continue to fire and the more Siberians we hit the more live ones storm from the back. . .We see how the Russians fall head-first, yet over every dead one ten men storm on. . .Many a battle was hard during the four years. But the living battle of Volhynia is like a shining sword amongst colourful flowers and it has a calm glow [compare Hahn-Butry] .

He wanted to free the German bourgeois from the chimera of conscience, the *Stammtisch* politician Hitler once said to Hermann Rauschning; what was imagined over the glass of beer was to become bitter reality; fancy's flight became the bloody fight.

Notes

1. Friedrich List (1789-1846), German economist who spent part of his career as a refugee in the US and had great influence on the development of the German customs union.
2. See p.170, n.9.
3. Thodor Storm (1817-88), North German poet and novelist.
4. See p.85, n.2.
5. Wilhelm Raabe, see p.176, n.7.
6. See p.81, n.36.
7. *Travel Journals* (2 Vols., 1826/27).
8. Nazi term for the individual members of the German nation at home or abroad.
9. Köpenick, small township immediately east of Berlin where in 1906 a shoemaker, dressed in a captain's uniform arrested the mayor of the town and confiscated the municipal cashbox with the aid of a group

of commandeered soldiers; the escapade has been celebrated in drama and literature.

10. The *Spiesser*'s roundtable at the corner tavern. See p.124, n.4.
11. *Hainbund*, student association founded 1772 in Göttingen advocating patriotism and the love of nature. Also a group of lyrical poets.
12. One of his arms was deformed.
13. See p.105, n.2.
14. See p.16, n.15.
15. See p.50, n.2.
16. Chlodwig Fürst zu Hohenlohe-Schillingsfürst (1819-1901), German Chancellor 1894-1900.

8 OSSIFIED CHURCHES

For the bourgeoisie the nineteenth century brought an increasing loss of religious substance; the ethical co-ordinates no longer matched. 'Whatever once was good and decent in the bourgeois — independence, perseverance, foresight, prudence — has been utterly corrupted' (Adorno). The firm foundation of trust in God became a rhetorical flourish. This lack of religiosity has nothing to do with the despairing atheism and nihilism which manifested itself increasingly after the Romantic period; rather, it grew out of the internal indifference to all deeper problems of life. The churches themselves furthered this attitude during the nineteenth century because they were equally ossified, saturated and indifferent, as for example in the face of social wants. Contrary to the anti-bourgeois heretics of the nineteenth century, who in their revolt against the old church proved themselves to be the great *homines religiosi* of the new church, the petit bourgeois was comfortable in the prevailing shallowness; here the parasitical corruptors of the people could flourish too. A petit-bourgeois church was not in a position to offer decisive resistance to National Socialism and its army of petit-bourgeois followers. The newly forming forces, however, which developed due to the appeal of necessity, and which affected the later existential regeneration of the churches, proved for the time being to be still too weak.

In the world of protestantism, these efforts at regeneration were obstructed by the strong alliance of throne and altar, of reactionary authority and restorative church politics. The concept of the identity of God's realm with the German *Reich* had its roots in the pietistic-patriotic thinking of the eighteenth century.

> Development into a totalitarian state seems to have been confirmed in advance, in view of the fact that the religious patriots did not even shy away from placing religion in the service of the state. One's own position is liable to be reversed; the state no longer exists in reference to God, but God in reference to the state — he punishes the bad patriots and rewards the good ones [Kaiser].

Christ appears as the teacher of patriotism:

Who teaches like your Lord and Master,
of love for Christ and fatherland? Who was, like he, the laws'
great pastor
submitting to the people's hand?
the Master's word you must fulfill
your heart must be as pure as his: this be your earnest, firmest will,
to loyally serve your country's bliss [Lavater].

Religiosity and patriotism were similarly connected during the liberation wars and the Second Empire, in the anti-democratic circles of the Weimar Republic and the Third *Reich*. More than anything else, it was religious instruction with its central pedagogical-didactic role in the school of the nineteenth century which became 'a tool of the Prussian state's authoritarian politics' (Weymar). The faith in the national mission could gain this enormous influence only because it had been earlier laced with religious association or boosted by the churches. Chauvinism, too, virtually grew under the shield of religion.

Racial aspects were linked to this national Christianity: the German was Aryan; as Aryan he was the best patriot; and as Aryan patriot he was the best Christian; or, conversely, the best Christian was the patriotic Aryan; the Aryan was pre-eminently German. Since the German — Langbehn observed — 'by his innermost nature is a child, he is Christian in his innermost nature; Aryanism, the child's innocence and Christianity, these three factors of life complement each other.' Genuine religiosity, 'this deepest of German attributes', Wagner rhapsodized, 'is part of' German being 'in the highest and heretofore unmatched sense'. 'This is the essence of the German spirit, that it builds from within; the eternal God truly dwells within it, before he even builds himself the temple of his honour.'

The pedagogue Seibert[1] observed that the Germans are a people with a characteristic mode of thought, well-being and warm-heartedness: therefore they are really 'essentially a religious people, the theological people *per se* of modern humanity'.

The bible became the Aryan bible, the cross a sort of swastika. The lines seperating heathendom and Christianity were more and more wiped out; heathendom was represented as Christianity and Christianity as a hazy kind of heathendom. The German Christian had a nordic God — a concoction of Christ, Wotan and Thor[2] — a ramrod God who stood up for war, for German war and fought along on the German side. The Napoleonic wars appeared like a purgatory staged by God, intended to rekindle the martial spirit of the Germans in the wars of liberation.

As Bismarck edited the Ems dispatch in so provocative a fashion as to
make the war with France appear as most probable, Roon[3] and
Moltke,[4] who were with the chancellor, rejoiced: '. . .it caused in the
two generals a change of attitude into a joyful mood, which startled
me with its vivacity. Suddenly they regained their appetite to eat and
drink and they conversed in high spirits. Roon said: "The old God is still
alive, and he will not let us succumb in shame" ' (Bismark). The German
God fought for German living space, Germany's prestige as a world
power; he was present at Leipzig[5] and Königgrätz,[6] at Sedan[7] and
Langemarck;[8] he lived in the pages of the primer, in the national
sermon and the national oratory and even was represented on the
belt-buckless of the soldiers. The path to Christian-German culture was
opened by not making prisoners: 'We shall not give pardon' (Wilhelm II).
Friedrich Naumann[9] joyfully confessed that he was at the same time
Christian, Darwinist and enthusiast for the battleship fleet. 'Father I
call you/roaring the sound of cannon surrounds me,/encompassed by
the jagged flashes of lightning/Charioteer of battles to you I appeal/
You, Father, lead me!' (Körner). The German martial prayer did not
change: as passionate invocation of battles, it rose to the German
heavens or German providence in 1813, 1870, 1914 and also still in 1939.

> We assemble to pray and all, officers and enlisted men find ourselves
> together in a confession: 'God with us' – and from the tower. . .
> the vesper bells carry the quiet prayers to the Lord of the worlds,
> who once again is sending the empires of the world to take measure
> of each other [Heuler].

The soldier facing the enemy prayed to God for a 'good shot' [Flex].

> Imagine the displeasure when platoons watched for days and still
> no enemy, not even a spy appeared. In such half-angered mood the
> following nice verse came to be: 'Shall there be no end to this
> night?/I'm ashamed of my God's spirit and might./Good God, let
> a few spies into the land/and give one single Russian throat into
> my healthy hand' [Heuler].

In the sign of cross and sword the Potsdam pastor pledged eternal
loyalty more to his people than to his God. 'In the field, in the field',
there the pastor too was worth more – 'An artillery man loves his
cannon like a mother her child. He caresses it, calms it when it
becomes hot and praises it when it lands a hit. To be with the comrades
of the big gun was the epitome of well-being' (Kessler). It was

considered 'sublime grace' that the German-national pastor was given the opportunity to meet Hitler, to experience 'his fascinating youthfulness, his great elasticity, his fresh naturalness, and above all his noble humility'. Now he could die in peace. For reasons of race, too, Hitler had to appear to the German-national pastor as a special apostle of Christ. During the nineteenth century – in a way in reference to the expulsion of the merchants from the temple – the expulsion of the Jews had been prepared in 'genuine Christian spirit'. For Stoecker,[10] the 'most stormy and quarrelsome political agitator and demagogue of the Second *Reich'* (Pinson), anti-Semitism was the most powerful weapon in his agitation. He did his best 'to oppose the toll taken by Judaism of German life, this worst of all tolls'.

The collapse of 1918 left the majority of the pastors, for whom the war had further fused nationalists and Christian thinking, with 'massive nationalistic and monarchistic frustrations', which deepened the chasm between the 'Christian' and the democratic-socialistic forces.

A far-reaching 'pastoral nationalism', which was rooted in the deep connections with the fallen throne, was reflected in the tenor of church synods, church annuals, announcements and sermons. It manifested itself in the form of the stab-in-the-back legend and emnity to republicanism. At the same time it obstructed the connection of the 'bourgeois' protestant church with democratic-socialistic elements of the population. Only gradually, and on the whole only in isolated instances, could more constructive impulses break through this basically negative attitude. It was an attitude which showed how strongly the church was connected with the fallen powers, not only in an institutional sense, but more than anything spiritually and intellectually. In spite of all the good-will offered by the new parliamentary democracy, the reconstruction of the relationship of church and state took place in an atmosphere of mistrust, for which the regressive attitude of the church leadership and the majority of the pastors were largely responsible. The general church synods usually ended on a note of 'patriotic proclamations' but evaded constructive answers for the concrete relationship of the political responsibility of the Christian in the democratic-parliamentary state of the present. By the same token, the continued rejection of the Weimar republic dominated, and the conviction became ever firmer that Christian-evangelical, and more or less German-national, conservative ways of thinking naturally complemented each other. A basic nationalistic attitude and the

perpetuation of the hero-worshipping terminology of the
Wilhelminian era continued to dominate in the clerical realm; many
sermons and pamphlets adhered to the Bismarck and Emperor cult.
The religious sanctification of ancient national symbols was retained.
The meetings of veterans' and SA associations were provided with
field-services. Black-White-Red[11] flags were flown at evangelical
meetings and one held on to the memory of the great era of the war
and the time before it in the spirit of a romantic cult [Bracher].

The life of the Pastor L. Muenchmeyer can serve as biographical
illustration, even though it is an extreme example; this 'national
Christian' and pastor was one of the most successful speakers of the
NSDAP during the Weimar Republic. For his 'brother in Christ', the
Führer Adolf Hitler, the powerfully verbose preacher travelled
249,485 kilometers, 'a distance six times the circumference of the
earth'; a grand total of three million people visited his meetings.
In appreciation of his services he was even made an honorary guest on
the island of Borkum, where a street was named after him because of
'the successful battle to keep Borkum free of Jews'. His sermons were
monarchistic, nationalistic, chauvinistic and later on national-socialist
in spirit. At the death of the former empress Auguste Viktoria, he gave
a 'visionary sermon on the 93rd psalm (1-4)' — 'at the shores of the
German North Sea . . .a memorial speech for Germany's unforgettable
mother of the country. Dedicated to German women and mothers as
most beautiful story for children.' At Christmas of 1923 he proclaimed:
'We Germans desire the realization at last of the ancient Christmas
evangelicalism: "Glory to God in the Highest, and peace on earth to
all men of good will." In this sense the word should also be interpreted:
'By German kind the world one day shall be healed!"' In his sermons
Münchmeyer cited more popular German phrases than bible words; the
part of the press inclined to a 'non-German' attitude therefore was
'convulsively trying to present pastor Münchhausen as a wild phantast
and rabble-rouser'; this is exactly what he was — a phantast and
rabble-rouser — but such phenomena were not unusual in German-
national protestantism.

   The year 1933 made it overwhelmingly clear that the larger part of
the protestant clergy had a positive or at least not a hostile attitude
toward National Socialism; the capacity to differentiate between the
Christian and the un-Christian had been lost. The 'un-Christianity' of
Hitler and National Socialism in programme and practice could not
have been overlooked had one not already been blind. The movement

of the 'German Christians'[12] here only was the culmination of a
development which began in the nineteenth century and then
increasingly affected the petit-bourgeois decomposition of the church.
The parade of the 'SA Christi' as Hossenfelder[13] described the German
Christians ('One *Reich,* one *Führer,* one church'), as for example at the
typical assembly of 13 November 1933, showed all the catch-phrases
of the awful religious-ideological stock of the nineteenth century in
striking concentration: there is a German-national Luther who either
shows the gate to a softened, un-German (Semitic) Christ or provides
him with a more nordic cast; there is dogmatic confusion which escapes
into a 'generic' kind of God experience; there is an atheistic biologism
concealed as worship in the church. Even the raving of a Rosenberg[14]
murmuring myths or an Ernst Bergmann[15] as a 'nordic herald of God'
could no longer sink below the level of the German Christian movement.

On November 13, 1933, twenty thousand people were assembled in
the sports palace, amongst them many German-Christian Church
leaders, who gave an official stamp to the assembly, amongst them
Hossenfelder and his group. . .Chairman of the assembly was a friend
of Krause,[16] the party official Johann Schmiedchen. Following the
ceremonial entrance of the flags and the songs 'Praised be God in the
Highest' and 'A mighty fortress is our Lord', Schmiedchen opened
the assembly. He emphasized that the faith movement had only
apparently reached the aim of its aspirations, that it had to follow
the old spirit of Gneisenau[17] in pursuing the beaten enemy to the
last breath of man and horse, until his flight would become a
disorganized rout. Then Hossenfelder spoke and made it known that
he had given orders to the High Council of the Church to execute the
Aryan Clause.[18] Then came the great address of Dr Krause dealing
with the folkish mission of Luther, and here he gave vent to his
radical feelings without inhibition. Luther, he observed, had left a
precious heritage, that is, the consummation of the reformation in
the Third *Reich:* The emerging people aspires to form a new
church. . .the German folk church. The new *Reich*-church never
would feature a dogmatic tie. Rather, it could only be the large
framework, the great organization which could now provide the
great outline. The result of the second German Reformation should
not be an authoritarian pastoral church with confessional ties, but
only one German peoples' church, which would give room for a
whole world of generic God-experience. A first step to make people
feel at home in the new church would be the elimination 'of all

up-Germanness in service and confession. Emancipation from the Old Testament with its Jewish morality of rewards, these tales of cattle traders and procurers.' All obviously distorted and superstitious accounts also would of course have to be removed, and one would have to get along without all the guilt-ridden inferiority theology of the Rabbi Paulus. One would also have to beware of the exaggerated exposition of the crucified [Buchheim].

Krause received 'prolonged applause'. Thereupon sixty new flags of the faith-movement were blessed. Voting on a resolution supporting Krause's words, only one of about 20,000 present cast his voice against it. At the elections to the Prussian church in November of 1932, the German Christians had won one third of all votes.

In the Catholic Church of the nineteenth century the anti-liberal current predominated: Pius IX not only proclaimed the dogma of papal infallibility, he also defined the intellectual-spiritual realm of Papal power with a clarity never attained before. He declared war to the spirit of modernity: a reconciliation of the Church with 'progress', liberalism and modern culture he considered impossible. Since, however, the liberal state in Germany progressively became national liberal, and since publicly sanctioned 'modern' culture here proved to be reaction and restoration in modernistic garb, the reserve of Catholicism toward the new Germany, growing out of its conservative thought, could indirectly serve to promote progressive elements. This development was furthered by the ultramontanism of South-German Catholicism, which found itself in diametrical opposition to Prussian-protestant nationalism and centralism. Finally, as a consequence of Bismarck's *Kulturkampf* Catholicism, contrary to its character, was pushed into the anti-conservative camp to form common front with democrats and 'genuine' liberals. The *Zentrum*[19] in the end even had a left wing (fluctuating very much in strength and influence), which the Protestantism of the day lacked. Here the Machiavellianism of the state, Manchesterism[20] and the power of Prussianism were opposed — that is to say, one supported the obligations of natural law, social responsibility and a balanced federal system. The situation was different in Austria where, because of a different societal and political situation, the reactionary, anti-liberal and especially also anti-Semitic circles dominated political Catholicism and in part also the internal aspects of church policy.

Three characteristic features of German Catholicism were open to a liberal reinterpretation: the struggle against ideological so-called

'libertarian materialism', which later on was understood as the struggle
against totalitarian dogmatic communism; efforts for equal rights of
the church *vis-à-vis* the state could be interpreted as a struggle against
totalitarian *Gleichschaltung*[21] tendencies; ultramontanism changed to
the concept of a Christian Europe based on the foundation of an
occidental universalism. At the same time — and this was the reverse
side of this type of 'progressive' thinking — the struggles against
totalitarian communism, for the right of church independence and for
the concept of organic Western unity, could be used to convey
absolutist Catholic demands in a 'Christian-liberal' garb. The year 1933
revealed ideological confusion and moral crisis in the Catholic Church
too. Nevertheless, national-socialist tendencies did not appear in as
concentrated organized form as in the German Christian movement;
moreover, tactical considerations, could be claimed in view of an
impending concordat[22] as mitigating circumstances. But the
responsibility to historical truth does not tolerate graded standards. So
observed Ernst Wolfgang Böckenförde,[23] who produced a gratifying
pioneering analysis of German Catholicism of the years 1932-3; 'not
to avoid it [historical truth] has in the end always proven to be the
best service of a cause one wishes to serve.'

> 'Under their [the bishops'] guidance, we cannot go wrong.' These
> words of a brave centre-party deputy of the may-days of 1933
> characterized the expectations German Catholics held of their
> spiritual leaders. The German Catholics, of course, could not surmise
> that these very leaders would ask them to affirm and support the
> National Socialist state.

The opportunistic attitude of the prelate Kaas,[24] making up with the
ambitious politician von Papen who had recently been expelled from
the Centre Party, was characteristic of the political tendencies of that
party toward the end of the Weimar Republic. He supported the
enabling law[25] decisively, contrary to the opinion of Brüning,[26] who
incidentally was the only prominent Catholic politician warning the
Vatican against the conclusion of the concordat. The pastoral letter of
all German bishops of 3 June 1933 paid respect to the new authority
in the German body politic; in his letter of thanksgiving written on
behalf of the Fulda bishops' conference, Cardinal Bertram confirmed
the 'sincere and joyful readiness' to co-operate with the new
government. Suffragan bishop Burger declared: 'The aims of the *Reich*
government have for long been the aims of our Catholic church.' At

the Catholic Youth assembly in the Cologne stadium on 20 August 1933, the Capitular Vicar Steinmann remarked: 'What all of us have yearned and striven for has become reality. We have a *Reich* and a leader, and we follow this leader loyally and conscientiously.' The intellectual confusion can be documented with many separate citations. Though opposed by a strong regenerative movement such as the 'confessing church'[28] in protestantism, it amounted to an affirmation and endorsement of the NS regime; one believed oneself to sense a harmony of Catholic with National-Socialist thought, and here a deeply rooted anti-liberalism again came to the fore which knew itself as one with National Socialism in the 'rejection of democracy and modern society' and 'the leaning toward authoritarian government, leadership and "an organically ordered people".' 'Added to this was the declared enmity to Bolshevism, which was considered as an immediate threat, and the annoyance over the widespread "public immorality".'

Carl Amery has traced the failure of German Catholicism — and his argumentation essentially also applies to German Protestantism — to the predominance of the milieu, the petit-bourgeois system of 'virtues' which since the nineteenth century has placed the church in a state of internal ossification. The primary Christian virtues of faith, humility, charity and ascetic efforts were overshadowed by secondary virtues such as diligence, cleanliness, punctuality, reliability, mistrust of modernity and obedience to authority. Yet these were 'virtues' which in themselves entailed no aspirations but had to be directed toward specific aims.

> I can arrive punctually in the parish house as well as in the Gestapo cellar; I can be fastidious in office work pertaining to the 'final solution' as much as in matters of social welfare; I can wash my hands after an honest day's work in the fields as well as after working in the concentration camp crematorium. So it came that Himmler could praise his murderous squads for remaining decent, engulfed as they were in their difficult duties. Of course, Herr Himmler is not exactly a most qualified witness for moral or ethical standards; but there is a hint of method noticeable in this mad observation.

Thus, secularized religiosity was an 'adorn-your-home-religiosity', which respected any kind of mediocrity more highly than the exceptional as long as it was 'clean' and proper. This applied even when the exceptional functioned on a much higher moral level. It was a religiosity which was satisfied and 'fulfilled' as long as the external framework of life remained unchanged. The milieu-Christianity of Catholicism as well as Protestantism therefore reacted only then with sensitivity and offered resistance only when the National Socialists threatened the milieu itself. The struggle against National Socialism was not officially begun when the dignity and humanity of man was offended and destroyed, but only when Catholic or Protestant human dignity — or often only the 'adorn-your-home-religiosity' — was threatened in all its saturation.

It is true that a good part of German Catholicism showed that it would not tolerate certain things; so it insisted on crucifixes in classrooms, supported the bishops in their fight against scandalous trials, and prevented the arrest of Galens.[29] But democracy? The Jews? The parties and men of the left? They would never have been defended by the milieu. They were opposed by it anyway — they would have to see how they got along alone. The milieu neither was prepared for this kind of resistance nor did it possess, like the bourgeoisie of the West, the intellectual traditions needed if imaginative improvisation was to function effectively. The authorities (and here we speak of the authorities over the world of ideas) had therefore from the beginning the choice only of two alternatives: On the one hand they could place themselves at the head of a small but determined minority to wage the war for justice and Europe's most sacred goods against a sea of plagues; or, on the other hand, they could capitulate to the silent but obvious desires of the Catholic majority and make the best of this capitulation [Amery].

The ossification of the churches during the nineteenth century, their failure in the face of the totalitarian powers during the twentieth century, was bitterly avenged on the churches themselves. It took most severe convulsions and bitterest pain before the forces of regeneration could again break through to the primary virtues of Christianity.

Have the churches with their moral self-examination found response in the German people? Has a moral reversal followed the year 1945? Has the restorative, reactionary, conservative, petit-bourgeois milieu-consciousness been conquered? The level of morality can be measured only within a free democratic order. Therefore, does the societal, cultural and political situation of the Federal Republic justify the assumption that the fateful *Spiesser* mentality has finally been eliminated, a mentality which flourished in Germany for decades and helped to prepare the fall into the abyss?

Such questions will have to be answered positively and negatively: there is much to incline the observer in either direction. Argumentation, accounts, assumptions and prognoses to answer them would fill another volume. One can notice with relief the outlines of a moral renaissance ahead; but it must also be noted with anguish that characteristics of the old German philistinism have been preserved in 'unspoiled freshness'. The future then must be regarded with mixed feelings: the crisis of the Federal Republic has not yet begun. But perhaps this wounded land will be spared the crisis for a few decades. So it is that, especially in regard to German political anthropology, the 'principle of hope' will have to play a not insignificant role.

Notes

1. The author of the popular treatise *Deutsche Abende* (Barmen, 1857).
2. Germanic God of thunder.
3. Albrecht von Roon (1803-79), Prussian and later (1871) German Minister of War 1859-73.
4. See p.199, n.14.
5. The 'Battle of the nations' defeat of Napoleon in 1813.
6. Decisive defeat of the Austrians by Prussia in 1866.
7. Major defeat of the French, September 1870.
8. Suicidal attack by inexperienced German volunteers in November 1914 in Belgium. It resulted in heavy losses.
9. See p.125, n.5.
10. See p.125, n.4.
11. The colours of the German flag from the time of the Second Empire which recurred in the emblem and flag of the Nazi party.
12. German Nationalist Christians organized during the Nazi period.
13. Joachim Hossenfelder, Protestant minister who helped to bring the 'German Christians' (the auxiliary of the Nazis) into existence.
14. See p.40, n.7.
15. Ernst Bergmann, author of *Deutschland das Bildungsland der neuen Menschheit* (Germany, the Cultural World of the New Humanity, Breslau 1936).
16. Reinhold Krause, Hossenfelder's rival who further radicalized the 'German Christians' and gave them a racist, anti-Semitic complexion.
17. August Neidhardt von Gneisenau (1760-1831), Prussian general and hero of the War of Liberation against Napoleon.
18. Anti-Semitic restrictions.
19. Catholic political party of the Second Empire and the Weimar Republic.
20. Classical English economic liberalism.
21. Gleichschaltung, levelling of undesirable distinctions of person and group to meet the standards and fulfill the purposes of the party.
22. The 1934 Concordat of the Catholic Church and the Third *Reich*.
23. E.W. Böckenförde, 'Der deutsche Katholizimus in Jahre 1933', *Hochland*, Feb. 1961, p.254.
24. Ludwig Kaas (1881-1952), Catholic prelate and leader of the Centre Party.
25. The law giving Hitler four years of virtually unrestricted power in 1933.

26. Heinrich Brüning (born 1885), Centre Party politician and German Chancellor 1930-32.
27. Adolf Cardinal Bertram (1859-1945).
28. Established in 1933 in opposition to Hitler.
29. Clemens August Cardinal von Galen (1878-1946), Bishop of Münster 1933-46.

BIBLIOGRAPHY

Abraham, L.U. 'Lied und Liederbuch in der Schule'. In: *Frankfurter Hefte*, 6/1963.

Ackermann, J. *Himmler als Ideologe*. Göttingen, 1970.

Adler, H.G. *Die Juden in Deutschland. Von der Aufklärung bis zum Nationalsozialismus*. München, 1960.

Adler, H.G. *Jews in Germany*. Notre Dame (Ind.), 1969.

Adorno, Th.W. *Minima Moralia*. Frankfurt, 1951.

——,*Versuch über Wagner*, München, Zürich, 1964.

——/E. Frenkel-Brunswik. *The Authoritarian Personality*. New York, 1950.

Ahrens, H. *Die deutsche Wandervogelbewegung von den Anfängen bis zum Weltkrieg*. Hamburg, 1939.

Alexander, F.G. *The Western Mind in Transition*. New York, 1960.

Alldeutscher Verband. *Grundzüge des völkischen Staatsgedankens*. 1923.

Allen, W.S. *The Nazi Seizure of Power. The experience of a single German town 1930-35*. Chicago, 1965.

Amery, C. *Die Kapitulation oder Deutscher Katholizismus heute*. Reinbek, 1963.

Amery, C. *Capitulation*. New York, 1967.

Apter, D. *Ideologie and Discontent*. London, 1964.

Arendt, H. *Elemente und Ursprünge totalitärer Herrschaft*. Frankfurt, 1955.

——, *The Origins of Totalitarianism*. New York, 1966.

Aris, R. *History of Political Thought in Germany 1789-1815*. New York, 1965.

Arndt, E.M. *Germanien und Europa*. Altona, 1803.

——, *Geist der Zeit*. Altona, London, Berlin, 1807.

——, *Lieder für Teutsche*. 1813.

Arnsberg, P. 'Heinrich Heine als linksintellektuelles Anti-symbol'. In: *Tribüne*, 6/1963.

Aron, R. *Opium of the Intellectuals*. New York, 1962.

——, *German Sociology*. New York, 1964.

Arp, W. *Deutsche Bildung im Kampf um Begriff und Gestalt unseres arteigenen Menschentums*. Leipzig, 1943.

Assel, H.G. *Die Perversion der politischen Pädagogik im*

Nationalsozialismus. München, 1969.

Avenarius, F. *Hausbuch deutscher Lyrik.* München, 1903.

Baeyer-Katte, W.v. *Das Zerstörende in der Politik. Eine Psychologie der politischen Grundeinstellung.* Heidelberg, 1958.

Bartels, A. *Geschichte der deutschen Literatur.* 1901.

——, *Jüdische Herkunft und Literaturwissenschaft.* Leipzig, 1925.

Barth, O.-H. *Masse und Mythos. Die Theorie der Gewalt.* Hamburg, 1959.

Barzun, J. *Darwin, Marx and Wagner.* Magnolia (Mass.), 1958.

——, *Race. A Study in Superstition.* New York, 1965.

Baumann, H. *Morgen marschieren wir.* Potsdam, n.d.

Bechstein, L. *Wollen und Werden. Teil 1: Berthold, der Student.* Halle, 1850.

Becker, K. 'Führerschaft'. In: *Deutschlands Erneuerung,* 4/1920.

Bensley, E.R. *A Century of Hero-Worship.* Boston (Mass.), 1957.

Beradt, C. *Das Dritte Reich des Traums.* München, 1966.

Berend, A. *Die gute alte Zeit. Bürger und Spiessbürger im 19. Jahrhundert.* Hamburg, 1932.

Berger, K. In: *Völkischer Beobachter.* 14 November 1931.

Bergmann, E. *Deutschland – das Bildungsland der neuen Menschheit.* Breslau 1936.

Berning, C. 'Die Sprache des Nationalsozialismus'. In: *Zeitschrift für deutsche Wortforschung,* 16/1960; 17/1961.

Beumelburg, W. *Douaumont.* Oldenburg, 1925.

——, *Sperrfeuer um Deutschland.* Oldenburg, 1929f.

Biesalski, K. 'Erinnerungen'. In: *Deutsche Corpszeitung,* 2/1961.

Bischoff, R.E. *Nazi Conquest through German Culture.* Cambridge (Mass.), 1942.

Bismarck, O.v. *Gedanken und Erinnerungen,* n.d.

——, *Die gesammelten Werke. Briefe,* 1936.

——, *Reflections and Reminiscences.* New York, 1968.

Bleuel, H.P. *Deutschlands Bekenner. Professoren zwischen Kaiserreich und Diktatur.* Bern, München, 1968.

Bley, F. *Die Weltstellung des Deutschtums.* 1897.

Bloch, E. *Erbschaft dieser Zeit.* Frankfurt, 1962.

Blüher, H. *Die Rolle der Erotik in der männlichen Gesellschaft.* Neudruck. Stuttgart, 1962.

——, *Werke und Tage.* Neudruck. 1953.

——, *Wandervogel – Geschichte einer Jugendbewegung. 1.Bd.: Heimat und Aufgang. 2.Bd.: Blüte und Niedergang.* 1919.

Böckenförde, E.W. 'Der deutsche Katholizismus im Jahre 1933'. In: *Hochland.* Februar 1961.

Boehlich, W. (Hrsg.) *Der Berliner Antisemitismusstreit.* Frankfurt, 1965.

——, 'Ein Pyrrhussieg der Germanistik'. In: *Der Monat,* no.154, 1961.

Boehn, M.v. *Biedermeier. Literatur, Kultur, Zensur in der guten alten Zeit.* 1924.

—— /O. Fischel, *Modes and Manners of the Nineteenth Century.* New York, n.d.

Bölsche, E. *Was muss der deutsche Mensch von Naturwissenschaft und Religion fordern?* Berlin-Charlottenburg, n.d.

Boelsche, W. *Das Liebesleben in der Natur. Eine Entwicklungsgeschichte der Liebe.* Leipzig, 1901.

Bollnow, O.F. *Mass und Vermessenheit des Menschen.* Göttingen, 1962.

Bonhard, O. *Geschichte des Alldeutschen Verbandes.* 1922.

Borinski, F./W.Milch. *Jugendbewegung, the story of German Youth 1896-1933.* London, 1945.

Bornkamm, H. *Luthers Bild in der deutschen Geistesgeschichte.* Stuttgart, 1958.

Bowle, J. *Politics and Opinion in the Nineteenth Century.* New York, 1964.

Bracher, K.D./W.Sauer/G.Schulz. *Die nationalsozialistische Machtergreifung.* Köln und Opladen, 1960.

Bramsted, E.K. *Goebbels und die nationalsozialistische Propaganda 1925-1945.* Frankfurt, 1971.

Brenner, H. *Die Kunstpolitik des Nationalsozialismus.* Reinbek, 1963.

Breuer, H. *Der Zupfgeigenhansl.* Leipzig, 1912.

Brinton, C. *Ideas and Men: The Story of Western Thought.* New York, 1963.

Broszat, M. *Der Nationalsozialismus. Weltanschauung, Programm und Wirklichkeit.* Stuttgart, 1960.

——, 'Betrachtungen zu Hitlers Zweitem Buch'. In: *Vierteljahrshefte für Zeitgeschichte,* 4/1961.

Broszat, M. (Hrsg.). *Kommandant in Auschwitz. Autobiographische Aufzeichnungen des R. Höss.* München, 1963.

Broszat, M. *German National Socialism 1919-1945.* Santa Barbara (Calif.), 1966.

Buchheim, H. *Glaubenskrise im Dritten Reich.* Stuttgart, 1953.

——, 'Der deutsche Katholizismus 1933. Eine Auseinandersetzung mit Ernst Wolfgang Böckenförde'. In: *Hochland,* August 1961.

——, *Totalitäre Herrschaft. Wesen und Merkmale.* München, 1962.

——, *Totalitarian Rule: Its Nature and Characteristics.* Middletown

(Conn.), 1968.

Buchholz, E. 'Was ist Kunst? Ein Jahrhundert obrigkeitliche Proklamationen und Definitionen'. In: *Die Zeit,* 22, 29 June 1962.

Bücherkunde. Organ des Amtes Schrifttumspflege bei dem Beauftragten für die gesamte geistige und weltanschauliche Erziehung der NSDAP und der Reichsstelle zur Förderung des deutschen Schrifttums, n.d.

Büchmann, G. *Geflügelte Worte – Der Zitatenschatz des deutschen Volkes.* Volksausgabe. Berlin, 1941.

Bullock, A. *Hitler. Eine Studie über Tyrannei.* Düsseldorf, 1959.

——, *A Study in Tyranny.* New York, 1964.

Burger, H.O. *Annalen der deutschen Literatur.* Stuttgart, 1952.

Burschenschaftliche Blätter vom 6 März 1933.

Busch, W. 'Die fromme Helene'. In: *Sämtliche Werke.* München, 1943.

Butler, R. *The Roots of National Socialism 1783-1933.* New York, 1968.

Carossa, H. *Wirkungen Goethes in der Gegenwart.* Leipzig, 1938.

——, Rede: 'Einsamkeit und Gemeinschaft'. Dezember 1938.

——, 'Gedicht'. In: *Dem Führer. Worte deutscher Dichter* (Tornisterschrift des Oberkommandos der Wehrmacht, Abt. Inland). Zum Geburtstag des Führers 1941. Ausgewählt von A.F. Velmelde. Mit Photo und Vorspruch von Adolf Hitler und Geleitwort von Hermann Göring.

——, *Führung und Geleit, Werke Bd.1.* Wiesbaden, 1949.

——, *Ungleiche Welten.* Wiesbaden, 1951.

——, *Der Tag des jungen Arztes.* Wiesbaden, 1955.

Chamberlain, H.St. *Die Grundlagen des 19. Jahrhunderts, 2. Hälfte.* München, 1909.

——, *Foundations of the Nineteenth Century.* New York, 1968.

Cohen, H. *Ein Bekenntnis zur Judenfrage.* Berlin, 1880.

Cohn, N. *Die Protokolle der Weisen von Zion.* Köln, 1969.

Conrad-Martius, H. *Utopien der Menschenzüchtung. Der Sozial-darwinismus und seine Folgen.* München, 1955.

Conze, W. *Die deutsche Nation. Ergebnis der Geschichte.* Göttingen, 1963.

Copalle-Ahrens. *Chronik der freien deutschen Jugendbewegung. Bd.1: Die Wandervogelbünde von der Gründung bis zum ersten Weltkrieg.* Bad Godesberg, 1954.

Croce, B. *Geschichte Europas im 19. Jahrhundert.* Stuttgart, 1950.

——, *History of Europe in the Nineteenth Century.* London, 1934.

Dahrendorf, R. *Gesellschaft und Freiheit.* München, 1962.
——, *Society and Democracy in Germany.* New York, 1967.
Daim, W. *Der Mann, der Hitler die Ideen gab.* München, 1958.
Dam, H.G.v./R. Diordano (Hrsg.). *Kz-Verbrechen vor deutschen Gerichten. Dokumente.* Frankfurt, 1962.
Daniel, H.A. *Handbuch der Geographie.* 3 Bde. Leipzig, 1859-62.
Darré, W. *Das Schwein als Kriterium für nordische Völker und Semiten.* 1927.
——, *Neuadel aus Blut und Boden.* München, 1930.
Darwin, Ch. 'Die Abstammung des Menschen und die geschlechtliche Zuchtwahl'. In: *Texte der Philosophie.* München, 1961.
——, *Origin of the Species.* New York, 1967.
——, *Descent of Man.* New York, n.d.
Das Dritte Reich in Dokumenten. Schallplatten des Christophorus-Verlages Freiburg.
Detjen, C. *Rufst du, mein Vaterland. . .Irrungen und Wirrungen um Nation und Volk.* Konstanz, 1966.
Deuerlein, E. 'Zur Gegenwärtigung der Lage des deutschen Katholizismus 1933'. In: *Stimmen der Zeit,* no.7,8,9/1961.
——, *Hitler. Eine politische Biographie.* München, 1969.
Diehl-Thiele, P. *Partei und Staat im Dritten Reich – Untersuchung zum Verhältnis von NSDAP und allgemeiner innerer Staatsverwaltung 1933-1945.* München, n.d.
Dilthey, W. *Gesammelte Schriften.* Leipzig and Berlin, 1914.
——, *Pattern and Meaning in History.* New York, n.d.
Dühring, E. *Die Judenfrage als Frage der Rassenschädlichkeit.* 1886.
Düntzer, H. *Erläuterungen zu den deutschen Klassikern. Hermann und Dorothea.* Jena, 1855.
——, *Erläuterungen zu den deutschen Klassikern. Faust 1.* Teil, Jena, 1859.

Eck, B. 'Adolf Hitlers "Mein Kampf" – Das Buch der Deutschen'. In: *Bücherkunde – Organ des Amtes Schrifttumspflege bei dem Beauftragten des Führers für die gesamte geistige und weltanschauliche Erziehung der NSDAP und der Reichsstelle zur Förderung des deutschen Schrifttums.* Oktoberheft 1938.
Eich, H. *Die unheimlichen Deutschen.* Düsseldorf, Wien, 1963.
——, *Unloved Germans.* New York, 1965.
Eilers, R. *Nationalsozialistische Schulpolitik. Die Schule im Zugriff des totalitären Staates.* 1963.

Emmerich, W. *Zur Kritik der Volkstumsideologie.* Frankfurt, 1971.

Entartete Kunst. *Ausstellungskatalog (Jubiläumsausstellung).* München, 1962.

Enzensberger, H.M. *Einzelheiten.* Frankfurt, 1962.

Erikson, E.H. *Kindheit und Gesellschaft.* Stuttgart, 1965.

Errell, R. *Bilderbuch für Vergessliche.* Frankfurt,

Ewers, H.H. *Alraune.* München, 1911.

Eyck, E. *Bismarck. Leben und Werk.* 1941.

——, *History of the Weimar Republic.* Cambridge (Mass.), 1963.

——, *Bismarck and the German Empire.* New York, 1964.

Falk/Gerold/Rother. *Deutsche Geschichte für das 6. und 7. Schuljahr.* Nürnberg, 1936.

Fehrenbach, E. *Wandlungen des deutschen Kaisergedankens.* München, 1969.

Fest, J.C. *Das Gesicht des Dritten Reiches. Profile einer totalitären Herrschaft.* München, 1963.

Fichte, J.G. *Sämtliche Werke.* Berlin, 1845.

——, *Vocation of Man.* La Salle (Ill.), 1906.

——, *Reden an die deutsche Nation. Eingeleitet von R. Eucken.* Leipzig, 1909.

Fichte, J.G. *Adresses to the German Nation.* New York, 1968.

Fick, L. *Die deutsche Jugendbewegung.* Jena, 1939.

Finke, L.E. *Gestatte mir Hochachtungsschluck. Bundesdeutschlands korporierte Elite.* Hamburg, 1963.

Fischer, H. *Körners sämtliche Werke in vier Bänden.* Stuttgart, um 1885.

Flex, W. 'Die Dankesschuld'. In: *Deutsche Balladen (Anthologie).* Leipzig, 1939.

——, *Der Wanderer zwischen beiden Welten,* München, n.d.

Fliegende Blätter. Jahrgang 1893.

Fraenkel, H./R. Manvell. *Himmler – Kleinbürger und Massenmörder.* Berlin, Frankfurt, 1965.

Frantz, K. *Literarisch-politische Aufsätze.* München, 1876.

Franz, G. 'Der Parlamentarismus'. In: *Führungsschicht und Eliteproblem. Konferenz der Rankegesellschaft – Vereinigung für Geschichte im öffentlichen Leben.* Frankfurt, Berlin, Bonn, 1957.

Franz-Willing, G. *Die Hitlerbewegung. Der Ursprung 1919-1922.* Hamburg, Berlin, 1962.

Freud, S. *Civilisation and Its Discontents.* New York, 1962.

Freytag, G. *Gesammelte Werke.* Leipzig, 1897.

Friedell, E. *Kulturgeschichte der Neuzeit.* München, 1928.

Friedell, E. *Cultural History of the Modern Ages.* New York, 1954.

Fritsch, Th. *Antisemiten-Katechismus, Eine Zusammenstellung des wichtigsten Materials zum Verständnis der Judenfrage.* Leipzig, 1892.

Fromm, E. *Escape from Freedom.* New York, 1969.

Funke, A. *Schönings Ausgaben deutscher Klassiker. Goethes Hermann und Dorothea. Erläuterungen von A.F. Paderborn.* 1907.

Frymann, D. [=Claß]. *Das Kaiserbuch.* Berlin, 1935.

Gabriel, W. *Martin Luther – Von den Jüden. Luthers christlicher Antisemitismus.* 1936.

Gamm, H.J. *Der braune Kult.* Hamburg, 1962.

Ganghofer, L. *Gesammelte Schriften,* 2. Serie, Bd.2. Leipzig,

——, *Das Schweigen im Walde.* 1899.

——, *Eiserne Zither – Kriegslieder.* Stuttgart, 1914.

——, *Die stählerne Mauer. Reise zur deutschen Front.* Berlin, Wien, 1915.

Gartenlaube, Die. Jahrgang 1853, 1856, 1866, 1869, 1871, 1876, 1879, 1883.

Geibel, E. *Gesammelte Werke in acht Bänden.* Stuttgart, 1883.

Geißler, R. *Dekadenz und Heroismus. Zeitroman und völkisch-nationalsozialistische Literaturkritik.* Stuttgart, 1964.

Gembruch, W. 'Fichtes Gedanken über Gesellschaft, Staat und Erziehung'. In: *Gesellschaft, Staat, Erziehung.* 5/1962.

George, St. *Poems.* New York, 1967.

Gerber, W. *Zur Entstenhungsgeschichte der deutschen Wandervogelbewegung.* Bielefeld, 1927.

Glaser, H. '"Mein Kampf" als Spießerspiegel'. In: *Deutsche Rundschau,* 4/1960.

——, *Das Dritte Reich – Anspruch und Wirklichkeit.* Freiburg, 1961.

——, 'Ein deutscher Denker. Hans Blüher oder Von der Perversion des deutschen Geistes'. In: *Tribüne,* 4/1962.

——, *Weltliteratur der Gegenwart. Dargestellt in Problemkreisen.* Frankfurt.

——/J. Lehmann/A. Lubos. *Wege der deutschen Literatur – Eine geschichtliche Darstellung.* Frankfurt, 1962.

——, *Adolf Hitlers 'Mein Kampf' als Spiesserspiegel.* In der Beilage zur Wochenzeitung 'Das Parlament': Aus Politik und Zeitgeschichte 24. Juli 1963.

Gobineau, A. Graf. *Die Ungleicheit der Menschenrassen.* Berlin, 1934.

——, *The Inequality of the Races.* Los Angeles (Calif.), 1966.

Göring, H. *Reden und Aufsätze. Hrsg. von E. Gritzbach.* München, 1939.

Goertz, H. *Preussens Gloria. 66 Jahre deutscher Politik 1848-1914 in zeitgenössischer Satire und Karikatur.* München, 1962.

Goethe, J.W. *Gedenkausgabe. Hrsg. von E. Beutler.* Zürich, 1949.

Goldschmidt, D. *Zur Soziologie des Antisemitismus. Schriften der Akademie für politische Bildung.* Reihe A, Heft 3. Tutzing, 1960.

Gollwitzer, H. *Forderungen der Freiheit.* München, 1962.

——, 'Weltbürgertum und Patriotismus'. In der Beilage zur Wochenzeitung 'Das Parlament': Aus Politik und Zeitgeschichte, 12 September 1962.

Grass, G. *Hundejahre.* Neuwied, 1963.

——, *Dog Years.* Greenwich (Conn.), 1969.

Grebing, H. *Der Nationalsozialismus – Ursprung und Wesen.* München, 1959.

Gregori, F. (Hrsg.). *Lyrische Andachten. Natur- und Liebes-stimmungen deutscher Dichter. Buchschmuck von Fidus.* Leipzig, n.d.

Gress, F. *Germanistik und Politik. Kritische Beitrage zur Geschichte einer nationalen Wissenschaft.* Stuttgart, 1971.

Grimm, H. *Volk ohne Raum.* München, 1928.

Grosse, F.G. *Die falschen Götter, Vom Wesen des National-sozialismus.* Heidelberg, 1946.

Grosser, D. *Grundlagen und Strukturen der Staatslehre Friedrich Julius Stahls.* Köln, 1963.

Gundolf, Fr. *Goethe.* Berlin, 1920.

Gurlitt, C. *Im Bürgerhause.* Dresden, 1888.

Haas, R. *Mutter Berta. Ein deutsches Frauenleben.* München,

Härtle, H. *Nietzsche und der Nationalsozialismus.* München, 1937.

Hahn-Burry, J. *Die Mannschaft. Frontsoldaten erzählen vom Front-Alltag.* 3.Bd. Berlin, Dresden, n.d.

Hallgarten, G.W.F. 'Mein Mitschüler Himmler'. In: *Germania Judaica.* no. 2/1960-61.

Hamerow, Th.S. *Restoration, Revolution, Reaction, Economics and Politics in Germany.* Princeton (N.J.), 1958.

Hamm-Brücher, H. (MdL.). *Denkschrift zu den bayerischen Lese- und Geschichtsbüchern.* 1963.

Hanfstaengl, E. *Zwischen Weissem und Braunem Haus. Memoiren eines politischen Aussenseiters.* München, 1970.

Harms, K. *Schleswig-Holsteinigscher Gnonom – Allgemeines Lesebuch.* Kiel, 1854.

Hartlaub, G.F. *Der Gartenzwerg und seine Ahnen.* Heidelberg, 1962.
Hartshorne, E.Y. *The German Universities and National Socialism.* Cambridge (Mass.), 1937.
Hauser, A. *Sozialgeschichte der Kunst und Literatur.* München, 1953.
——, *Social History of Art.* New York, London, 1951.
Hausmann, M. *Lampion küsst Mädchen und kleine Birken.* München, 1955.
Heer, F. *Der Glaube des Adolf Hitler. Anatomie einer politischen Religiosität.* München, Esslingen, 1968.
——, *Europa – Mutter der Revolutionen.* Stuttgart, 1964.
Heiber, H. *Joseph Goebbels.* Berlin, 1962.
——, *Walter Frank und sein Reichsinstitut für Geschichte des neuen Deutschlands.* Stuttgart, 1967.
Heiber, H. (Hrsg.). *Himmler, H.L.: Reichsführer!. . .Briefe an und von Himmler.* Stuttgart, 1968.
——/H. Kotze (Hrsg.). *Querschnitt durch das Schwarze Korps.* München, 1968.
Heidegger, M. *Die Selbstbehauptung der deutschen Universität.* Bresslau, 1933.
Heigert, H. *Deutschlands falsche Träume.* Hamburg, 1968
Heine, H. *Selected Poems.* New York, 1965.
——, *Lyric Poems and Ballads.* Pittsburgh (Penn.), 1969.
Heller, E. *The Disinherited Mind. Essays in Modern German Literature and Thought.* Cambridge (Mass.), 1952.
Helmers, H. *Geschichte des deutschen Lesebuchs in Grundzügen.* Stuttgart, 1970.
Helwig, W. *Die blaue Blume des Wandervogel.* Gütersloh, 1960.
Hentschel, C. *The Byronic Teuton. Aspects of German Pessimism 1800-1933.* London, 1940.
Hermann, G. *Das Biedermeier im Spiegel seiner Zeit.* Berlin, Leipzig, Wien, Stuttgart,
Herzstein, R. *Adolf Hitler and the Third Reich 1933-1945.* Boston (Mass.), 1971.
Herzog, R. *Hanseaten.* Berlin, 1909.
——, *Gesammelte Werke.* Stuttgart, Berlin, 1920.
Hesse, H. *Der Steppenwolf.* Frankfurt, 1961.
——, *Der Steppenwolf.* New York, 1963.
Heuler, F. *In den Gluten des Weltbrandes. Berichte und Erzählungen aus dem grossen heiligen Kriege um Deutschlands Ehr' und Österreichs Recht.* Würzburg, 1914.
Heyl, F. 'Des Deutschen Volkes Ehrentag. Eröffnung des

Niederwalddenkmals'. *Die Gartenlaube.* Jahrgang 1883.

Himmler, H. 'Erlaß über die Heiratsgenehmigungen der SS. Müchen 31.Dez. 1931'. In: *Wehrhaftes Volk. Der organisatorische Aufbau,* Teil II. Hrsg. von P. Meier-Benneckenstein. Berlin, 1939.

——, 'Wesen und Aufgaben der SS und Polizei. Rede vom Januar 1937'. In: *Wehrhaftes Volk.* Berlin, 1939.

Hitler, A. *Mein Kampf.* München, 1934.

——, *Mein Kampf.* Boston (Mass.),

——, Rede auf einer Wahlkundgebung im Sportpalast Berlin am 10.Feb. 1933. Tondokument T C 916. Lautarchiv des deutschen Rundfunks.

——, Rede in der Garnisonkirche zu Potsdam. 21.März 1933. Tondokument T C 1175. Lautarchiv des deutschen Rundfunks.

——, Tischgespräche. Hrsg. von H. Picker. Bonn, 1951.

——, *Speeches of Hitler.* New York, 1969.

Hofer, W. *Der Nationalsozialismus. Dokumente 1933-1945.* Frankfurt, 1957.

Hofmann, W. *Das irdische Paradies. Kunst im 19. Jahrhundert.* München, 1960.

——, *Art in the Nineteenth Century.* Boston (Mass.),

Hofmannsthal, H.v. *Das Schrifttum als geistiger Raum der Nation.* München, 1927.

——, *Prosa II.* Frankfurt, 1951.

——, *Selected Writings.* 3 vols. Princeton (N.J.), 1952-63.

Hohenlohe-Schillingsfürst, Chl.v. *Memoirs.* New York, 1906.

Hohlfeld, J. *Dokumente der Deutschen Politik und Geschichte von 1848 bis zur Gegenwart.* Berlin, München, 1951.

Hornung, K. 'Etappen politischer Pädagogik in Deutschland'. In der Beilage zur Wochenzeitung "Das Parlament": Aus Politik und Zeitgeschichte. 1. und 8. März 1961.

Hühnerfeld, P. *In Sachen Heidegger. Versuch über ein deutsches Genie.* München, 1961.

Huss, H./A. Schröder (Hrsg.). *Anti-semitismus.* Frankfurt, 1965.

Jacobsen, H.A./W. Jochmann. *Ausgewählte Dokumente zur Geschichte des Nationalsozialismus 1933 bis 1945.* Bielefeld, 1961.

Jäckel, E. *Hitlers Weltanschauung.* Tübingen, 1969.

Jäger, O. *Aus der Praxis. Ein pädagogisches Testament.* Leipzig, 1930.

Jahn, F.L. *Briefe.* Hrsg. von W. Meyer. Leipzig, 1913.

——, *Deutsches Volkstum.* Lübeck, 1910.

——, *Deutsches Volkstum.* Lübeck, 1806.

Jantzen, W. Die soziologische Herkunft der Führungsschicht der deutschen Jugendbewegung 1900-1933'. In: *Führungsschicht und Eliteproblem.* Konferenz der Rankegesellschaft für Geschichte im öffentlichen Leben. Frankfurt, Berlin, Bonn, 1957.

Jens, W. 'Völkische Literaturbetrachtung heute'. In: *Bestandsaufnahme.* München, 1961.

Joachimsen, P. *Vom deutschen Volk zum deutschen Staat.* Göttingen, 1956.

Johann, E. (Hrsg.). *Innenansicht eines Krieges.* Frankfurt, 1968.

Jünger, E. *In Stahlgewittern.* Berlin, 1922.

——, *Der Kampf als inneres Erlebnis.* Berlin, 1929.

Jünger, F.G. *Aufmarsch des Nationalismus.* Leipzig, 1926.

Jung, E.J. *Die Herrschaft der Minderwertigen.* Berlin, 1930.

Kaehler, S.A. *Studien zur deutschen Geschichte des 19. und 20. Jahrhunderts.* Göttingen, 1961.

Kaiser, G. *Pietismus und Patriotismus im Literarischen Deutschland.* Wiesbaden, 1961.

Kalkschmidt, E. *Biedermeiers Glück und Ende.* München, 1957.

Kampmann, W. *Deutsche und Juden.* Heidelberg, 1963.

Kaufmann, G. 'Die Hitler-Jugend'. In: *Wehrhaftes Volk. Der organisatorische Aufbau,* Teil II. Hrsg. von P. Meier-Benneckenstein. Berlin, 1939.

Keller, E. *Der unpolitische Deutsche.* Bern, München, 1965.

Kessel, E. 'Adolf Hitler und der Verrat am Preußentum'. In der Beilage zur Wochenzeitung "Das Parlament": Aus Politik und Zeitgeschichte. 15 November 1961.

Kessler, H. Graf. *Walther Rathenau.* Mit einem Kommentar von H. Fürstenberg. Wiesbaden, n.d.

Kessler, J. *Ich schwöre mir ewige Jugend.* Auflage, 1935. Neuauflage. München, 1962.

Killy, W. 'Zugelassen zum Gebrauch in Schulen'. In: *Neue Hefte.* Jahrgang 3/156/57.

——, *Deutsches Lesebuch.* Bd.3. Frankfurt, 1959.

——, *Deutscher Kitsch.* Göttingen, 1961.

Klages, L. *Der Geist als Widersacher der Seele.* 3 Bde. Leipzig, 1929-32.

Kleist, H.v. 'Katechismus der Deutschen'. In: *Sämtliche Werke.* München, 1954.

Klemperer, K.v. *Konservative Bewegungen zwischen Kaiserreich und Nationalsozialismus.* München and Wien, 1962.

Klemperer, K.v. *Germany's New Conservatism.* Princeton (N.J.), 1957.

Klönne, A. *Hitler – Jugend. Die Jugend und ihre Organisation im Dritten Reich.* Hanover, Frankfurt, 1956.

Klopstock, F.G. *Sämtliche Werke.* Leipzig, 1854.

Kluckhohn, P. *Das Ideengut der deutschen Romantik.* Tübingen, 1953.

Klüter, H. (Hrsg.). *Facsimile Querschnitt durch die Gartenlaube.* Bern, Stuttgart, Wien, 1963.

Körner, Th. *Sämtliche Werke.* Stuttgart, n.d.

Kogon, E. *Der SS-Staat.* Frankfurt, 1959.

——, *Theory and Practice of Hell.* London, 1950.

Kohlrauch, F. *Deutschlands Zukunft. Sechs Reden.* Elberfeld, 1814.

Kohn, H. *Idea of Nationalism.* New York, 1961.

——, *Prophets and Peoples: Studies in Nineteenth Century Nationalism.* New York, 1961.

——, *Wege und Irrwege. Vom Geist des deutschen Bürgertums.* Düsseldorf, 1962.

——, *Age of Nationalism.* New York, 1962.

——, *Absolutism and Democracy 1814-1852.* Princeton (N.J.), 1965.

——, *Nationalism and Realism 1852-1879.* Princeton (J.J.), 1968.

Kotowski, G./W. Pöls/G.A. Ritter. *Das Wilhelminische Deutschland. Stimmen der Zeitgenossen.* Frankfurt, 1965.

Kralik, R. *Karl Lueger und der christliche Sozialismus.* Wien, 1923.

Kraus, K. *Die Dritte Walpurgisnacht.* München, 1952.

——, 'Beethoven und Goethe – Vorbilder und Lebensführer'. In: *Auswahl aus dem Werk.* München, 1957.

Krausnick, H. 'Unser Weg in die Katastrophe 1945'. In der Beilage zur Wochenzeitung "Das Parlament": Aus Politik und Zeitgeschichte. 9.Mai 1962.

Krebs, A. *Nationalsozialistische Morgenfeiern.* Stettin, 1939.

Krieck, E. *Nationalpolitische Erziehung.* Leipzig. 1933.

Krieger, L. *The German Idea of Freedom. History of a Political Tradition.* Boston (Mass.), 1957.

Kruck, A. *Geschichte des alldeutschen Verbandes 1890-1939.* Wiesbaden, 1954.

Künneth, W. *Der grosse Abfall. Eine geschichtstheologische Untersuchung der Begegung zwischen Nationalsozialismus und Christentum.* Hamburg, 1947.

Kz-Verbrechen vor deutschen Gerichten. Dokumente. Hrsg. von H.G.v. Dam und R. Diordano. Frankfurt 1962.

Lagarde, P.de. *Deutsche Schriften.* Göttingen, 1886.

Lagebesprechung im Führerhauptquartier. Hrsg. von H. Heiber.
München, 1963.

Langbehn, J. *Rembrandt als Erzieher – von einem Deutschen.* Leipzig,
1891.

Lange, K. *Hitlers unbeachtete Maximen.* Stuttgart, 1968.

Laqueur, W. 'Jugendbewegung'. In: *Der Monat,* 142/1960.

——, *Young Germany.* New York, 1962.

——/G.L. Mosse (eds.). *International Fascism 1920-1945.* New York,
n.d.

Lasky, M.L. 'Warum schrieb Mommsen nicht weiter?' In: *Der Monat,*
no.19/1950.

Lebovics, H. *Social Conservatism and the Middle Classes in Germany
1914-1933.* Princeton (N.J.), 1969.

Leers, J.v. *14 Jahre Judenrepublik. Die Geschichte eines Rassenkampfes.*
2.Bd. Berlin, 1933.

Lemberg, E. *Ideologie und Gesellschaft.* Stuttgart, Berlin, Köln, Mainz,
1971.

Lenartz, W. *Vaterländische Feiern.* Düsseldorf, 1936.

Lenk, K. 'Das tragische Bewußtsein in der deutschen Soziologie der
zwanziger Jahre'. In: *Frankfurter Hefte,* 5/1963.

——, *Volk und Staat.* Stuttgart, Berlin, Köln, Mainz, 1971.

Leppmann, W. *German Image of Goethe.* New York, 1961.

——, *Goethe und die Deutschen. Vom Nachruhm eines Dichters.*
Stuttgart, 1962.

Lesser, J. *Von deutscher Jugend.* Berlin, 1932.

——, *Germany: The Symbol and the Deed.* London, New York, 1965.

Lessing, G.E. *Die Erziehung des Menschengeschlechts.* Berlin,
1780.

Lewy, G. *The Catholic Church and Nazi Germany.* London, n.d.

Ley, R. *Durchbruch der sozialen Ehre.* Berlin, 1935.

——, *Wir alle helfen dem Führer.* München, 1937.

——, *Soldaten der Arbeit.* München, 1938.

Lilge, F. *The Abuse of Learning: The Failure of the German University.*
New York, 1948.

Lion, F. *Romantik als deutsches Schicksal.* (Neudruck) Stuttgart, 1963.

Lippmann, W. *Public Opinion.* New York, 1965.

List, F. *Gesammelte Schriften.* Stuttgart, 1850.

Litt, Th. 'Hochschule und öffentliches Leben in der Weimarer
Republik'. In: *Kulturverwaltung der zwanziger Jahre.* Hrsg. von
W. Zilius und A. Grimme. Stuttgart, 1961.

Loewenstein, H.v. *The Germans in History.* New York, 1969.

Loewenstein, R. *Christians and Jews.* New York.

Löwith, K. *Einleitung zu Friedrich Nietzsche: Vorspiel einer Philosophie der Zukunft.* Frankfurt, 1959.

——, *From Hegel to Nietzsche: The Revolution in Nineteenth Century Thought.* New York, n.d.

Loewy, E. *Literatur unterm Hakenkreuz. Das dritte Reich und seine Dichtung.* Frankfurt, 1966.

Lohalm, U. *Völkischer Radikalismus.* Hamburg, 1970.

Ludendorff, E. *Vernichtung der Freimauerei durch Enthüllung ihrer Geheimnisse.* München, 1933.

Ludwig, E. *Wilhelm der Zweite.* München, 1925.

Lübbe, H. *Politische Philosophie in Deutschland.* Basel, Stuttgart, 1963.

Lütkens, Ch. *Die deutsche Jugendbewegung. Ein soziologischer Versuch.* Frankfurt, 1925.

Lukács, G. 'Deutsche Literatur im Zeitalter des Imperialismus'. *Literatur.* Berlin, 1953.

——, *Die Zerstörung der Vernunft. Der Weg des Irrationalismus von Schelling zu Hitler.* Berlin, 1955.

Luther, M. *Von den Jüden und ihren Lügen.* Hrsg. von H.L. Parisius. Volksausgabe, München, 1933.

——, *Kampfschriften gegen das Judentum.* Hrsg. von W. Linden. Berlin, 1935.

Mann, G. *Deutsche Geschichte des 19. und 20. Jahrhunderts.* Frankfurt, 1958.

——, *History of Germany Since 1789.* New York, 1968.

Mann, H. *Der Untertan.* Leipzig, Wien, 1918.

Mann, Th. *Friedrich und die Grosse Koalition.* Berlin, 1915.

——, *Betrachtungen eines Unpolitischen.* Berlin, 1918.

——, *Zu Lessings Gedächtnis. Gesammelte Werke.* Berliner Ausgabe, Bd.XI. Berlin, 1929.

——, *Tristan.* Stuttgart, 1950.

——, *Bekenntnisse des Hochstaplers Felix Krull.* Berlin, 1954.

——, *Versuch über Schiller.* Frankfurt, 1955.

Mannheim, K. *Man and Society in an Age of Reconstruction.* New York, London, 1940.

Marcuse, H. *Reason and Revolution: Hegel and the Rise of Social Theory.* Boston (Mass.), 1960.

Marcuse, L. *Mein 20. Jahrhundert.* München, 1960.

——, *Obszön. Geschichte einer Entrüstung.* München, 1962.

——, *Das denkwürdige Leben des Richard Wagner.* München, 1963.

Marcuse, H. *Obscene. The History of Indignation.* New York, 1965.
Marr, W. *Der Judenkrieg, seine Fehler und wie er zu organisieren ist.* Chemnitz, 1880.
——, *Der Sieg des Judentums über das Germanentum.* Bern, 1879.
Marsani, A.R. *Frauen und Sehönheit. Ein Bilderbuch gestaltet von A.R.M.* Berlin, 1941.
Maschmann, M. *Fazit. Kein Rechtfertigungsversuch.* Stuttgart, 1963.
——, *Account Rewarded: A Dossier on My Former Self.* New York, 1965.
Maser, W. *Adolf Hitler.* München, 1971.
Maste, E. 'Hugo Preuß — Vater der Weimarer Verfassung'. In der Beilage zur Wochenzeitung "Das Parlament": Aus Politik und Zeitgeschichte. 26.Okt. 1960.
Mau, H. 'Die deutsche Jugendbewegung 1901-1933'. In: *Jahrbuch der Jugendarbeit.* München,
Mau, H./H. Krausnick. *German History 1933-1945: An Assessment of German Historians.* New York, 1963.
Maurer, E.H. *Der Spätbürger.* Bern, München,
——, *Richard Wagner.* Reinbek, 1959.
Mehring, F. 'Zur Geschichte der Sozialdemokratie'. In: *Die Gartenlaube.* Jahrgang, 1879.
Meinecke, F. *Die deutsche Katastrophe. Betrachtungen und Erinnerungen.* Wiesbaden, 1946.
——, *German Katastrophe.* Boston (Mass.), 1963.
Menzel, W. *Denkwürdigkeiten.* Bielefeld, 1877.
Michel, K.M. 'Rinnen muß der Schweiß oder Wie wir Schillers 200. Geburtstag feierten'. In: *Frankfurter Hefte,* 12/1960.
Minder, R. 'Soziologie der deutschen und französischen Lesebücher'. In: *Minotaurus.* Hrsg. von A. Döblin. Wiesbaden, 1953.
——, *Kultur und Literatur in Deutschland und Frankreich.* Frankfurt, 1962.
Minoque, K.R. *Nationalism.* New York, 1967.
Mitscherlich, A. *Auf dem Wege zur vaterlosen Gesellschaft.* München, 1963.
——, *Society without the Father: A Contribution to Social Psychology.* New York, 1969.
Moeller van der Bruck, A. *Das Dritte Reich.* Hrsg. von H. Schwarz. Hamburg, 1932.
——, *Germany's Third Empire.* New York.
Möbus, G. *Realität oder Illusion. Zum Problem der unbewältigten Vergangenheit.* Osnabrück, 1961.

Mörike, E. *Werke.* 1.Bd. Leipzig, Wien, 1914.
Mohler, A. 'Konservativ 1962'. In: *Der Monat,* no.163/1962.
——, *Die konservative Revolution 1918-1932.* Stuttgart, 1950.
Mommsen, Th. *Auch ein Wort über unser Judentum.* Berlin, 1880. 1880.
Mosse, G. *The Crisis of German Ideology, The Intellectual Origins of the Third Reich.* New York, 1964.
Muchow, H.H. *Jugend und Zeitgeist.* Reinbek, 1962.
Müller, A.H. *Die Elemente der Staatskunst.* Berlin,1809.
Münchmeyer, L. *Kampf um deutsches Erwachen. Zusammengestellt von Th. Fuchs.* Dortmund, 1935.
Muschg, W.J. 'Nadlers Literaturgeschichte'. In: *Die Zerstörung der deutschen Literatur.* München, 1960.

Nadler, J. *Literaturgeschichte der deutschen Stämme und Landschaften.* Regensburg, 1912.
——, *Literaturgeschichte des deutschen Volkes.* Berlin, 1938.
Naumann, B. *Auschwitz.* New York, 1966.
Neeße, G. 'Von der deutschen Erneuerung'. In: *Wille und Macht. Führerorgan der nationalsozialistischen.* Jugend, 16/1935.
Neumann, F.L. *Behemoth. The Structure and Practice of National Socialism.* New York, 1963.
Neurohr, J. *Der Mythos vom Dritten Reich.* Stuttgart, 1957.
Niekisch, E. *Das Reich der niederen Dämonen.* Hamburg, 1953.
Nietzsche, F. *Wrke* in 3 Bden. Hrsg. von K. Schlechta. München, 1956.
——, *Basic Writings.* New York, n.d.
——, *Portable Nietzsche.* New York, 1959.
Nigg, W. *Religiöse Denker.* Berlin, München, Zürich, 1948.
Nipperdey, Th. 'Die deutsche Studentenschaft in den ersten Jahren der Weimarer Republik'. In: *Kulturverwaltung der zwanziger Jahre.* Stuttgart, 1961.
Noack, P. *Die Intellektuellen. Wirkung, Versagen, Verdienst.* Mümchen, 1961.
Nolte, E. *Der Faschismus in seiner Epoche.* München, 1963.
——, *Three Faces of Fascism.* New York, 1969.
Norden, G.v. *Kirche in der Krise. Die Stellung der Evangelischen Kirche zum Nationalsozialistischen Staat im Jahre 1933.* Düsseldorf, 1963.

Paetel, I.O. *Das Bild vom Menschen in der deutschen Jugendführung.* Bad Godesberg, 1956.

Paetel, K.O. *Jugendbewegung und Politik.* Bad Godesberg, 1961.

Paul, J. *Ernst Moritz Arndt.* Göttingen, 1971.

Pauls, E.E. *Der politische Biedermeier.* Lübeck, 1925.

Pauls, Th. *Luther und die Juden.* 1939.

Pecht, W. *Geschichte der Münchner Kunst im 19. Jahrhundert.* 1888.

Petersen, J. *Die Sehnsucht nach dem Dritten Reich in deutscher Sage und Dichtung.* Stuttgart, 1934.

Petzet, M.u.D. *Die Richard Wagner-Bühne König Ludwig II.* München, 1970.

Pinson, K.S. *Pietism as a Factor in the Rise of German Nationalism.* New York, 1934.

Plessner, H. *Die verspätete Nation.* Stuttgart, 1959.

Plewnia, M. *Auf dem Wege zu Hitler. Der völkische Publizist Dietrich Eckart.* Bremen, 1970.

Poliakov, L.J. *Das Dritte Reich und die Juden.* Berlin-Grunewald, 1955.

——, *Das Dritte Reich und seine Denker.* Berlin-Grunewald, 1959.

Pross, H. *Die Zerstörung der deutschen Politik. Dokumente 1871-1933.* Frankfurt, 1959.

——, 'Vom Wandervogel zum Jungenstaat'. In: *Die Zerstörung der Deutschen Politik. Dokumente 1871-1933.* Frankfurt, 1959.

——, 'Das Gift der blauen Blume. Eine Kritik der Jugendbewegung'. In: *Vor und nach Hitler – Zur deutschen Sozialpathologie.* Olten, Freiburg, 1962.

——, 'Studenten, Verbindungen, Politik'. In: *Vor und nach Hitler – Zur deutschen Sozialpathologie.* Olten, Freiburg, 1962.

——, *Dokumente zur deutschen Politik 1806-1870.* Frankfurt, 1963.

Pulzer, P.G.J. *The Rise of Political Anti-Semitism in Germany and Austria.* London, New York, 1964.

Pundt, A.G. *Arndt and the Nationalist Awakening in Germany.* New York, 1935.

Raabe, F. *Die bündische Jugend.* Stuttgart, 1961.

Raabe, W. *Sämtliche Werke.* Freiburg, Braunschweig, 1951.

Ranulf, S. *Moral Indignation and Middle-Class Psychology.* Copenhagen, 1938.

Rauschning, H. *Gespräche mit Hitler.* Zürich, 1940.

Rehm, W. *Experimentum medietatis. Studien zur Geistes- und Literaturgeschichte des 19. Jahrhunderts.* München, 1947.

Reichmann, E.G. *Hostages of Civilization. The Social Sources of National Socialist Anti-Semitism.* Boston (Mass.), 1951.

Reichmann, E.G. *Die Flucht in den Hass. Die Ursachen der deutschen Judenkatastrophe.* Frankfurt, 1956.

Reichstagung in Nürnberg 1933. Hrsg. im Auftrage des Frankenführers Julius Streicher. Berlin 1933.

Rein, G.A. *Die Reichsgründung in Versailles.* München, 1958.

Reinhardt, H.K.F. 'Akademisches aus zwei Epochen'. In: *Die Krise des Helden — Beiträge zur Literatur- und Geistesgeschichte.* München, 1962.

——, *Germany: Two Thousand Years.* New York, 1961.

Richter, A. *Unsere Führer im Lichte der Rassenfrage und Charakterologie.* Leipzig, 1933.

Richter, H.E. 'Mörder aus Ordnungssinn. Warum viele NS- Verbrecher so schnell zu braven Kleinbürgern wurden'. In: *Die Zeit.* 19 Juli 1963.

Richter, u.a. *Alte und neue Studenten-, Soldaten- und Volks-Lieder.* Leipzig, 1847.

Rießer, G. *Zu Schillers 100. Geburtstag.* Hamburg, 10 November 1859.

Rilke, R.M. *Briefe und Tagebücher aus der Frühzeit. 1899-1902.* Leipzig, 1933.

——, *Letters.* New York, 1969.

Ringer, F. *The Decline of the German Mandarins. The German Academic Community 1890-1933.* Cambridge (Mass.), 1969.

Ritter, G. *Vom sittlichen Problem der Macht.* Bern, 1961.

——, *Das deutsche Problem.* München, 1962.

——, *The German Problem.* Columbus (Ohio), 1965.

——, *Sword and the Scepter: The Problem of Militarism in Germany.* Coral Gables (Fd.), 1969.

Roeder, P.M. *Zur Geschichte und Kritik des Lesebuchs der höheren Schule.* Weinheim, 1961.

Roh, F. *Entartete Kunst- und Kunstbarbarei im Dritten Reich.* Hannover, n.d.

——, *German Art in the Nineteenth Century.* Greenwich (Conn.), 1968.

Rosenberg, A. *Das politische Tagebuch aus den Jahren 1934, 1935 und 1939.* Hrsg. von H.G. Seraphim. Göttingen, 1956.

——, *Der Mythus des 20. Jahrhunderts.* München, 1934.

Rothe, C. 'Hans Carossa'. In: *Merkur,* Februar, 1957.

Roxan, D./K. Wanstall. *The Rape of Art. The Story of Hitler's Plunder of the Great Masterpieces of Europe.* New York, n.d.

Rudolf, E.V.v. *Georg Ritter von Schönerer, der Vater des politischen Antisemitismus.* München, 1936.

Rudolph, L.v. *Die Lüge, die nicht stirbt. Die 'Dolchstosslegende' von*

1918. Nürnberg, 1958.

Rüdiger, K. 'Auslese und Bewegung'. In: *Wille und Macht. Führerorgan der nationalsozialistischen Jugend.* 12/1936.

Rüstow, A. *Ortsbestimmung der Gegenwart.* Erlenbach-Zürich, 1950.

Saliger, R. *Braune Universität. Hochschullehrer zwischen gestern und heute.* München, 1964.

Salin, E. *Vom deutschen Verhängnis. Gespräch an der Zeitenwende: Burckhardt-Nietzsche.* Hamburg, 1959.

Saller, K. *Die Rassenlehre des Nationalsozialismus. Wissenschaft und Propaganda.* Darmstadt, 1961.

Sandvoss, E. *Hitler und Nietzsche.* Göttingen, 1969.

Santayana, G. *The German Mind. A Philosophical Diagnosis.* New York, 1968.

Sauberzweig, D. 'Die Hochschulen im Dritten Reich'. In: *Dei Zeit,* 4 Folgen. März 1961.

Schäfer, W. *Die dreizehn Bücher der deutschen Seele.* München, 1922.

Schallenberger, H. *Untersuchungen zum Geschichtsbild der Wilhelminischen Ära und der Weimarer Zeit.* Ratingen, 1964.

Scheffel, J.V.v. *Der Trompeter von Säckingen.* Stuttgart, 1854.

——, *Ekkehard.* New York, 1965.

Scheler, M. 'Der Mensch im Weltalter des Ausgleichs'. In: *Ausgleich als Aufgabe und Schicksal.* Berlin, 1929.

Schemm, H. *Seine Reden und sein Werk.* Hrsg. von G. Kahl-Furthmann. Bayreuth, 1935.

Scherer, W. *Deutschland im Liede vaterländischer Dichter.* Paderborn, 1876.

Scherr, J. 'Johann Gottlieb Fichte'. In: *Gartenlaube.* Jahrgang, 1862.

Scherrer, H. *Deutsche Soldatenlieder.* Leipzig, 1914.

Scheuer, O.F. *Burschenschaft und Judenfrage.* Berlin, 1927.

Schiller, F.v. *Sämtliche Werke in zwei Bänden.* 2.Bd. Leipzig, Wien, Teschen, 1870.

——, *On the Aesthetic Education of Man.* New York, 1965.

——, *Naïve and Sentimental Poetry.* New York, 1966.

Schlechta, K. *Nietzsches Werke.* München, 1956.

Schmeer, K.H. *Die Regie des öffentlichen Lebens im Dritten Reich.* München, 1956.

Schmidt, H.W. *Feiern des Jahres.* Frankfurt, 1940.

Schmitt, C. *Politische Romantik.* München, Leipzig, 1925.

Schmitz, M. *Die Freund-Feind-Theorie.* Köln, Opladen, 1965.

Schmolck, H. *Rückkehr der Kunst.* Freiburg, 1935.

Schneller, M. *Zwischen Romantik und Faschismus.* Stuttgart, 1971.

Schonauer, F. *Stefan George.* Reinbek, 1960.

——, *Deutsche Literatur im Dritten Reich.* Olten, Freiburg, 1961.

Schorn, H. *Der Richter im Dritten Reich. Geschichte und Dokumente.* Frankfurt, 1959.

Schüssler, W. *Kaiser Wilhelm II – Schicksal und Schuld.* Göttingen, Berlin, Frankfurt, Zürich, 1962.

Schultze-Naumburg, P. *Die Kunst der Deutschen.* Stuttgart, Berlin, 1934.

Schuppe, E. *Der Burschenschaftler Wolfgang Menzel. Eine Quelle zum Verständnis des Nationalsozialismus.* Frankfurt, 1952.

Schwabe, K. 'Zur politischen Haltung der deutschen Professoren im Ersten Weltkrieg'. In: *Historische Zeitschrift,* 3/1961.

Schwaner, W. *Germanenbibel.* Berlin, 1904.

Schwarz, H.P. *Der konservative Anarchist. Politik und Zeitkritik Ernst Jüngers.* Freiburg, 1962.

Schwedhelm, K. (Hrsg.). *Propheten des Nationalismus.* München, 1969.

Schweitzer, A. *Die Nazifizierung des Mittelstandes.* Stuttgart, 1970.

Schwerte, H. *Faust und das Faustische. Ein Kapitel deutscher Ideologie* (mit dem Anhang: Dürers 'Ritter, Tod und Teufel' – Eine ideologische Parallele zum 'Faustischen'). Stuttgart, 1962.

Schwierskott, H.J. *Arthur Moeller van den Bruck und der revolutionäre Nationalismus in der Weimarer Republik.* Göttingen, 1962.

Seibert, C.G. *Deutsche Abende.* Barmen, 1857.

Seidelmann, K. *Bund und Gruppe als Lebensformen deutscher Jugend. Versuch einer Erscheinungskunde des deutschen Jugendlebens in der ersten Hülfte des 20. Jahrhunderts.* München, 1955.

Seidelmann, K. 'Der Generationsprotest der Jugendbewegung'. In: *Beilage zur Wochenzeitung "Das Parlament": Aus Politik und Zeitgeschichte.* 10 Januar, 1962.

Seidlmeyer, M. 'Das Lutherbild im Wandel der Zeiten'. In: *Ein Leben aus freier Mitte. Beiträge zur Geschichtsforschung. Festschrift für Ulrich Noack, von seinen Kollegen, Schülern und Freunden zum 60. Geburtstag.* Göttingen, 1961.

Shafer, B.C. *Nationalism. Myth and Reality.* New York, 1955.

Simplizissimus. 'Ein Rückblick auf die satirische Zeitschrift'. Auswahl und Text von E. Roth. Hannover, 1954.

Simplizissimus-Facsimile-Querschnitt. Bern, Stuttgart, Wien, 1963.

Siemering, H. *Die deutschen Jugendverbände.* Berlin, 1931.

Snell, E. *Neun Tage Latein.* Göttingen, 1956.

Snyder, L.L. *The Dynamics of Nationalism*. New York, 1964.

Soldatengeist. *Eine Deutung aus Bekenntnissen der Front*. Berlin, 1942.

Sombart, W. *Händler und Helden*. München, 1915.

——, *Jews and Modern Capitalism*. New York, 1969.

Sontheimer, K. *Thomas Mann und die Deutschen*. München, 1961.

——, *Antidemokratisches Denken in der Weimarer Republik*. München, 1962.

Speer, A. *Erinnerungen*. Berlin, 1969.

——, *Inside the Third Reich. Memoirs*. New York, 1970.

Spengler, O. *Urfragen*. München, 1965.

——, *Preussentum und Sozialismus*. München, 1919.

——, *Jahre der Entscheidung. Neuauflage*. München, 1961.

——, *Hour of Decision*. New York, 1963.

——, *Decline of the West*. London, 1926-29.

Stählin, W. *Der neue Lebensstil. Ideale deutscher Jugend*. Hamburg, 1925.

Stahl, F.L. *Staatslehre*. Berlin, 1910.

Stapel, W. *Antisemitismus*. Hamburg, 1920.

——, *Der christliche Staatsmann. Eine Theologie des Nationalismus*. Hamburg, 1932.

Sterling, E. *Er ist wie du. Aus der Frühgeschichte des Antisemitismus in Deutschland 1815-1850*. München, 1956.

——, *Judenhass. Die Anfänge des politischen Antisemitismus in Deutschland 1815-1850*. Frankfurt, 1969.

Stern, F. *Kulturpessimismus als politische Gefahr. Eine Analyse nationaler Ideologie in Deutschland*. Bern, Stuttgart, Wien, 1963.

——, (ed.). *Path of Dictatorship 1918-1933*. New York, 1967.

——, *Politics of Cultural Despair: A Study in the Rise of German Ideology*. Berkeley and Los Angeles, 1961.

Sternberg/Storz/Süskind. *Aus dem Wörterbuch des Unmenschen*. Hamburg, 1957.

Sternberger, D. *Panorama oder Ansichten vom 19. Jahrhundert*. Hamburg, 1955.

——, *Über den Jugendstil und andere Essays*. Hamburg, 1956.

Stippel, F. *Die Zerstörung der Person*. Kritische Studien zur nationalsozialistischen Pädagogik. Donauwörth, 1959.

Stoecker, A. *Christlich-Soziale Reden und Aufsätze*. Bielefeld, 1885.

Stöwe, G. 'Einer Dichterin zum Gruß'. In: *Bücherkunde*. April, 1941.

Stolberg, L.v./Ch.v. *Gesammelte Werke*. Hamburg, 1820.

Strachwitz, M. Graf. 'Germania'. In: *Sämtliche Lieder und Balladen mit Lebensbild und Anmerkungen.* Hrsg. von H.M. Elster. Berlin, 1912.

Strothmann, D. *Nationalsozialistische Literaturpolitik. Ein Beitrag zur Publizistik im Dritten Reich.* Bonn, 1960.

——, 'Die gehorsamen Mörder. Das Heuser-Verfahren in Koblenz'. In: *Die Zeit,* 7 Juni, 1963.

——, 'Hölderlin zwischen den Exekutionen'. In: *Die Zeit,* 14 Juni, 1963.

Stürmer, Der. Jahrgang 1934, no.1.

Stürmer, Der. Jahrgang 1943, no.30.

Stumpfe, O. 'Professoren, Reaktion und Männerbünde zwischen 1870 und 1933'. In: *Politische Studien,* 145/1962.

Talmon, J.L. *Origins of Totalitarian Democracy.* New York, 1970.

Teut, A. *Architektur im Dritten Reich.* Frankfurt, Wien, 1967.

Thieme, K. (Hrsg.). *Judenfeindschaft. Darstellungen und Analysen.* Frankfurt, 1963.

Thoma, L. *Gesammelte Werke.* München, 1956.

Timm, A. *Der Kyffhäuser im deutschen Geschichtsbild.* Göttingen, 1961.

Töpner, K. *Gelehrte Politiker und politisierende Gelehrte – die Revolution von 1918 im Urteil deutscher Hochschullehrer.* Göttingen, Zürich, Frankfurt, 1970.

Treitschke, H.v. *Fichte und die nationale Idee.* Leipzig, 1862.

——, 'Ein Wort über unser Judentum'. In: *Preussische Jahrbücher.* 1879.

——, 'Zum Gedächtnis des großen Krieges'. In: *Auswahl für das Feld.* Hrsg. von Freytag-Loringhoven. Leipzig, 1917.

——, 'Luther und die deutsche Nation, 1883'. In: *Historische und politische Aufsätze.* Leipzig, 1920.

——, *Politics.* New York, 1963.

——, *History of Germany in the Nineteenth Century.* 7 vols. New York, 1915-19.

Tremel-Eggert, K. *Barb. Der Roman einer deutschen Frau.* München, 1939.

Troeltsch, E. *Protestantism and Progress.* Boston (Mass.), 1958.

Ueberhorst, H. *Elite für die Diktatur – die Nationalpolitischen Erziehungsanstalten 1933-1945.* Düsseldorf, 1969.

Unger, E./R. Schottländer/L. Zahn (Hrsg.). *Texte der Philosophie – Kommentar.* München, 1961.

Velmede, F. *Ewiges Deutschland.* 1.Bd. Braunschweig, 1939.
Vermeil, E. (ed.). *The Third Reich.* London, 1955.
Viereck, P. *Metapolitics. From the Romantics to Hitler.* New York, 1941.
Vogelsang, E. *Luthers Kampf gegen die Juden.* Tübingen, 1933.
Vondung, K. *Magie und Manipulation. Ideologischer Kult und politische Religion des Nationalsozialismus.* Göttingen, 1971.

Wachtel, J. *Herzgeliebte Gartenlaube.* Feldafing, n.d.
Wagener, H. *Staats- und Gesellschaftslexikon.* 5.Bd. Berlin, 1861.
Wagner, R. *Das Judentum in der Musik.* Leipzig, 1869.
——, 'Wieland der Schmied, als Drama entworfen'. In: *Auswahl seiner Schriften.* Leipzig, 1920.
——, *Prose Works,* 8 vols. New York, 1893-1899.
Wahl, A. 'Die Ideen von 1789 in ihren Wirkungen auf Deutschland'. In: *Zeitwende,* 1/1925.
Warnke, M. (Hrsg.). *Das Kunstwerk zwischen Wissenschaft und Weltanschauung.* Gütersloh, 1970.
Weinländer, K. *Rassenkunde, Rassenpädagogik und Rassenpolitik. Der naturgesetzliche Weg zu Deutschlands Aufstieg.* Weißenburg, 1933.
Weltgeschichte im Aufriß. Arbeits- und Quellenbuch. Bd.3: Von der Französischen Revolution bis zur Gegenwart. Frankfurt, Berlin, Bonn, 1957.
Werner, B.E. 'Literatur und Theater in den zwanziger Jahren'. In: *Die Zeit ohne Eigenschaften. Eine Bilanz der zwanziger Jahre.* Hrsg. von L. Reinisch. Stuttgart, 1962.
Werner, K.F. *Das NS-Geschichtsbild und die deutsche Geschichtswissenschaft.* Stuttgart, Berlin, 1971.
Westphalen, L. Graf v. *Geschichte des Antisemitismus in Deutschland im 19. und 20. Jahrhundert.* Stuttgart, 1962.
Weymar, E. *Das Selbstverständnis der Deutschen. Ein Bericht über den Geist des Geschichtsunterrichts der Höheren Schulen im 19. Jahrhundert.* Stuttgart, 1961.
Whiteside, A.G. 'Nationaler Sozialismus in Österreich vor 1918'. In: *Vierteljahrshefte für Zeitgeschichte,* 4/1961.
Wilamowitz-Moellendorff, F. Gräfin v. *Carin Göring.* Berlin, 1934.
Wittek, E. (Hrsg.). *Die soldatische Tat – Berichte von Mitkämpfern des Heeres.* Berlin, 1942.
Wolters, F. *Stefan George und die Blätter für Kunst.* Berlin, 1930.

Wucher, A. *Eichmanns gab es viele.* München, Zürich, 1961.
——, *Theodor Mommsen-Geschichtsschreibung und Politik.*
 Göttingen, Berlin, Frankfurt, 1956.
Wulf, J. *Die bildenden Künste im Dritten Reich.* Güterloh, 1963.

Young, E.J. *Gobineau und der Rassismus.* Meisenheim, 1968.

Zeimer, G./H. Wolf. *Wandervogel und Freideutsche Jugend.* Bad
 Godesberg, 1961.
Zipfel, F.v. *Kirchenkampf in Deutschland 1933-1945.* Berlin, 1965.
Zmarzlik, H.G. 'Der Sozialdarwinismus in Deutschland'. In:
 Vierteljahrshefte für Zeitgeschichte. 3/1963:
Zöberlein, H. *Der Befehl des Gewissens.* München, 1938.

INDEX

Adams, Henry 24-5, 34n
Adorno, Theodor 206, 220, 227,
  229n., 235, 246
aestheticism 19, 45-57, 186
agrarian policies 154f
Ahlwardt, Wilhelm 226f., 230n.
d'Alquen 132
Amery, Carl 254-5
Anacker 196-7
Andreas Hofer League 169
anti-democratism 14, 27, 32, 53-4,
  106-7, 111-20, 122, 134, 167,
  195, 203, 208
anti-humanitarianism 14, 116ff., 203,
  210, 220ff.
anti-intellectualism 22, 25-6, 98-100,
  103, 117, 202
anti-rationality 98-100, 155
anti-semitism 33, 103-4, 109, 115,
  169, 177, 197, 202ff., 217-8,
  220-9, 236, 249, 252
anti-socialism 28, 121-5, 167
anti-Westernism 101-5, 116, 167
apoliticism 231-45
Arminius 196, 199n.
Arndt, E.M. 65, 99, 101, 114, 127,
  140, 164f., 174, 193
Arp, W. 104, 117
Aryanism 47, 103f., 141, 144ff., 203,
  247
Auschwitz 10, 19, 34, 54, 96, 188,
  206, 237ff.
Austria 124, 167, 226f., 252

Bach, Johann Sebastian 43, 198
Bade, Wilfried 43
Bamberg, Knight of 43, 80, 133, 196
barbarism 12, 37, 136-41, 215
Barbarossa, Friedrich I 128, 129n.,
  133
Barlach, Ernst 55, 56n., 160
Baroque period 33, 142, 211f.
Bartels, Adolf 104, 160
Bartsch, Wolfgang 20
Bauer, L. 101
Baumann, H. 89
Bavarian Homestead and Royal
  League 169; Monarchist

Party 169; Veterans Association
  169; see also NSDAP
Beard, Charles 23
Bechstein, L. 201
Becke, K. 133
Beckstein, Helena 189
Beethoven, Ludwig van 42, 198
Belsen 206
Benn, Gottfried 118, 138
Berens-Totenohl, Josefa 158f., 160,
  162n.
Berger, K. 160
Bergmann, Ernst 133, 197, 251
Berning, C. 152
Bertram, Adolf Cardinal 253, 257n.
Bertram, Ernst 143, 150n.
Beumelburg, W. 69, 159, 194, 197
Biedermeier period 13, 82, 87f.,
  90, 156, 166, 181, 188, 231, 233f.
Biermystik 32, 200-7
Biesalski, K. 151
Binding, Rudolf G. 96
Bismarck, Otto von 26, 95, 106, 108,
  112, 124, 145f. 167f., 185, 196ff.,
  226, 248, 250, 252
Bley, F. 173
Bloch, Ernst 90f., 95, 138, 241
blood and race 29-30, 53, 116, 131,
  151-3; and soil 154-61, 195f., 216
Blubo poets 158ff., 187
Blüher, Hans 45, 50n., 131f., 137,
  140, 208, 243
Blunck 160
Böckenförde, Ernst Wolfgang 253
Böcklin, Arnold 44, 50n
Bölsche, E. 64, 67, 80, 95, 159, 174
Bölsche, Wilhelm 186-7, 192n.
Bormann, Martin 191
Böttischer, Paul see Lagarde, Paul
  Anton
bourgeoisie, petit 10ff., 14, 18, 28f.,
  51f., 86, 94-6, 124ff., 133, 136,
  156f., 166, 171-6, 177ff., 186,
  206, 217, 220, 237, 246, 254;
  see also Spiessertum
Bracher, K.D. 109, 250
Brecht, Bertolt 47
Breker, Arnold 48

282